R.E.M.

Enjoy!!

Thanks for being
a great friend!

Jerry Kubawski

♪ There are scratches all around the
coin slot like a heartbeat, baby ♪♪
trying to wake up, but this machine
can only swallow money. You can't
lay a patch by computer design. It's
just a lot of stupid, stupid signs.
Tell her she can kiss my ass, then laugh
and say that you were only kidding. That
♪♪ way she'll know it's really, really, really,
really me.
Album: Automatic for the People
Song: The Sidewinder Sleeps Tonight ♪
Artists: Berry/Buck/Mills/Stipe '92

R.E.M.

FROM "CHRONIC TOWN" TO "MONSTER"

DAVE BOWLER & BRYAN DRAY

A Citadel Press Book
Published by Carol Publishing Group

Carol Publishing Group Edition, 1995

Previously published as *R.E.M. Documental*

A Citadel Press Book
Published by Carol Publishing Group
Citadel Press is a registered trademark of Carol Communications, Inc.

Editorial Offices: 600 Madison Avenue, New York, NY 10022
Sales & Distribution Offices: 120 Enterprise Avenue, Secaucus, NJ 07094

Queries regarding rights and permissions should be addressed to:
Carol Publishing Group, 600 Madison Avenue, New York, NY 10022

Picture credits
Andy Catlin/LFI: page 4 *top;* Kevin Cummins/LFI: page 8 *top;*
Alain Gales/LFI: page 4 *bottom;* Lawrence Lawry/LFI: front
cover; Kevin Mazur/LFI: page 6 *bottom;* Michael Linssen/
Redferns: page 5 *top;* Martina Raddatz/Redferns: page 7 *top;*
Ebet Roberts/Redferns: back cover, pages 1,2,3,
5 *bottom,* 6, 8 *bottom*

All quotes from *Rolling Stone* courtesy of
Straight Arrow Publishers, Inc.

Manufactured in the United States of America
10 9 8 7 6 5 4 3 2 1

Library of Congress Cataloging-in-Publication Data

Bowler, Dave.
R.E.M. : from Chronic time to Monster / Dave Bowler and
Bryan Dray.
p. cm.
Includes index.
ISBN 0-8065-1724-7 (pbk.)
1. R.E.M. (Musical group) 2. Rock musicians—United States—
Biography. I. Dray, Bryan. II. Title.
ML421.R22B6 1995
782.42166'092'2—dc20
[B]   95—22310
                                                      CIP
                                                      MN

CONTENTS

Dedication   vi

Acknowledgments   vii

Authors' Note   viii

Introduction   1

Chapter One: Elysian Fields   7

Chapter Two: Gained Momentum   21

Chapter Three: Beside Yourself   39

Chapter Four: Say What?   55

Chapter Five: Not Bound to Follow Suit   69

Chapter Six: Still a Ways Away   79

Chapter Seven: Forsight Has an E   93

Chapter Eight: No Sense of Decency   107

Chapter Nine: With Feathers   122

Chapter Ten: Timeless, Matchless, Fretless   139

Chapter Eleven: Cactus Field Hippies   158

Chapter Twelve: The Supreme Boner   175

Chapter Thirteen: Let Us Sort Out the Music From the Sound 189

UK Discography   193

Sources   201

DEDICATION

To Mom and Dad
A thousand books couldn't repay my debt to you.
And for Denise
I knew. It was like magic.
Always

David

To Trish, Emma and Rebecca for their love and support. And to Mum, Dad, Gran, Joyce and Wal without whom this would have been impossible.

Bryan

Acknowledgments

A number of people have been of sterling service in the compilation of this book. At the top of the list are R.E.M. and their organization for all the wonderful music that inspired it.

Our thanks must also go to our agents, Tanja Howarth and Charlotte Oldfield, who are responsible for us having to write this book in the first place and similar thanks must go to Clare Hulton at Boxtree for her assistance.

Denise Dean did a great deal of the necessary research, realizing all too late that it is virtually impossible to transcribe any interview featuring Peter Buck. Encouragement has come from many sources including Mrs Enid Fisher and other friends far too numerous to mention.

As far as the text goes, we are indebted to the following for the right to quote from their work: *Chronic Town*, *Cut*, *GQ*, *The Guardian*, *Hot Press* (the world's finest publication), *Lime Lizard*, *Melody Maker*, *Mojo*, *New Musical Express*, *Observer*, *Q*, *Rolling Stone*, *Select*, *Sounds*, *The Times*, *Sunday Times*, *Top* and *Vox*. Other sources were also helpful with background material.

Two R.E.M. fanzines worth sending an SAE to for details are *Chronic Town*, 27 Oriel Drive, Old Roan, Liverpool, L10 3JL and *Fretless*, 24 Westbrook Close, Park Gate, Southampton, Hampshire, SO3 7AU.

Authors' Note

What isn't this book going to be? Well, we don't intend to prove that Michael Stipe is currently the most intriguing performer in popular music nor that Bill Berry has rock's finest eyebrows – if you've read this far, you probably already accept these as givens. R.E.M. aren't to be deified as the greatest band since The Beatles – although they are – nor are they to be labelled as the saviours of rock'n'roll, because they aren't. Why should we be out to second guess them? There's no great desire to lapse into political polemic nor artistic adoration nor any other kind of alliteration though the temptation teases. Take all that away and you're left with 'Documental'.

When *Dead Letter Office* appeared in 1987, Peter Buck likened it to a musical junkshop, a tidying up package that comprised all manner of R.E.M. odds and ends. If this book can't offer anything as inspirational as the *Chronic Town* EP that appeared on the CD version, nor anything as stupid as 'Walter's Theme' or 'King Of The Road', at least it helps tidy up the detritus that has been building up over the years as a consequence of R.E.M.'s colourful interview technique. The only caveat to add is that Peter Buck has a penchant for embellishment while Michael Stipe tends to veer between disarming honesty and perverse self-mythologizing to enhance his already bizarre image.

INTRODUCTION

Labels are often pretty misleading, especially when applied to the arts, and popular music in particular. Rock'n'roll was divided into pop and rock, then came punk which was further sub-divided into the new wave. The independent scene of the late 1980s was split into indie-dance and retro-indie, while dance music has always had its own particular hierarchy of styles. One of the more confusing terms that has been employed in recent years, stolen from other artistic spheres, is 'postmodernism', a phrase that allegedly covers modern attitudes utilized within a traditional framework. It is this term that has been most regularly applied to R.E.M., and which most clearly indicates the futility of categorizing music: over the last decade and a half, R.E.M. have surfed most musical forms, ranging from the futuristic strains of 'King Of Comedy' on *Monster* to the arcane narratives that characterize *Fables Of The Reconstruction*.

Like many great artists before them, R.E.M. have contrived a form of presentation that has cloaked them in mystery while at the same time retaining a public face that is highly approachable and expresses their engaging personalities. Their grasp of media manipulation has stood them in good stead over their career, enabling them to ride the storm of publicity that has trapped so many other groups and destroyed their muse. Their background as inhabitants of Athens, Georgia has become an axiomatic cliché that has been rendered empty by repetition but, as we shall see, it has provided the group with an ideal base for their work. Firstly, it gave them the time to develop into a good band away from the glare of big city expectations that might have stifled them, and secondly it offered a rich tradition of fabulism, a heritage on which they have been able to draw.

1

It is ironic then that although they have been able to further their careers through their judicious use of the press interview, the rapid movement of the media monster has robbed them of the chance to approach a wider constituency. It's important to note that, unlike their most obvious contemporaries U2, R.E.M. as a group have never specifically set out to act as spokesmen nor have they presented any form of manifesto. The fact that they, Stipe in particular, have not been portrayed as the 'voice of a generation' in the way that Dylan or Lennon were in the '60s is not something they lose any sleep over.

Popular culture has changed – progressed seems to be a totally inappropriate word – and music is no longer the fulcrum of that culture as it was thirty years ago, but instead occupies a peripheral role. Contrast the reaction to Vietnam and to the Gulf War within the musical community and the impact of that reaction if you want an illustration of the shift. The intervening years have seen music move to the fringes, from where its role has become an educational one of 'think global, act local' rather than the clarion call to revolution which it might have been in the past. Perhaps that change represents the growing cynicism that has gripped the world, a recognition that the numbing naivety that an earlier age clung on to was hopelessly misplaced; or perhaps it is simply a dawning realization that most pop stars are barely qualified to tell us how to get out of bed, never mind how to run the world. Certainly Peter Buck has little time for that bygone era, insisting to *Melody Maker* that

the sixties was just a bullshit revolution that was advertised. You could have sold soap the way you sold hippies and revolution. I hate the sixties, I hate those people. It's garbage ... the only time anything was ever accomplished was by the people who worked with Martin Luther King, who were lower-class blacks. The middle class ... rich kids who pretend to be idealistic for a certain number of years until they reach reality, which is you've gotta have a job ... (they) never did anything. They were horrible times. Mean guys with short haircuts who beat up little kids for no reason, television was stupid – cars were nice – there was a war on, rioting in the streets, anyone who didn't look like everyone else was picked out of the pack and murdered. It was alright for The Byrds and The Beatles, they had limos and bodyguards. I know what it was like to get beaten up for having [long] hair in Georgia.

For R.E.M., the fringe seems to be a good place from which to operate and, as Buck suggests, they might be able to achieve something more concrete by virtue of not being a mere fashion accessory. Their position offers a degree of personal anonymity, except possibly in the case of Michael Stipe, as well as the freedom to work: to create timeless, evocative music that can move their audience, sometimes educating, or opening listeners' eyes to other concerns. Since R.E.M. have avoided the traps of celebrity, they have also maintained their freedom of speech, presenting themselves as defenders of common sense and morality. Their work with Amnesty International, Greenpeace and PETA, as well as other less celebrated civil liberty groups, has not been rewarded with the vocal criticism that Sting has run into for similar work.

In some ways it's a shame that R.E.M. do not possess the worldwide media clout that The Beatles or The Rolling Stones did in the '60s. But, paradoxically, it is their tangential frame of reference to mainstream culture that allows them to be so potent a force. Since R.E.M. rarely beat people over the head with political or environmental concerns, outsiders feel less daunted in approaching their music and more willing to embrace the philosophy it offers. They have been regularly criticized for a lack of linear lyricism, but it is still very clear just what R.E.M. stand for once you have begun to absorb their music.

Michael Stipe suggests that 'the one thing that R.E.M. can offer is music that you can dance to if you want, you can ignore it, you can use it like furniture, but there's also something there that you can listen to and say "this is intelligent" or at least "this is not stupid". We're not a message band but there's certainly things in the music and the way we present ourselves that hopefully people could take home with them.' If Stipe is presented as an enigma, an image with which he is happy to play on occasion, he is also a very down-to-earth character. He does not subject the group or their music to elaborate theories, nor does he raise impractical suggestions as to how people should improve the world and the lot of those who inhabit it. He does not profess to be a saint, and merely suggests that people take time to think about their lives, their behaviour and their actions a little more carefully, a viewpoint fully supported by R.E.M. as a group. The group's role is suggestive rather than authoritative.

It is a consequence of people's broader perceptions, exaggerated and encouraged by a voracious media, that Bill Berry and Michael

Stipe can say precisely the same thing and receive widely differing reactions. If Stipe talks of recycling, he is regarded as either endearingly quirky, dispensing homespun philosophy from the porch or as some messianic genius on a crusade to save the Earth from self-destruction. When Berry says the same thing he is seen to be talking mundane common sense. To arrive at any understanding of what R.E.M. do and how they achieve it, it's necessary to deconstruct the popular fables that have been constructed around them and focus instead on what they themselves have chosen to reveal over the years.

The Peter Buck of legend – and his own comic strip – is not necessarily the same Peter Buck that plays with R.E.M.. The Michael Stipe who frequents the pages of the music press is at times unrecognizable from the one that sings so affectingly, and is certainly not the be-all and end-all of the group as many would pretend. To the wider audience to which R.E.M. now appeals it is the powerful, beautiful songs and the band's performance that is the attraction, not the enigma that the press has built around Michael Stipe. For the 'serious' fans and for the press keen to get a story he may well be the most interesting facet of R.E.M., but it is the music, first and foremost, that has won R.E.M. their enormous success, something for which the credit is to be equally shared.

This differentiation between members of a group is not a new thing – for example, Talking Heads suffered from the same treatment, as David Byrne was viewed as some kind of alien. Talking Heads was also apparently more fractious, more prone to the internal bickering and egotistical arguments that have destroyed so many groups. If R.E.M. have had their moments on the road and in the studio, they seem better equipped than most to deal with the problem. Berry underlines the point: 'We're great friends. We started out as friends, we didn't find each other through newspaper clippings, it was just something that happened. It overrides everything else in the band right now. We're friends first, professional musicians second.'

There is a surprising lack of role definition in R.E.M., too. Although Stipe produces the vast majority of the lyrics, instrumental duties are diversely spread, with Buck occasionally playing drums, Berry using bass or mandolin and Mike Mills involved in keyboard parts or the accordion, as well as adding the vocal harmonies, sometimes in tandem with Berry. This willingness to swap instruments and to experiment has become an R.E.M.

trademark, and has paid musical dividends by ensuring that they do not fall into tired old habits which could lead to formulaic songs. It has also led each member of the band to appreciate the musical importance of the others, so that no-one can easily be taken for granted. R.E.M. have become a complete unit, ensuring that each is valued equally within their organization, even if the outside world is always quick to jump to erroneous conclusions.

If you were to call a rock'n'roll group 'intellectual', you could be accused of pushing things a little too far. There are certainly few stranger methods of making a living and much of the life of such a group is absurd; the music sometimes follows suit. However, there is certainly a theoretical level to R.E.M.'s work which implies a greater degree of thought and care above and beyond the normal cathartic thrashing beloved of so many bands, even if Stipe argues that 'the intuitive sense in the music comes out pretty strongly. R.E.M. intuit as a band much more than they analyse'. Perhaps part of their appeal lies in the fact that, like The Beatles before them, R.E.M. are completely in tune with, and attuned to, their times but they do apply a collective intelligence to their songs. This has helped them strike common, universal chords in 'Everybody Hurts' or 'Perfect Circle', the latter a song whose literal meaning is uncertain even to the other members of the band, but whose atmosphere is unmistakably moving. It may be no coincidence that both of these songs started with Bill Berry.

Long before U2's video walls were informing the world that 'contradiction is balance', R.E.M. were putting that idea into practice. This may indeed be their most attractive characteristic. In a musical and lyrical sense, certainly prior to *Monster*, they have managed to combine a sometimes wistful and nostalgic appreciation of the past in personal and global terms while simultaneously meeting the challenges of the future head on. Stipe agrees: 'I'm not a Luddite. I understand the advances ... give me a manual typewriter over a word processor, though.' They have worked with an oxymoronic language both musical and lyrical. On 'Get Up' from *Green* for instance, dreams both complement and complicate life within the same harmony part, an example of the push-me-pull-me way in which R.E.M. songs are completed. But the songs exist beyond a simple rendition of Stipe's words, something tacitly accepted by the refusal to provide lyric sheets and exemplified by such songs as 'Perfect Circle'. Stipe, for his part, accepts that their songs have an appeal beyond mere words, admitting that 'I personally find language quite stifling and, simultaneously, liberating'.

That in itself is a neat summation of R.E.M., a group that defies linear explanation yet which means the world to their audience. Seemingly, it means as much to the group themselves. Peter Buck told *Q*:

> on every record there's one of us who has less of an involvement than maybe the next record, but nobody needs to know that. By the time we write the bridges and intros and rewrite the stuff, it's all of ours anyway. Since we split the money equally, there's no real reason to get egotistical about it. Saying who wrote what is counter-productive, like family business. I like the idea of the four of us indivisible; you can't drive a wedge between us. That's how we stay together.

The unity of R.E.M. is proof positive once more that the most important ingredient in any great group is personal chemistry – once that is achieved, the rest is simply down to hard work. Like R.E.M., U2 formed as friends and then became a group and have had the intelligence to protect the sanctity of that line-up. Once The Beatles found Ringo Starr, they stayed together for eight years and changed the musical world. Led Zeppelin kept their volatile foursome together through thick and thin until death parted them. Those four bands have produced some of rock music's finest moments in the last thirty years. The stability of their personnel speaks volumes and is the reason why R.E.M. are not Michael Stipe & Co, but a real four-piece group. This book will treat them that way.

1

ELYSIAN FIELDS

'For better or worse, people are affected by popular entertainment and by the music they listen to, whether they're aware of it or not.' In recent years few have affected people so strongly as Michael Stipe and his colleagues in R.E.M.. That, of course, is the way in which we are encouraged to perceive the band by the media everywhere: Michael Stipe and his group. It is an indication of the increasing power of television, radio and the press to distort facts to their own ends that even media manipulators as skilled as R.E.M. have failed fully to transmit the idea that they are a group in every sense of the word, and have a commitment that stretches far beyond the simply musical.

Warner Brothers, the multinational corporation who eventually pushed R.E.M. into the global spotlight they deserved, are aware that here they have a rather different group from any other they might have represented. Contractually, there is no such group as R.E.M., as guitarist Peter Buck explained to *Sounds*.

With Warners we signed a contract with the five of us [including manager Jefferson Holt] and we provide them with services. We provide songs for records, videos, live performances but there's no guarantee that we're all going to appear on the record. We gave them a verbal agreement that most of us would play on the records ... but if we all agree that R.E.M.'s going to make a record and it's going to be Mike and Michael that'd be fine.

If on the surface that suggests that R.E.M. aren't concerned about working together, like so much else with the group, a lot is going on beneath mere words. Their most popular record to date, *Automatic For The People*, was recorded almost in that fashion, with the foursome often not playing together as a group, yet all having some input into what was possibly their most cohesive album. For Stipe, Buck, drummer Bill Berry and multi-instrumentalist Mike Mills, R.E.M. constitutes much more than a simple performing unit and therein lies their greatest strength.

R.E.M., sometimes presented as the least ambitious of groups, have managed to construct a highly efficient corporate lifestyle from their own staggering success; a success which has bought them the freedom to work or not, to experiment or not and to tour or not. Every facet of R.E.M. life bears the stamp of all four players, along with the indispensable back-room team of Holt and lawyer Bertis Downs, for whatever affects the band is everyone's responsibility, not just Stipe's or Mills's. That aside, R.E.M., especially as it progresses, is no longer the sole concern, maybe not even the central concern in their lives – Peter Buck has embraced fatherhood, something of a surprise to those outside who viewed him as their token rock'n'roller, while Bill Berry and his wife appear keen to start their own family too. Professionally, all four have long been wise enough to embark on other projects away from the group, be it Michael Stipe's involvement in film company C-00 or the others' work with Warren Zevon or The Troggs for instance. Before R.E.M. became a full-time commitment, Bill was a member of Love Tractor, and Michael experimented with a more typically Athenian art band, Tanzplagen, in 1981, a set-up that allowed him to indulge his more outlandish leanings. These brief sabbaticals provide fresh perspective on R.E.M. and what makes it so special, while allowing the band's members to pick up new ideas from other artists that can help refresh their creative process.

R.E.M. as a unit recognize that what makes them special is the unique chemistry which exists when they get together to work. They are sufficiently respectful of that magic ingredient to avoid abusing it – hence their retreat from the road in the early '90s – while they happily admit that should any member of the band leave, R.E.M. would be no more. Within such a comprehensive commitment to the 'band ethic', the four are able to protect one another from over-exposure or from inflated egos and can musically bail one another out when necessary. *Automatic For The People* illustrates that perfectly in its piecemeal construction, while

Monster shows that they can still cut it as a full-blooded rock'n'roll outfit which is, after all, how they started.

How did they start? As any fan of rock music is well aware by now, R.E.M. first got together in Athens, the small-town home of the University of Georgia in the Southern States. It was the university that initially attracted the individuals in the group to Athens. From a musical viewpoint, the basis of R.E.M. has long been Mike Mills and Bill Berry, an atypical rhythm section if ever there was one, but one which came to the group as a unit. Peter Buck noted that 'those years of playing Meters songs and stuff means they have a different, kind of less rock'n'roll slant on the rhythm section. Bill very rarely plays that kind of rock'n'roll 4/4 time, he's very subtle.'

Mike Mills was born in Orange County, California on 17 December 1958 but grew up in Georgia, his family having moved back to his father's home state while he was a baby. He had a musical background, grounded mainly in the classical idiom, as his father performed as a dramatic tenor while his mother sang and played both piano and guitar, an indication of the origins of Mike's musical dexterity and ability to handle a number of instruments. As a child, he learned to play piano and tuba before dabbling in sousaphone – not a rock'n'roll staple, it must be said. This musical outlet was important to Mike, who admitted later that once his family had moved to Macon in his early teens, his own shyness meant that he would rarely go out until he had developed firm friendships. His musical ability led him inexorably towards a place in his high school marching band where Bill Berry was already waiting.

Bill, born in Duluth, Minnesota on 31 July 1958, had already encountered Mike in school and had cultivated a seething dislike for his eventual colleague. 'I hated him from the first time I saw him,' he admitted to *Rolling Stone*, ''cause he had that same kind of nerd appeal that he has now ... we had the same Home Room, the first place you go in school every morning and he was very studious, really smart, very polite and we were just the antithesis of each other ... I was just starting to experiment with drugs and stuff. He was everything I despised; great student, got along with teachers, didn't smoke cigarettes or smoke pot ... we really did despise each other.' Mike accepts that he was something of a 'goody-goody' at the time.

Bill had only reached Georgia in 1972, having lived in a number of towns around America's Great Lakes before the family finally settled in the South. If his home wasn't quite the musical breeding ground that Mike's was, he still had plenty of opportunity to soak up the latest music from the collections of his elder brothers and sisters. Bill recalls that 'I'd sneak in [when they were playing records] and hide behind a chair and listen to them.' The natural consequence was to pick up an instrument and eventually, as a ten-year-old, he chose the drums.

Why the drums? Maybe Bill realized he had an interesting and highly individual sense of rhythm and could apply that usefully to the instrument. It's still an unusual choice given that as a child he'd begun to strum on a ukulele and shown a reasonable aptitude for stringed instruments. In future years with R.E.M., Bill would often play bass or guitar in rehearsals or even during live shows; on the *Out Of Time* promotional tour of mainland Europe, he spent as much time on guitar as on drums. Peter recalls that for the *Green* sessions, 'Bill wrote two of the songs on mandolin; "Hairshirt" is one of his riffs and "The Wrong Child" was him on mandolin and me on guitar.' In the light of later statements which have sometimes hinted at frustration with the limited scope of his chosen field, you're left to wonder if there was any other reason for his seemingly offbeat selection. Certainly, it's possible that Bill took to the drums because of their sheer physicality. He has confessed that because of the numerous moves his family made while he was a child, 'I was kind of mad at my folks for that, I was rebellious.' Perhaps the chance to thrash out some of that anger, channelling it in a more useful way, provided an allure. He might also have felt that the relative simplicity of the drums was the limit of his horizons: recently he has confessed to having had problems with low self-esteem since childhood, itself probably a legacy of moving around so much and not having a settled base from which to grow. If Bill was as hard on himself as he suggests, it's certainly reasonable to conclude that he may have felt daunted by the idea of playing guitar, given that he was growing up surrounded by the Southern boogie bands such as Lynyrd Skynyrd, where the guitar was the focal point of the show. Later experience has proved beyond doubt that he has more than enough ability to tackle any instrument, but as a child he clearly felt limited and uncomfortable with the idea of pushing himself into a starring role where he felt he might fail.

Unbeknown to Bill, Mike had traded in his sousaphone for the more portable and infinitely cooler bass guitar. Had Bill been more aware of this change of tack, R.E.M. might never have got off the ground. 'A friend of mine was a guitar player,' recalls Bill, 'and he lined up a jam session. He said, "Take your drums to this house," so I did. I spent half an hour setting up my drums and we were all there tuning up and waiting for the bass player – which is what we still do – and who should turn up but Mike Mills. I just thought, "Oh God!" If I'd played guitar, I'd have packed up and left but I looked at the drums and thought, "I'm stuck here, it's his house," so we made the best of it and had some fun and formed a band.' That band was, in best 1970s fashion, called Shadowfax, after Gandalf's horse in *The Lord of the Rings*. 'We just shook hands and said we'd put the past behind us and became best friends,' remembers Bill.

Shadowfax inevitably disbanded, but by now Mike and Bill had become an inseparable team, playing in covers bands around town, and in a lounge trio with a teacher, which may have been pretty trying at the time even though it paid well. Weddings were also catered for though this was short lived, as Mike fell down drunk at one such engagement. They started another covers group too, called the Back Door Band, playing Freddie King material; it was with this group that they first started to play their own songs. They quickly became frustrated with the local scene, which revolved around Southern boogie, and, on graduation in 1976, they quit playing. They left their respective homes and shared a flat in Macon, Mills taking a job at Sears department store while Berry worked at the Paragon booking agency where he spent time booking bands. This job was to prove important to the future of R.E.M., since Bill came into contact with Ian Copeland there, brother of Stewart from The Police, and their manager Miles, who was to set up the IRS record label. Copeland introduced Bill to a whole new kind of music, bringing from his London base all the punk and new wave offerings that were pouring out of Britain at the time. Bill took the records to play to Mike, and The Sex Pistols and their US counterparts The Ramones formed their staple listening for some time, firing them with the necessary enthusiasm to form a short-lived trio with Ian called The Frustrations, whose only gig was rained off.

Punk was the newest and most exciting musical form to hit the world in years – probably since The Beatles. If the rock output on British radio was uninspiring, major radio stations in the US were even worse because of their close ties to commercial sponsorship. To avoid losing the corporate dollar, mass appeal stations had to continually pump out soft rock, disco and standard AOR and MOR fare which meant that only the growing college radio network could dare to offer anything new. By 1978, they were playing Patti Smith, Television and Talking Heads, and were providing a genuinely innovative and stimulating mix of music while the mainstream continued to rot.

It's a little extreme to believe that college radio was the force that persuaded Mike and Bill to go back into the education system, but certainly their renewed musical ardour must have been a motivating factor – the free time that college life could provide might help them get a band off the ground or, at the very least, offer a few years away from the nine to five. In addition, Bill was keen to get involved in the music industry from an administrative standpoint and became interested in the idea of a law degree; Mike, on the other hand, was undecided and so took a general course when studies opened in January 1979. Naturally enough, they chose to enrol at the University of Georgia in Athens, about 100 miles from Macon.

The university has something of a reputation for being fairly relaxed in its attitude to students; if it wasn't quite the University Of Please Yourself, California made famous by The Rutles, it still allowed students a remarkable amount of latitude. In their first year, Mike and Bill barely attended school but spent their time staying up, sleeping in and getting drunk, which on the face of it isn't so very different from the college experience across the world. Bill was soon persuaded to pick up his drums again, at the behest of Kathleen O'Brien, a DJ at the college station, WUOG. There was a mutual attraction, and Kathleen asked Bill to play drums for her group The Wuoggerz, a fun group that extended Mike and Bill's musical tastes, now firmly grounded in the new wave.

Kathleen O'Brien was already something of a face on the Athens rock'n'roll circuit, a scene which had been promising much through the late '70s in the wake of the B52s. They were Athens' first musical heroes, formed to play at a Valentine's Day party in 1977, and quickly developing a following around the town. In August 1978 they pressed up 2000 copies of a single, 'Rock Lobster', which attracted record company interest. By the middle of 1979, they were signed to Warners in the US and Island elsewhere and were recording their first album in Nassau. Reactions to their success differed wildly in Athens. To some it was a once-in-a-lifetime deal; Athens had had its moment and it would never come again. Others

12

felt that the success of the B52s might pave the way for others to follow. Certainly, basking in the reflected glory, groups were springing up all over the town – good ones too, such as Pylon, The Tone Tones and The Method Actors while Love Tractor would soon follow. Why Athens? According to Mike Mills, 'There's a lot of young people with nothing to do,' while Michael Stipe suggests, 'It's pretty open to lots of different lifestyles.'

Contrary to popular opinion though, while Athens was playing host to lots of new bands, the whole town wasn't taken with the music, even though it was described as a popular music town as far back as the 1950s. Peter Buck was later to note that 'there was only about a hundred of us in Athens that would go and see the bands so you got to know everybody'. Peter was, inevitably enough, a friend of Kathleen's – they shared accommodation in Athens, of which more later. Peter was a little older than many of the crowd, born on 6 December 1956 near Oakland, California. By the time he was five his family had moved to San Francisco, putting them in the ideal place to observe the 1960s peace and love era which Peter later referred to with such distaste. Like most kids of his age, Peter was captivated by The Beatles and worked his way through all the other sounds of the '60s, tending towards the poppier end of the market occupied by groups such as The Supremes or The Monkees.

By the time he was ten, the Bucks had moved on to Indiana, and then to Roswell, Georgia when he was thirteen. Like Bill Berry and, to a lesser extent, Mike Mills, this constant moving gave him a sense of displacement and a slightly rebellious streak that was ideal in one fascinated by pop music: according to his own testimony he bought his first albums around 1970 based on reviews in the rock press simply because he hated to go out of the house, wouldn't go to record stores and so could only send away for titles that he knew all about. His next move in musical taste was into the harder end of glam rock with Slade and T-Rex, which pushed him in the direction of Iggy Pop, The New York Dolls and finally The Velvet Underground, although The Stones and The Beatles remained perennial favourites. One group that, allegedly, didn't make it to the Buck turntable was The Byrds, rather surprisingly given his later reputation as the king of jangly guitar in the mode of Roger McGuinn.

By this stage, at the age of seventeen or eighteen, Peter was a hardened music *aficionado*, absorbing the rock press and looking for records way beyond the normal radio fare, picking up as many interesting singles and albums as he could afford. As yet, he wasn't playing much guitar, his younger brother Kenny being the outstanding musician in the family, but Peter was certainly aware of the potential for doing more within the popular music format than the radio suggested. Having absorbed the lessons of The Velvets and their beautifully understated sound, born of imagination rather than technique, Peter was not at all surprised when punk exploded; he'd read the signs, seen the need for a new form that was about heart and soul rather than fingers and frets and sat back waiting for it to happen. When it did, Peter was there to witness it. He saw The New York Dolls in 1973 when they were supporting Mott the Hoople and was on hand to see the first US Sex Pistols show in Atlanta on 5 January 1978 – or, more accurately, to see a couple of songs before he was thrown out for not having a ticket.

A little earlier, in the summer of 1975, Peter had left high school and enrolled at Emory College in Atlanta – 'Being a student gave me some kind of rationale for existing,' he reminisced, adding, 'All the time I was supposed to be in classes just meant I had free time' – where he remained until spring 1978. He then dropped out and moved to Athens, armed with an impressive and highly contemporary record collection which featured the same albums and singles that Mike and Bill had discovered through Ian Copeland. That record collection had been honed by virtue of a part-time job he'd taken in Atlanta at Wuxtry Records, a second-hand record store near the college. At around the time he wanted to drop out of school, another of Wuxtry's stores, this time in Athens, found itself looking for help. Peter's brother was already at university in Athens, so Peter volunteered for the job – 'I used to play records I hadn't heard all day long' – and moved there, leaving his education behind. The excitement that the B52s were stirring up around the town was not a coincidence, for Peter was being inexorably drawn towards the idea of being in a band even if he was still refusing to countenance the idea publicly.

The Athenian arts/rock'n'roll community was a pretty small one and everyone within it was aware of one another. Peter took to the scene immediately, frequenting parties and concerts with great fervour, partly to get out of his accommodation, firstly an apartment in Milledge, and then a house that he had moved into on Oconee Street, a concrete building that he described as 'a dump'. This problem was soon to resolve itself when Dan Wall, co-owner of Wuxtry, offered him the lease of an old, run-down church on the same street, St Mary's Episcopal Church. Although the converted church was in a fairly awful state, with no heat or running water, it offered five bedrooms and a huge area that retained the pews and altar, doubling as a stage, which was ideal for holding parties and concerts. In retrospect, Peter remembers it as a lousy place to live but at the time it had its romantic, bohemian appeal. Peter took up the lease in the autumn of 1979 with Kathleen O'Brien, who had first met him in Atlanta. The only problem was the rent – a pretty prohibitive $350 – so he quickly persuaded his brother Kenny to move in too.

Another girl, Robin Bragg, also joined the house, but the rent was still too high, so it was fortunate that Peter had formed a close friendship with another newcomer to Athens, who jumped at the chance of moving in with them. Michael Stipe had pitched up in Athens in 1978, though he actually lived in Watkinsville, just outside the town itself. Again, as with his future colleagues in R.E.M., Stipe had led something of a nomadic existence as a child. He was born in the Georgia town of Decatur, an Atlanta suburb, on 4 January 1960, into a comfortably well-off family. His father was in the US Air Force, and his family moved around a lot while he was growing up, even living in Germany for a while when his father was posted to Vietnam, so he rarely made many friends. He became fairly introspective and mainly concerned with family life. These experiences may have led him to sharpen subconsciously those observational abilities which have served him so well as a lyricist, and provided him with the air of detachment that has been fundamental to so many of rock's finest performers.

Living on Air Force bases for much of the '60s and early '70s gave Michael little idea of the popular music of the time – understandably enough, as, given the anti-Vietnam sentiment that the 'counter-culture' displayed, pop music was given short shrift on these bases, whatever the Robin Williams' film *Good Morning, Vietnam* might suggest. It was not until the family really started to put down roots in the early part of the 1970s when they set up home in St Louis that Michael came out of his shell and began to listen to contemporary music. At high school he discovered a new musical form that he failed to take to. 'Heavy metal was real big and I tried really hard to like Ted Nugent and I couldn't, though I liked Aerosmith.' Like Peter Buck, Stipe began to investigate the music press via the *Village Voice* and 'found out what was going on in New York and that led to what was going on in England and that really excited me, the whole do-it-yourself attitude'.

In interviews, Michael has rather ingenuously suggested that he took the idea too literally, and actually believed that anyone could be in a band, claiming that it was just fate that he turned out to have a good voice. Further study of his work and character suggests that this is nonsense, that Michael Stipe is not the naively innocent Forrest Gump character that he sometimes chooses to hide behind but is a street-smart artist with a clear idea of what he wants and how to get it. It would be far more accurate to suggest that he was infected by the punk *zeitgeist* and was galvanized into musical action by the excitement of the times, recognizing a promising outlet for his artistic leanings which allowed him to hide behind a self-deprecating attitude. He is clear that Television's 'Marquee Moon', Wire's 'Pink Flag' – available only on import initially – and, especially, Patti Smith's 'Horses' were the records that changed his life, informing *Melody Maker*:

I kinda locked into that whole CBGBs thing when I was about sixteen. I had every article ever written about Television and The Velvets and it was listening to those bands that got me thinking about the personal possibilities of being in a band ... it was just me sitting in the Mid West wishing I was in New York ... I thought, 'If [Patti Smith] can sing, I can sing.' She was just real guttural. It was like all the body noises you make ... it wasn't a strained, perfect crescendo of notes. It was this howling mad beast.

Pretty soon Michael was singing in a group, turning into an extrovert almost overnight; his punk group Bad Habits got so far as to open for Rockpile in St Louis, but were unlikely to go further. Even so, Michael chose to remain there when his parents moved home again to Watkinsville in 1978, though he eventually followed a little later.

Although Michael was now on the fringes of the Athens community, he stepped back from his developing interest in music and spent a lot of time at home, refusing to go out in much the same way Peter Buck had. It's reasonable to suggest that periods of semi-solitude were very important to both of them, enabling them to evaluate themselves as people and set goals for the future. This period led Michael towards photography and a course in art at the university, though he argues that he chose art rather than geology simply because 'the building was walking distance from downtown

Athens'. His interest in photography is closely linked to his work as lyricist as well as image-maker for R.E.M.. The best photographers tend to be solitary figures who are sufficiently unobtrusive to be able to observe and take pictures without being noticed; there is a similar feeling of sympathetic intrusion in many of his songs, which he combines with an instinctive grasp of a lyric's cinematic potential.

Michael also knew the value of his personal image. A classmate of his was Linda Hopper who formed a group with Michael's sister Lynda and David Pierce called Oh Ok, an engagingly innocent trio who had no pretensions towards success. Linda, who later formed the excellent Magnapop, whose debut single was produced by Stipe, remembers him as looking 'really bizarre. His hair was really blond, bleached and long and very curly and he always wore sunglasses – a totally cool look, like someone who'd come down from the North. That stuff came down South really late.'

Given Michael's advanced musical tastes, it was natural, once he had come out of his voluntary hibernation, that one of his early ports of call should be the Wuxtry store where he and Peter struck up a strong friendship based on their love of the same records. Once Peter was ready to take up the lease on St Mary's, it naturally followed that Michael should move in with him to help cut costs; in fact, Peter's slightly vague recollection is that eighteen or so people, including Bill and Mike at various times, were eventually living in the church, though others put the figure at closer to a dozen. Even so, the two would regularly return home to find the church filled with people they didn't know – the church had been the party place before they took over and there was no changing its status.

Peter remembers that 'it was a kind of unspoken thing that we were gonna be in a band', though Michael did dabble in another Athenian outfit – a covers band called Gangster for whom he changed his name to Michael Valentine – before he and Peter began working properly together. Linda Hopper argues that his desire to perform was 'inspired by these professors at college who were discovering native folk artists around Georgia. That was something he really loved.' This was certainly true, as Michael, in his dual role as lyricist and visual co-ordinator, seized upon much that was rich in Southern culture, sights and sounds that would be unusual but have some resonance with observers outside Georgia. The cover of *Murmur* features a rampaging vine known as kudzu which overruns Georgia on the front and an Athenian railway trestle on the back;

Reckoning utilizes artwork by their friend Howard Finster (of whom more later), while *Fables Of The Reconstruction* deals with the Southern penchant for storytelling. The film *Left Of Reckoning* and the promotional video for 'Can't Get There From Here' also draw heavily on Athens and Georgia. As Linda Hopper noted in *Mojo*, 'I suppose R.E.M. helped galvanize opinion of the South through their visuals.'

Although Michael and Peter had started to work together, they still found the time to go to plenty of parties. At one of these – some suggest it was in the autumn of 1979, others place it in February 1980 – Kathleen O'Brien, who had become aware of Peter's work with Michael, felt that, since they would need a rhythm section at some point, she ought to introduce them to Bill Berry and Mike Mills. 'Mike wasn't there for some reason,' recalls Bill, 'but I met them at this party and said, "We've got the bass and drums, let's get together and see what happens." They'd started writing songs a week before. It turned out that somebody didn't make it so we bagged the idea but then I saw Pete in a bar a few weeks later and said, "Let's give it another shot." We got together and it was magic, but it nearly didn't happen.' Peter's version was, 'When we met Bill and Mike, within like an hour we were a band, wrote a couple of songs and were playing.'

Michael, of course, had a different take on it all, suggesting that he liked Bill purely because of his eyebrows and claiming that 'Buck couldn't really play the guitar and I couldn't sing. We were like a speed metal band,' but Mike's version is probably more accurate. Mike picked up on the way Peter's limited experience gave his playing a minimal quality around which Mike, as the more talented player, could play melodic rather than rhythmic bass lines, and was quickly taken by Michael's 'incredible ear for melody'. The quartet transformed a couple of songs that Bill and Mike had already written, leaving them in no doubt that they were a band in the making. Even so, given the community in which they were working, it was easily as important – probably more so – that they became close friends; they spent a month rehearsing and hanging around together before they got as far as a live show and, as Peter points out, 'We were friends before we were in a band. Some people try to put together a band then try to figure out if they're friends or not. It's like getting married to a stranger. It's been done and you can make it work, but I wouldn't like to do it.'

Michael's ear for melody is a vitally important component in

R.E.M.'s sound and success. He does pick up unusual melody lines, and the harmonic constructions that the group have used to such good effect over the years have been probably their most enduring and endearing characteristic. Whether this was merely a gift that Michael was born with, compounded by the sheer good fortune that he, Mike and Bill should have such compatible voices, is open to debate. It may be, however, that Michael's formative years explain his talent. Having missed out on the pop of the '60s, Michael was fed family radio staples, with the likes of George Gershwin a particular favourite in the household. Michael later told *Melody Maker* that '*Rhapsody in Blue* is one of the most impeccable pieces of music written this century, maybe of all time. I think it's just stunning', establishing his credentials as a man of great taste, but also paying due homage to one of the finest melody writers, from whom he has learned a great deal. In the same vein, as a vocalist Michael must have picked up on the singing styles of those who tackled Gershwin's songs: when he and Mike joined Larry Mullen Junior and Adam Clayton to play U2's 'One' at an inauguration party after Bill Clinton's election victory, Bono graciously accepted that the song had always needed a voice like Stipe's, calling him a 'great crooner' in the mould of Bing Crosby, who Michael must have heard many times at home. It's a less outrageous comment than you might at first think and certainly a complimentary one that sheds an interesting light on his subconscious influences: Peter Buck has added names like Skeeter Davis, Patsy Cline and Tammy Wynette to the list.

With this new group beginning to rehearse, some further consideration should be given to their adopted home. As a university town and a fairly laid-back one at that it's not surprising that the kids there could throw themselves into having a great time. The university's reputation in the arts helped too, meaning that Athens played host to a lot of creative people who wanted to express themselves while they still had the freedom to do so. That peer pressure in turn required R.E.M. to find their own distinctive voice because, as Peter recalls, 'When we started the idea was that if you sounded like another band, that was horrible. Most bands in Athens [tried] not to sound like one another . . . like Pylon, where did they come from? Where did the B52s come from? That was just something they pulled out of the air. The whole idea in Athens at the time was to express yourself originally.'

It was a combination of these creative factors, the advent of catalysts such as the B52s, the free and easy attitude of the college and the mysterious quality of the South's folklore that gave rise to the Athens scene. Michael Stipe has subsequently suggested that the climate had something to do with it too – the intense heat in the South encouraged people to stay out late drinking and partying, coming home when lower temperatures made sleeping more comfortable. Whatever the case, Athens was a combustible mix of talents who happened to be in the right place together at the right time. That openness to new ideas and experiences also meant that the small band of musical cognoscenti there were aware of the new wave in both its British and American forms, and were able to pick and choose what they wanted from that. Michael noted that 'rock'n'roll is just a skeleton that you can hang a whole lot of meat on' and it was that lack of any purism that gave the Athens scene its charm and diversity; as with the earliest rock'n'roll, you could take what you liked, mix and match with a variety of other ideas, mutate it and call it your own. The mutual support that groups gave one another was equally important too, given that their ideas were often so off the wall in tone and that their followings were quite limited.

Excited by the possibilities of their new hobby, Mike, Bill, Michael and Peter now spent most of their free time working together. The party area of the church provided them with an ideal and huge space in which to rehearse their cover versions, a very un-Athenian activity, although they compensated for this by simultaneously trying to write their own material. At this stage though, it was pure fun, with no other aim. Kathleen O'Brien had naturally seen them perform, since she still lived in the church and was intrigued by the music they were making. She was keen to see them progress, and in her unofficial role as the guardian angel of what would become R.E.M., she provided them with their first goal. On 5 April 1980, she would be twenty and was holding a huge party at the church. She wanted the boys to provide the soundtrack as a present. How could they refuse?

2

GAINED MOMENTUM

Looking at R.E.M. now, with their long record of political activity, it's surprising how apolitical the Athens community was as they were starting their rise to prominence. Certainly there was no evidence to suggest that anyone was doing much more than having a good time, serious issues being put to one side, and in the climate of all-out fun and celebration that existed at the start of the '80s, R.E.M. were the perfect band. Few contemporaries had seen them in rehearsal: those that had sometimes watched with a sneer, enjoying the music in spite of themselves, while others simply used it as a drinker's soundtrack. Peter Buck told *Melody Maker*, 'We were kinda laughed at because we had a sound that people could relate to.'

Each Athens band prior to R.E.M. prided themselves on trying to contrive a sound that was plucked from the ether and was totally rootless, with no real connection to anything that had gone before. Yet R.E.M. never felt the need to go in that direction. Certainly they tried to be original, but they were equally happy to work inside a relatively conventional rock'n'roll format, Linda Hopper offering the opinion that 'everything they've ever done has been very subtle and classic . . . it was very success-oriented'. Peter's slant was that 'there was the post-punk thing with guys with Les Paul guitars doing three-chord fast songs, new wave which was just dumb disco dance with skinny ties and then there was dinosaur rock. We were trying to invent a more literate, evocative and more harmonically complex structured kind of rock'n'roll.'

Southern boogie wasn't on the agenda but with Peter's thorough grounding in rock history and a rhythm section which addressed the

21

music from an almost R'n'B rather than rock'n'roll angle they covered a number of familiar bases. Stipe admitted to *Sounds* early on in 1983 that, 'We're certainly not a retro band, I don't think. We're not doing anything really new ... we're not stretching the boundaries of music, forging paths for generations to follow! We mean what we do. I guess that sometimes is kind of rare. And I'm very sincere in saying that, it might sound kind of ridiculous and self-proclaimed but we really do mean that we're doing.' Mike added, 'We grew up with all types of music from the '50s to the '80s ... that's a heritage we draw on.' The cleansing aspect of the punk experience helped keep them rooted in economy, with Michael topping off the package with his eccentric performance and iconoclastic approach. Essentially, R.E.M. were presenting a traditional rock sound with a twist.

The four were not really keen to play Kathleen's party, and Peter was especially unhappy about performing in public when they still had so little to offer by way of original material, but they were pushed into a corner from which they couldn't escape. They began rehearsing for five hours every day, as all four had taken up residence in the church. While they worked, preparations were going on for the party itself – five kegs of beer were brought in and two more groups lined up. The party was to be opened by The Side Effects with, according to your source, Turtle Bay or, more likely, Men In Trees acting as second band. The still nameless R.E.M. would play last, although there are hazy recollections that they performed as The Twisted Kites.

The group were trying to work up their share of originals so that they could safely take their place among the pantheon of Athenian talents but time was against them. Peter Buck recalls that they played about eighteen songs during that first-ever concert, of which 90 per cent were originals, yet Mike Green of The Fans recounts that they played 'Hippy Hippy Shake', 'Shakin' All Over', 'Stepping Stone', 'There She Goes Again', 'God Save The Queen', 'Secret Agent Man', 'Needles And Pins' and 'California Sun'. The most significant thing about their performance was, according to Green, that every song seemed like it might have been a cover version, an admission that here was a band with a highly tuned commercial ear working within classical boundaries. It was a sound and an attitude that won approbation and opprobrium in equal measure. Curtis Crowe was Pylon's drummer and he remembers liking R.E.M. despite his better instincts, since he and the Athens movement felt that they represented a retrograde step.

The party itself was a monumental success. Having worked out that around 125 people would turn up, the church was packed with something like 400 or 500 bodies all enjoying the free beer and music. It was R.E.M.'s great good fortune to be able to play on an evening that quickly became legendary around the town; they were equally lucky to be able to play their brand of music to such a large crowd. As has already been established, the Athens musical community had its own very clear ideas about what did and what didn't constitute a progressive, forward-looking unit – rhythm was especially important, all the more so in the wake of Talking Heads with their astoundingly powerful rhythm section and apparently intellectualized take on dance music. Blatant commercialism was not a trait that won too many friends. Had R.E.M. played their first shows to the small coterie of 100 avid music followers, they might not have earned such a rapturous response, but their introduction to the out-and-out revellers who were already well watered and just looking for a fun band was ideal. R.E.M. knew how to give an audience a great time and they had found an audience that wanted it.

Yet another element of good fortune was in the mix that night: Mike Hobbs from Tyrone's, a club in Athens, was on hand to see the band perform. He was looking for an opening act to support The Brains, an Atlantan band who were playing Tyrone's the following month, and felt that this new group might fit the bill. Playing in front of drunken friends was one thing but playing a real show at a real concert was something they didn't feel prepared for until they heard they'd get $100. As the taps on the beer kegs on which Kathleen had paid a deposit had been stolen after the party, they played the gig as a benefit, not for the last time.

Though participants in the Athens scene might not choose to look at it this way and R.E.M. might resent the idea too, they really were the culmination of the whole explosion of creativity that the B52s had started, the group that everything had been leading towards. For three years, groups had been springing up all over the town, playing a few shows and then splitting up or making a record for friends. An infrastructure of sorts was in place for any group of musicians that fancied their chances as a band; there were venues to play, spaces to rehearse and a captive audience of like-minded music fans who were interested in seeing new bands with something to offer. As a consequence, Athens was attracting some attention from the larger cities in the South, notably Atlanta, with the promise of greater things in store. For an Athens group, playing outside Athens itself was almost unthinkable because the whole experience was geared to enjoyment and sharing time with your friends.

Because of this, and the fact that individuality held such integral importance, few of the groups would appeal to a broader audience which could not appreciate the cultural nuances and in-jokes that surrounded these bands. Until R.E.M. surfaced, Athens had not produced a group who, while still endearingly quirky, had a musical agenda that was limitless. Bill stated that, 'We always stood apart from the rest of the bands that made up the Athens scene . . . we were the first to cross the gap between fraternities and the biker bars. We weren't really ostracized by the trendies but we never really fitted in either.' Their later success caused a little bitterness among some people who felt that R.E.M. were the beneficiaries of the foundations laid by others but, in fairness, they were the only group to look beyond the Athens horizon. Their dedication to rehearsing and improving illustrated their unwillingness to look inept in public, even if they didn't mind looking dumb every now and then. The group started out as fun, but pretty soon R.E.M. would take on an altogether different character and a far more important role in the lives of the four musicians.

Perhaps it's overstating things, but in hindsight it seems that that first gig at Tyrone's – getting it, playing it and the response – was the pivotal point in the history of R.E.M.. In the first instance, it gave them their name. If they did play the party as The Twisted Kites, it was never an official title, and so, in the ensuing weeks, the band played around with a variety of titles including Cans of Piss and Negro Eyes which, had they been adopted, might have done very little for the quartet's longevity. Eventually, they settled for R.E.M., 'rapid eye movement', the movement of the eyeballs during the deepest period of sleep when a person is dreaming. The band have regularly argued that there was no rationale behind the choice and that it was certainly nothing to do with dreams. Whether that's true or not, it's an apposite name for a group whose early work in particular had a dreamlike quality, an elusive nature that gave the illusion of songs shrouded in mist with only the occasional shard of clarity cutting through. Buck has often specifically stated that R.E.M. is not an abbreviation of rapid eye movement but is just an appealing set of letters, Michael adding, 'It stands for nothing but we'll lie down for just about anything. We just like the dots.' This doesn't explain how they came to be billed as Rapid Eye Movement on some of their early tour handbills. A little more expansively, Stipe explains, 'We wanted a name that wouldn't put us in any particular category musically and at the time we got together bands pretty much didn't have names that were just letters.'

The show at Tyrone's was a triumph for R.E.M.. They were already the main attraction despite the fact that The Brains were nominally the headliners. The good people of Athens had taken R.E.M. to their hearts and Mike Hobbs, realizing he was on to a good thing, gave them a headline show of their own a fortnight later. At this gig they were paid according to bar takings, and took $343, cementing their place as Athens' most popular band in the process, just six weeks after their debut. The show was packed, attracting a crowd three times the size any other band from the town would pull in, simply because R.E.M. offered an experience that no other group in town could match. Their eclectic choice of classic cover versions allowed the crowd to participate in their set, a piece of crowd pleasing that other bands in town frowned on. If Pylon or The Method Actors were on the 'cutting edge' of modern music with an artistic and intellectual agenda of their own, R.E.M. came at music from a different perspective. Peter said that music provided 'people's chance to forget how dismal life is and how bored they are. It's something to take your mind off things. It's a very important outlet. There's nobody in the world who doesn't listen to music.'

In a fairly tight-knit and musically incestuous community such as Athens, such talk was tantamount to heresy. The bands themselves might well be enjoying what they were doing and having as much fun as Buck, Berry, Mills and Stipe but it was just as crucial that they should be fashioning something new and different. This remains a thoroughly commendable idea, for such experimentation always points the way forward, but in the initial stages, before the rough edges have been smoothed down, such pioneering work is rarely rewarded with commercial acclaim. Pylon might have been causing a critical stir but they weren't packing the clubs simply because their performances were so novel and alien to those not in the know. Groups such as this tended to create cliques, their own exclusive circles of admirers, while the more casual music fans wanted something they could recognize.

R.E.M. provided that familiarity and that sense of fun that was missing. As Linda Hopper told *Mojo*, 'The art-school crowd in the town looked down on them for being more straight-ahead and fashionable ... but Michael was totally bizarre on stage. He threw his back out every night. He was compulsive to watch, a real focal point. In fact they all were, they used to get offstage and horse around.' Michael backed that assertion up later by remarking, 'I have the most oblique rhythm, I don't dance. I just have the most sideways rhythm that's ever been put before the public. It's not deliberate, I just can't keep a beat.'

Having played just a handful of shows, it would be harsh to suggest that R.E.M. were already honing their sound along careerist lines. The music they played was merely an amalgam of their tastes. If lines were to be drawn between them and the rest of the Athens crowd, the demarcation was that Buck, Mills and Berry in particular were music fans and played that way, while the other groups were attacking their music from a more oblique standpoint, viewing their work almost as some form of conceptual art. You don't win a prize for guessing which is likely to fall on the more popular side.

The element which securely placed one foot in the 'art' camp for R.E.M. was Michael Stipe, who had some understanding of that abstract style and was a little more sympathetic towards it than the other members of the band. In the future Michael and the rest of the group showed the influence of the 'art' bands by appropriating some of the esoteric clothes from the likes of Love Tractor in an attempt to keep the mainstream at arm's length until they were ready to submerge themselves in that wider culture. It is Stipe who has given R.E.M. the enigmatic status that has so pricked the critical sensibilities, carving out a niche for them to inhabit, and it was his performance as singer, lyricist and front man that marked R.E.M. out from the commercial crowd of very good bands in the years to come. However, the ability of the three musicians in the band to provide a fresh take on conventional forms first brought the group to wider attention.

Few contemporaries seem to remember Michael Stipe as being the eccentric that he is portrayed as nowadays, though observers such as Linda Hopper are ready to concede that his onstage routines were both odd and affecting. As he studied art and photography, and was so taken by the artistic leanings of the CBGBs scene in New York in the '70s, it's difficult to know how much is his own natural performance and just how much is manufactured for effect. As all the group have confessed at one time or another, Michael most volubly, 'Live, there is an energy level that we reach on a really good night . . . the stage thing, whenever I get up there and I know Peter feels the same way and Mike and Bill too, the whole thing about being in a band is so ridiculous and I get up there and I kind of realize what I'm doing and it's kind of silly – it makes me laugh.' There is a sense in which Michael's occasionally demented performance provides him with an escape hatch, a separate persona that he can observe and laugh at without exposing too much of himself or becoming too self-conscious at the innate absurdity of his chosen profession. Not that it's any more absurd than any other career: 'I think on the ladder of important things in this world being in a band is probably on a low rung; but then again being Secretary of State is probably down there too, just below dishwashing I guess.'

As performers, Mike and Peter were pretty energetic too, throwing themselves into the concerts with a passion and forcing Michael to formulate a means of establishing himself as the focal point above and beyond this straightforward exuberance. From the earliest days of R.E.M., Michael was experimenting with his own image and that of the group. He has often noted that his visual sense is his strongest suit and his studies at university were not put to waste: one of his teachers there was Jim Herbert, who was to play a large part in helping Stipe fashion R.E.M.'s videos and who had been instrumental in ensuring that the university art department was the finest in that corner of the USA. It was this academic reputation that helped create the thriving artistic community in the town in which R.E.M. were able to create and develop. Michael drew on artistic spheres other than the purely musical and this in turn marked him out as someone worthy of special attention – his aesthetic imagination rubbed against the group's tougher musicality, the resulting friction producing a high octane mix.

Stipe the enigma is largely a media invention, the flames of which Michael has been happy to fan, safe in the knowledge that it makes the band all the more interesting to outsiders, who are intrigued by the sense of mystery. Mystery is the R.E.M. signature and it's apparent that very early on, Michael was keen that the good-time simplicity which their concerts offered should be tempered by a measure of inscrutability which would retain the attention of any crowd. Given his preoccupation with the New York scene that spawned Television and Patti Smith, it's clear that Michael would also have come across Talking Heads very early on in his musical apprenticeship. It's a comparison that isn't often broached, but the similarities between Michael Stipe and David Byrne are sometimes quite striking. Both approach interviews in a highly distinctive manner, mixing the distracted with the obsessively fascinated, using quaint colloquialisms to make their point and occasionally mouthing the most prosaic of statements in such a way as to make them seem alien. In live performance too, Byrne's apparent embarrassment, which is progressively shaken off during a show as he approaches an almost religiously ecstatic condition, manifests itself in Stipe's performances at times. If there are no direct references, there are plenty of inferences, although Stipe would say that his shyness sometimes makes him uneasy with the audience in front of him, so that he tries to block them out.

Having played a few local, highly successful concerts, R.E.M. were clearly a group that could grow beyond Athens. They got their chance in July when Pylon had to cancel a couple of shows in Carrboro and one in Raleigh, North Carolina; the promoter tried to secure the services of The Method Actors as replacements but eventually had to settle for this band called R.E.M. of whom he had never heard. As all the best legends go, R.E.M. tore the place up over the weekend they spent there; but this is just an aside compared with the real lasting import of their trip to Carrboro.

The promoter who had been forced to book the band and who had to accommodate the group and their camp followers, Linda and Kathleen, went by the name of Jefferson Holt. Like Peter Buck, he was working in a record store and booking bands mainly for his own enjoyment in the midst of a dead-end musical scene. He later recalled that seeing R.E.M. for the first time 'was like what I would have imagined of seeing The Who when they first started. They blitzkrieged through some incredibly pop covers, then they had some of their own songs that were real pop but also some stuff that wasn't pop.' That synthesis of styles eventually helped R.E.M. touch both the pop fans and the more theoretically inclined followers of music alike and it was something which certainly alerted Jefferson to their potential. Initially he became a big fan of the group in the same way that Linda and Kathleen were, but he clearly had his mind on higher things.

It was fortunate indeed that R.E.M. were looking to spend some time on the road, for in the summer of 1980 their lease ran out on the church and, following one last triumphant attempt at trashing the place, the band had to move out. Kathleen and Bill took a flat together while the rest of the group moved into an apartment, though pretty soon their itinerant lifestyle meant they were living out of cars and friends' houses. If moving home was one worry, school was another. Bill in particular was on a knife-edge as far as his place at university was concerned, having spent his first eighteen months in Athens doing everything but attending school. As the band were starting to pick up pace right from the off, Bill was torn between getting his head down and doing some work to preserve his academic status or throwing in his lot with the band. As he recalled later,

> As students, we were barely hanging on, though I think Michael was doing okay. In fact, I flunked out because we started playing round Athens and then we went out to Atlanta. So we were booking small tours starting on Friday so we'd take Friday off and maybe the following Monday and that started to turn into Thursday to Tuesday and eventually we were doing quite poorly and more than one of us was invited to leave. That was when we had the choice to apply again or to get into the band. We were just having so much fun we decided to do that.

Their staple by the summer of 1980 was playing shows in Athens at Tyrone's or at the newly opened 40 Watt Club. With his past experience at Paragon behind him, the newly liberated Berry was put in charge of the group's organization, attempting to book as many dates as he possibly could: he did a pretty good job, calling in favours from all those people he'd met through that now defunct company. From the ashes of Paragon, Ian Copeland had set up his own agency, FBI; inevitably he got the call from Bill about this new group he was in, though he remembers that first Bill 'asked to get on the guest list for The Police show at the Fox Theatre in Atlanta. He said he had this little band and I said, "Well why don't you just be the support band and save me the hassle?"' In a long list of strokes of good fortune, this was to be a particularly impressive one. Taking the stage on 6 December 1980, Ian remembers that 'they went down so well that the crowd demanded an encore and it got me in a big deal of trouble because they weren't supposed to play one'. Quite what Sting thought of this new band is anybody's guess though the chances are that he would have been engaged in a backstage fight while the support group were on if the stories which surround The Police have any truth in them.

The reaction that R.E.M. got that evening wasn't atypical. Just eight months into their career, they were tearing up venues across the South and constructing a nice little reputation for themselves. Fired by an enviable self-confidence, they simply felt that they were good enough to play anywhere with anyone. Peter Buck later told *Melody Maker*,

> In our naïve way, we were kinda arrogant. We were like head-hunters. Sometimes we'd open for some cool bands, but usually we opened, you know, for just some nobodies who weren't very good and we'd go in and say, 'Man, let's blow them off stage.' The whole idea was to walk on and do like a 50-minute set that was like a hurricane blowing off the stage. We wanted to present those people with something that was just undeniable. By the time we were finished we wanted them to think that everything else was irrelevant. I just loved that challenge.

Although in itself the sheer excitement from approaching gigs in that way was enough to sustain the band, it was also evidence that they had further aspirations. It's unrealistic to accuse R.E.M. of having been mercenary at any time – as we'll see, their dealings with record companies totally refute that argument – but the band seem, right from the very start, to have set their sights on creating a legacy of some excellent work both on record and as a live group, in the firm knowledge that the other rewards of a large audience and financial security would naturally follow. R.E.M. haven't compromised in order to win fans, but have simply placed considerable faith in their own talents and the old-fashioned idea of a slow but steady increase in the size of their fan base.

That steadfast refusal to make concessions is a feature of all four as individuals. When they came together as a band, there was never any question that they might water down their sound to reach a mass audience; indeed, they have at times wilfully avoided commercialism by the simple device of turning the vocals down a little or using a 'difficult' song title such as 'Swan Swan H' to which many just could not relate. R.E.M. from their very first show were aware that they had a commercial sound; it was alternative given the prevailing musical fashion of the early '80s but they were aware that such trends were cyclical and that their time would come. By refusing to affiliate themselves with fads, they were taking care to set down roots for longevity rather than burn out. As a careful student of rock history Peter knew the traps they could fall into and set out some firm guidelines: 'We were writing on our own originally and so I said that unless we published the songs as a four-way split, I wouldn't be in the group. To do it any other way is counter-productive, it's greed that splits bands up.'

They were fortunate, too, that the group consisted of four fairly level-headed guys. Buck was a little cynical, unimpressed by the idea of glitz and glamour and the music industry in general, although, paradoxically, he was simultaneously attracted by it. Berry had already had some dealings with its periphery and was wise to some of the scams that could go on. In addition, he was to be the driving force that got R.E.M. off the ground by booking gigs and pushing the others into taking the group seriously. Stipe was articulate and able to ask the right questions at the right time; the popular perception of him as other-worldly founders when you consider that he knows what he wants and how to get it and realizes all the repercussions of any business dealings the band might enter into. No band becomes as big as R.E.M. are now without knowing the ins and outs of the record business and the studious Mills helped complete a self-contained unit with his thorough study of just how a group might grow towards a greater level of success. However, as the group's work rate picked up, it was all that Bill could do to keep up with practice on the one hand and administration on the other, to the point where something had to give.

Jefferson Holt, who had booked them in Carrboro, was so taken with their performance that he had moved to Athens in October 1980 on the pretext of opening his own record shop, though in reality this was merely a cover story which helped him see more of his favourite group. To begin with he helped out the group by working as a roadie, but gradually he took more and more of the workload from Bill and was devoting his time exclusively to the band. Once his store went bust at the beginning of 1981, Jefferson was offered and accepted the position as R.E.M.'s manager. As such, he became a non-musical director of the R.E.M. corporation with earnings sliced equally among the five.

Freed from the onerous duties of booking work for themselves and with someone else to drive the van for them, they threw themselves ever more conscientiously into their work. By now they had left the pretence of doing this just for fun behind them and were, instead, embarking on an apprenticeship that they hoped would bear fruit in later years. It's an old cliché about genius being 10 per cent inspiration and 90 per cent perspiration but in the case of R.E.M., that's been the case. Any success that they've had over the years has been earned because they worked damned hard to get it, rehearsing rigorously, writing prolifically and touring exhaustively.

It was their contention that to be in a rock band did not mean taking on airs, behaving like stars and becoming remote. Their version of the rock'n'roll experience was to play anywhere and everywhere that would have them, making themselves available to their fans at the same time. Live work was an integral part of the early R.E.M. since they had no records to sell but, they were also intelligent enough to see that it was an environment in which they could improve their presentation, their musicianship and their songwriting without any pressure; their knockabout attitude effectively masked their more earnest musical ambitions.

This extensive touring all over the South took R.E.M. right through 1981 and into the following year, by the end of which they were able to play further afield. The logic beyond it was simple – build a fan base, get better at your craft and then make a record. Buck has a certain fondness for those early days, reminiscing that, 'We musta played like 800 bars all over the South. We'd go in and there'd be maybe thirty people if we were headlining or maybe a cheap drink night – we always tried to play cheap drink nights 'cause that would cram 'em in – and by the end of the set we'd always be able to kinda go, "See, tell your damned friends about this!"' This self-belief carried the band through several years of hard times, as he concedes: 'When I think back, I just remember all the garbage we had to go through like five people to a bed, not being able to afford hotel rooms, sleeping as we drove overnight, driving all night all the time to get to the next show on time. Not being able to bathe. Not having money for food.'

Nevertheless, being on the road and the attendant air of adventure did appeal to the group and to their romantic Jack Kerouac sensibilities, as Peter told *Melody Maker*:

Whatever happened, it was like one more story for us . . . we played some weird places. Weird bars where the audience had to check in their guns at the door, where crazy, drunken guys

would come down front 'n' yell and scream at us and threaten
to kill us, y'know. Mind you we were getting pretty rowdy
ourselves, getting drunk and falling off stage and fighting
people in the audience, punching some guy if he was bothering
us ... they weren't real pleasant places but we were never in a
situation that I thought was incredibly life-threatening.

Michael for his part recalls the times as 'harrowing' but, 'Peter and
I certainly had romantic notions about [being on the road] and
damned if it didn't pay off.'

R.E.M. have a fund of stories about their early days on the road,
some of which may be apocryphal such as Buck's assertion that
they played second on the bill to a puppet show just like Spinal
Tap, but there's plenty of truth in many of them. The main aspect
of it all was the evidence it provided of their formidable tunnel
vision, their dedication to the cause of R.E.M. which puts the lie to
suggestions that they weren't out to turn the group into some kind
of career, even if only in the short term. Their cultural aspirations
were at least the equal of their material ambitions but they realized
that the two went hand in hand. They were not shy of doing the
groundwork but their language – the 'blowing bands off stage' –
illustrates that they were taking no prisoners either, that as far as
they were concerned they were already a great band, though they
were wary of pushing themselves too far too soon. Peter later noted,
'We decided right from the start that we'd take our time rather than
rush things and make mistakes. We actually held off signing
contracts and doing tours that took us to New York until we were
absolutely certain about what we were doing.' In fact, they did a
showcase in New York with Gang of Four in June 1981 which won
them a good review in the *Village Voice*, starting a buzz around the
band further afield.

While things were picking up speed, one area which did initially
give cause for concern was songwriting. Their travelling itinerary
didn't give them a huge amount of time to write material, while
back in Athens their rehearsal space was 'so cold that we couldn't
work there' according to Mike. With their perennial ability to
fashion the best from difficult situations, R.E.M. chose to write
songs in soundchecks, a habit that has persisted to the current day
with 'Belong' and 'Low' from *Out Of Time* having been tried out
on the *Green* tour, for instance. Early songwriting was fraught with
difficulty from a technical viewpoint, too, as initially, the band

really didn't know how to go about the process. It was only by playing covers together that they developed a musical direction.

Peter explained to *NME* that they became 'known as a guitar band but to me the thing that's interesting is the way the rhythm section works; the drums and bass are locked in, like Motown, but the bass is doing this melodic stuff against what I'm doing . . . it's more of a lead instrument . . . I play the beat more than he does, he does melodies, harmonies, the guitar goes more with the bass drum which is completely the opposite of what you should do in rock'n'roll.' Returning the compliment, Mike argued, 'I wouldn't be able to play this really melodic bass if it wasn't for Peter's guitar . . . [he] plays a constant solo so rather than have a thumping bass, I'm just as free to work around the melody as he is.' The mutual support that each offered was indicative of both their affection for one another and their refusal to accept starring roles, playing down the absurdity of the situation. That was apparent in the verdict of the group's nominal 'star turn', Michael Stipe: 'The background vocals really carry this band. Mike and Bill both have this amazing harmonic idea about vocals. A lot of the time I think the lead vocals take the place of the drums and the drums are there providing some sort of rhythm, along with the vocal and Mike is providing melody with the bass and Peter is doing this rhythm on top.'

Essentially, R.E.M.'s early approach to songwriting was to make the most of their strengths and dismiss their limitations. By playing concert after concert, ideas began to take shape but it still remained difficult for them. Michael remembered later that the first thirty or so songs they wrote were 'dry runs', though the R.E.M. work ethic ensured that they kept on writing as many songs as they could. After about three or four months, they produced the first song with which they were reasonably satisfied, 'Gardening At Night', which was to appear on the debut *Chronic Town* mini album. This was Michael's first stab at the non-linear lyricism for which he later became so celebrated; prior to this his words had been pretty much standard pop fare, a convention from which he was desperately keen to break free – as Peter advised, 'Don't tell people what they already know.' Stipe was expressing his own artistic leanings as well as giving R.E.M. a highly distinctive personality. In honour of this success the band named their publishing company Night Garden and it was a reasonably impressive first step which augured well for their future, a strikingly original number couched in traditional terms. It showcased all the elements that were to finally bring the group to prominence: Peter's guitar had the same ringing clarity that The Edge had achieved for U2, though in a very different style; Bill's drum pattern was engagingly odd; and Mike's bassline was the centre of attention. On top of these diverse instruments, all of which appeared to be doing precisely what they shouldn't, Michael's adumbrative vocal both irritated and intrigued as the listener tried to come to terms with what he was saying and what it meant anyway. Peter eventually explained it as covering the futility of everything.

As R.E.M. began to add more and better material to their sets, their popularity steadily increased, even in Athens itself, where the art crowd was starting to come to terms with the band's sound and approach. Paradoxically, their original material was going down well elsewhere, too. 'We were always the anomaly,' stressed Buck to *Sounds*. 'A bar band that played originals. We just liked to turn up, do our three sets and see what happened ... Playing in bars really teaches you how to do it. I remember one time we're in this bar and these guys are shouting for "Sweet Home Alabama" by Lynyrd Skynyrd. I just shouted, "We don't play songs by dead bands!" That coulda got ugly. Mind you, there were only four in the audience at the time.'

This eighteen months of constant touring around the South was the making of R.E.M.. The hard knocks that a working band has to take threw them closer together as people; the workload provided them with excellent practice, turning them into a stunningly powerful live force; and their songwriting improved on the way, as they took on board what did and didn't work in front of an audience. But the South was of far more value to them than its generous offer of glorified rehearsal opportunities. As Buck later accepted:

It's a place where you don't have to be professional right away, you can take a few years and play in clubs and bars. It's not like playing in New York where people are there right from your first show. We played pizza parlours for a year and a half before anyone heard of us. It gave us time to become a good band ... we [did] this four days a week playing throughout the South and nobody hears about it 'cause it's the South. But that's equally valid, if not more so. The people in New York who like us one month might not like us the next.

Mike concurred with these sentiments, adding, 'I think being able to grow in the anonymity of the South was very constructive.'

The environment was also creatively stimulating. Michael in particular developed a great affinity for the area, possibly because it was the first time in his life when he had been able to take stock of one area for any prolonged period, or perhaps it was because of his ancestry. 'My great-grandfather and his wife [a Cherokee Indian] lived on Black Mountain [North Carolina] ... I go up to Black Mountain every now and then. It makes me feel really good ... my grandfather was a South Georgia preacher, very backwoods churches, and as a child that interested me, gave me an extroverted front. It has seeped into the way that I perform I think, there's a preacherly quality in there.' However he avers, 'I'm not a Christian, I don't follow any organized religion *per se*.' Michael wasn't the only member of the group to be attracted by aspects of religious ceremony. Peter explains, 'I'd probably be a Christian if I was black because the music is so exciting I would never have got past that. It's full of exactly what you want from rock'n'roll, the passion, the involvement, the excitement ... that's part of what religion, for that part of the culture, is for; it's a reconciliation of a tough world with something that's better.' That established strain of exuberant religious teaching was allied to the traditions of the area itself as Michael confirms: 'There's a very wonderful tradition of old storytelling, I think it comes with every culture but in the South it's been kind of built up into a wonderful thing. In a way, I think I am carrying on that tradition. Although I'm not really telling stories because I've never been fond of songs which have a storyline.'

He was happy to go further in his warm appreciation of his adopted home, telling Adam Sweeting in *Melody Maker*:

> I'm a great believer in colloquialism and not only in language. If I came from Los Angeles I would definitely have some very different ideas about particular things, just because living in such different places as a small town in the South or Los Angeles or New York or Philadelphia – or even a large town in the South ... there's so many differences just in day-to-day living.

Black Mountain had a part to play in that history:

When Hitler took over Germany a lot of people from the

Bauhaus movement came to America and settled in Black Mountain working for the college. The place was a breeding ground for the forerunners to Ginsberg and Kerouac ... it's kind of amazing to me that first the Indians were attracted to the place. Then all these artists and poets arrived. And later the Bauhaus people settled, probably the most inspired group of architects and artists. They all wound up there.

This cross-pollination of cultures adds another clue as to how R.E.M. came up with such an unusual collection of European and American styles in their work.

Musically too, the rich heritage of the South has provided R.E.M. with much from which to draw. Certainly their leanings towards a folkier feel in their earlier days were totally out of keeping with the times, and much of this inspiration came from the world around them, although Peter also insisted that it was as much the influence of Richard Thompson, his favourite musician, as anything else. Whatever the case, in the early '80s R.E.M. were restoring a degree of humanity to a musical landscape that was increasingly mechanized, and it was perhaps this quality, together with the all-consuming energy with which they approached live performance, that made them such a popular live group. Mike summed it up, remarking, 'I just think rock'n'roll is the coolest thing in the world. Not all of it, but a lot of it.'

If the rest of the group were fans of The Band and of English equivalents such as Fairport Convention, Michael's folk roots were a little more esoteric, leading him towards the indigenous cultures that surrounded him in the South. 'I do like that kind of homespun feeling and I'm glad it shows. I'm proud of it,' he told *Melody Maker* in 1985. A little later, he remarked, 'There's a man I know who plays the guitar outside Columbus, Georgia, and has an Appalachian porch band together. He's a seventy-five-year-old and he's probably been playing for fifty years. He's always been there and I respect anything that's absolutely genuine. I truly admire the primitive and raw compared to the kind of homogenized sounds we're inundated with ... we try to carry on the traditions of something simpler and felt, traditions that are lost like storytelling.' Though this was to become clearest with *Fables Of The Reconstruction*, R.E.M. have always carried that cultural fascination.

'I listen to a lot of Appalachian mountain music, it's very strong in my past and it has a real, direct appeal to me,' Michael informed *Hot Press*. 'A lot of my older friends play folk instruments and they're totally unabashed about picking up a fiddle or harmonica and just blasting out their entire repertoire of songs at you on any given occasion. It can be very numbing and alarming sometimes but it's also very entertaining and very beautiful . . . it's becoming more rare. Because Georgia is so rural, there is a real propensity for people to create their own entertainment.' The influence of his surroundings is plain to see in those words, hinting at the roots for the band's support of environmental concerns, having been so close to a natural setting, rather than an urban one, in Athens.

Such is Stipe's affection for the South, he and the rest of the group have become virtual ambassadors for the area. He has often reacted angrily – or as near to angrily as his extreme courtesy will allow him to show – when confronted with stereotypes such as the South's supposedly insidious racism.

> It's something that's really not quite fair. I think that culturally speaking, blacks and whites have lived together for a long, long time and even the Native Americans too. The way the cultures have swapped with each other historically in that part of the world makes it difficult to make that easy a division. I would go so far as to say that there were a lot of places in the United States and certainly in the world that have much worse and much more obvious racial problems than the South.

R.E.M. came across as gentlemen, in the old Southern meaning of the term, and it has shaped their philosophy which Michael was happy to outline, 'R.E.M. aren't an overtly political band but their sentiment is an elegy for the simple man.' The next step in making that elegy available beyond their immediate locale was to make some recordings.

3

BESIDE YOURSELF

A hundred gigs or so had certainly toughened up the young R.E.M., and by now they had a healthy number of original songs. Their songwriting had advanced considerably; the first weeks of 1981 presented them with 'Radio Free Europe' which surpassed anything else they'd written, pointing them in the direction of the studio. They had already made one tape back at Tyrone's in the autumn of 1980 comprising eight songs, 'Dangerous Times', 'All The Right Friends', 'Different Girl', 'Narrator', 'Just A Touch', 'Baby I', 'Mystery To Me' and 'Permanent Vacation'. This was primitive even by garage band standards and was merely used as a calling card to get gigs out of Athens.

The tape was totally unrepresentative of the band by early '81, so a new demo was urgently recorded. On 8 February 1981, they travelled to Atlanta to spend a day working on eight songs at Joe Perry's Bombay Studios where they recorded 'Sitting Still', 'Gardening At Night', 'Radio Free Europe', 'Shaking Through', 'Mystery To Me', 'Rockville', 'Narrator' and 'White Tornado'. Naive about the tricks of the studio trade, R.E.M. later reported that their performance had been 'inept' and, having had thoughts about releasing a single from these recordings, they quickly shelved the tape on Jefferson's recommendation. He simply refused to send it to booking agencies and record companies, feeling that it might do more harm than good.

With the band maintaining their concert profile, money remained in short supply as everything they earned was eaten up by the running costs incurred on the road. Desperate to compile a demo that carried the same impact as a live show, Jefferson contacted

Peter Holsapple from The dBs, who was later to augment R.E.M.'s live sound. On his suggestion, Jefferson called Mitch Easter who had opened the Drive-In studio in Winston-Salem in North Carolina, which had a sixteen-track facility. Easter's initial attraction was that his studio was cheap, he understood their musical drive and was easy to work with, having played in a number of bands himself. Their lesson learned from the Bombay session, this time, on 15 April, the band chose to work on just three songs, 'Radio Free Europe', 'Sitting Still' and 'White Tornado'.

Having given themselves time to record properly, the results matched the quality of the raw material and around 400 promotional tapes were made up and distributed to various journalists and venue owners; it was this tape that alerted the *Village Voice* to R.E.M.'s New York gig with Gang of Four, ensuring favourable reviews. It's to their credit that the rave response they got in New York didn't go to their heads; many bands might have moved North to capitalize on their new-found fame, but R.E.M. still felt that they weren't ready for the spotlight and that they still had much to learn. Even so, given the impressive reception accorded to the tape, they were looking to put out a debut single to spread the word still further and to help band funds.

'Radio Free Europe' was the obvious choice as a single, but first they needed to find a company to produce it for them. Wisely, they had no truck with any of the big record companies that had already expressed an interest on the basis of the New York shows. To sign a long-term deal at such an early stage in their careers might have left them submerged within a huge roster and without the promotional attention required to help them cross over to a larger audience. Instead, they wanted to release the single as a one-off deal. Around the same time, an Atlanta law student, Jonny Hibbert, was toying with the idea of launching his own record label. He'd heard all about R.E.M. and the way in which they were staking out a claim to being Georgia's finest. Thoroughly unimpressed by the group, he was taken by the fervour of the crowd and, doing a few mental calculations, realized that a single by this group might sell well and give his new label a healthy start.

R.E.M. liked the idea of working with local people and were also taken by the idea of an independent trying to make his way in the world. Once Hibbert approached them with the idea of the Hib-Tone label they were completely sold on it, and gave him the publishing rights to both 'Radio Free Europe' and 'Sitting Still' in return for further studio time to re-record these two tracks for the single. In the studio on 25 May they didn't start from scratch, but merely tinkered with the mix of the original Drive-In songs, coming up with a version that both the group and Mitch Easter disliked but which excited Hibbert. Easter later sent a further mix on to the band which they much preferred, but Hibbert used his casting vote – based on financial clout – to go with the May mix.

With a group as committed to their own sense of what was right and wrong as R.E.M. were, it was pretty obvious that the relationship with Hibbert would not survive this argument: this was the only record they made together. Further frustrations crept in: it was frequently unavailable in record shops, and often had to be repressed since Hibbert couldn't afford to make too many at one time. However, it was the choice of take that ruined things for R.E.M.. Peter later complained:

We hated it. It wasn't anyone's fault, it was lack of money, but it was mastered by a deaf man apparently – that's what it sounds like! The thing is none of us could afford to re-do it and it was like, 'God, this isn't what it should be.' At least it wasn't our first album. A lot of bands have their first albums come out awful, this was just our first single which sold zero and a half copies. It was a nice calling card and I think the version that ended up on CD is a little clearer than the one that was the single. The actual single just sounded like valleys of mud, it was just depressing.

One of the things that has helped R.E.M. in their remorseless march to success has been their solidarity and their willingness to act once a decision has been taken. Initially happy to have struck the deal with Hibbert, they pressed on with the remix and made the best of things. Once they discovered that his view of the group wasn't in unison with their own, however, Hibbert was quickly banished from the scene. They took their Hib-Tone contract to a fan from Athens, lawyer Bertis Downs, who was horrified at the implications of the contract, explaining that the band's publishing rights were their greatest asset. Downs' advice was probably the most prescient the band ever received. Working for free to begin with, although he became their official lawyer later on, he set up their own publishing company – Night Garden; their own corporation – R.E.M./Athens Limited; and registered the band's name. These building blocks ensured that when R.E.M. became a hot property all the corporate mechanisms were in place to ensure that they got the best possible deals.

Despite their reputation as nice guys, they could be tough too. After their defection from Hib-Tone and in the wake of other record industry interest in the group, Hibbert found himself in straitened financial circumstances. He started to tout the publishing rights for the two songs to other interested parties for $10,000. R.E.M. were furious, feeling that he'd not only taken advantage of their naivety earlier on but had sabotaged their first single release with his poor mix selection. Wanting to ensure that there were no loose ends trailing in their wake should they go on to greater glory, they offered Hibbert $2000 for the publishing rights and the rights to the single. Hibbert asserts that he was 'persuaded' by a friend of Peter's, who was now writing for *Rolling Stone*, to accept the offer. In return he was granted a reputation for fair dealing. He was now history and the group could forge ahead, unfettered by worries of old tapes coming back to haunt them. It's undeniable that R.E.M.'s action was justified; had they left the rights with Hibbert, he would almost certainly have exploited them to the full in subsequent years, but the aggressive swiftness of their actions clearly revealed an iron resolve behind their friendly exterior. Similarly, Peter Buck's absolute refusal to ever record 'Radio Free Europe' again without the return of their publishing rights also indicates a group completely assured of their eventual commercial success.

Even if the mix could have been better on 'Radio Free Europe', they did Hibbert something of a disservice, for it was this release that paved the way for their future. In time, 'Radio Free Europe' came to be seen as one of those great, seminal singles and it certainly laid down an R.E.M. archetype that ran through the early years of their recording career. As first recorded evidence of their songwriting ability and their extraordinarily defined sound, the Hib-Tone single crashed through preconceptions of some hick Southern group. Peter vented his spleen on that front, saying, 'Everyone in the North still thinks we wear bib overalls and chew tobacco and burn crosses on people's lawns all night long. I think they were kinda surprised that we put out a record that didn't necessarily bear out Southern stereotypes.' By the end of 1981 *Village Voice* had named the single as one of America's greatest ever, and the *New York Times* more soberly placed it among their Top Ten singles of the year. Suddenly, R.E.M. began to find themselves the centre of record company attention.

Stipe's lyrics were almost entirely incomprehensible, which upped the enigma stakes right away. Forced into listening to the record more intently than most standard rock fare, those who took the trouble were rewarded with a dense mixture of sounds that gradually released surprise after surprise on each subsequent airing, Easter's excellent production allowing sounds to overlap while still charting out their own distinct space. In the light of the rich music on offer, it was an adroit decision not to detract from that with any overbearing vocal pyrotechnics, though Michael insisted, 'I purposely did not want any of the lyrics understood. The main reason for that was that I hadn't written any of the words yet so I just kind of blabbed over the whole single.' Mitch Easter demurs however, telling *Mojo*, 'Michael's lyrics really were lyrics – they really were written down ... but because everybody liked the band's mysteriousness they blew it up even more. Maybe there was a bit of vocal improvising but for the most part he had lyrics.'

Michael wasn't the only star of the show, as all four contributed equally to the single's impact. Peter's jangling twelve-string presented him with a straitjacket labelled 'King of Byrds' from which it took him years to wriggle free, Bill's drums were almost a lead instrument at times and Mike's melodic bass just jumped out of the speakers. Most interesting of all were the vocals being cooked up in the background. Certainly they didn't get the prominence that they would later receive, as they were almost buried beneath layers of sound, but they nagged away, insisting that they might actually be the core of the track. What was equally startling was the understated nature of what was, after all, a real rock song. At the time of its release, new wave had deteriorated into wimpy synthesized drivel, while the rock format was formularized into hectoring noise that did away with the need to think or process any further musical information. R.E.M. had studied popular music history enough to know that in the long run, subtlety usually wins. All the accolades that have been heaped on 'Radio Free Europe' over the years are deserved, even if there was a degree of cynicism in its release – radio stations just love records that mention them. Once 'Radio Free Europe' was released, it was no longer a question of 'if' for R.E.M.. It was 'when'.

The 'when' was of course a little further in the future, but the single's release in July helped them engineer more and more bookings, taking them on to the road in earnest. Touring proved to be the R.E.M. way to gain respect and improve their music, although it was hard work. As Peter explained:

We're just determined not to get ripped off and not to be turned into something that we're not ... I don't want to be like Van Morrison, just sit on a ranch and put out one record a year with a horrible cover. I don't mind devoting seventy hours a week to what I do. I don't mind doing fifteen-hour drives from Georgia to New York for a gig ... if R.E.M. wanted to be one of those bands that got rich quick we could bend over enough ways to do it. But that's not the idea ... we're still basically a touring band, that's what we do.

Concerned with the 'authentic' nature of their rock'n'roll muse, there were no quick fixes as far as they were concerned. If 'Radio Free Europe' had brought in more concerts, the extra money they made was ploughed back into the group in the form of better instruments, or set aside to fund further recording sessions. Not that all their concerts were lucrative money-spinners, however, for, as Buck reflected later, 'We toured just to play, we had a natural organic growth.' More candidly he admitted, 'We had to [tour]. We were broke and had to sell some fucking records so, "Sure, we'll play the pizza parlour" ... we played more gay bars than you could shake a stick at.' Other Spinal Tapesque stories inevitably surfaced as Buck was only too pleased to relate.

We played in an Air Force base in Wichita Falls, Texas and we were getting death threats. They were passing notes 'If you play one more song like this, you die faggots!' So me and Michael kissed one another. After that though we probably played the best show of the tour ... we were also playing a lot of semi-biker bars, places where when Blackfoot doesn't tour any more you can maybe get a gig on a Tuesday night. We had to beat them over the head with the beat because if they didn't know who you were, they didn't want to hear no love songs. We've never been beaten up at a club. But boy have we been threatened.

This view of themselves as a working group gave them an anchor and proved that they were dedicated to their craft. Buck said, 'Whether or not we're successful, we're going to be around for quite a while.' By this stage though, his self-effacing modesty was applied for effect rather than from any uncertainty, for by October 1981 they were back in tandem with Mitch Easter to record another set of songs. Surprisingly, the sessions took place with a view to another small label release, this time on Dasht Hopes, owned and run by David Healey. Like Jefferson, he'd seen R.E.M. at an out-of-town show, this time in New Jersey, and almost immediately decamped to Athens. The difference between Healey and Hibbert was one of friendship. Healey was already close friends with the group before the idea of a record label came up and promised them artistic control. The fact that he had greater resources to pay for the recording and manufacture of records did not escape the group's attention either.

With experience of the studio behind them by now, they were happy to break the rules, egged on by the iconoclastic Easter, and five songs were put together over four days. 'Ages Of You', '1,000,000', 'Stumble', 'Gardening At Night' and 'Carnival Of Sorts (Box Cars)' were committed to tape, virtually the *Chronic Town* set that would be released the following year, while '9-9' was abandoned part way through the sessions. This desire to record coupled with their feverish songwriting pace began to betray the fact that R.E.M. were beginning to tire of concerts and wanted to push their career up to the next level. Working on the basis that the record companies wouldn't go South to see them in their natural habitat and given that gigs in the North were harder to come by, the band felt that further demos would do the trick – after all, the release of 'Radio Free Europe' had lit a fire among those interested in music a little beyond the usual. R.E.M. had as a result become something of a college radio staple, having themselves spent years listening to the form. Among the more astute members of the record industry there was a dawning realization that this kind of radio might just be showcasing the coming wave of music that would dominate the second half of the '80s.

Jefferson and the band were gradually focusing on the national rather than local horizon and, in hindsight, you have to question whether or not they were ever really sincere about releasing anything through Dasht Hopes. It may be that they were simply using Healey's enthusiasm and money as a tool to help them accumulate studio experience and compile a new set of original material to hawk around the larger companies. Certainly they didn't pull out of any prospective deal with him until they had assured their future elsewhere, whereupon he was dropped without ceremony. By this time, he had financed two further Drive-In sessions, one each in January and February, which yielded the tapes that would make up *Chronic Town*.

The treatment of Hibbert and Healey was rough, to say the least, since each had been only too willing to put up some money to help an impoverished R.E.M. on their way. How badly this reflects on the band is a moot point. As brand new labels, neither Hib-Tone nor Dasht Hopes were ever going to take R.E.M. beyond the circuit they had already conquered and so, artistically, the group had to move on. Playing the same places over and over would have led to creative atrophy and might even have split the group. Nevertheless, the merciless way in which they despatched the two to the history books was at odds with their perceived image and gave a firm sign that these boys weren't to be trifled with. To prevent artistic compromise they would do whatever they had to do in the business field to get ahead. That has been good news for the listening public who have been privileged to hear a group that have kept their musical integrity intact, but it has caused a lot of anguish to a few people the band encountered on the way up.

Even though the Dasht Hopes tapes were impressive fare, RCA were the only one of the big boys to bite. Though they went as far as to put R.E.M. into the studio to make further demos in February 1982. This was R.E.M.'s first experience of a New York studio, and RCA house producer Kurt Monkacsi was pleasantly surprised by their ability and experience. He in turn spruced up the band's sound, making them a more readily identifiable rock'n'roll band, free of any studio trickery and presented in an almost live fashion. The sound was more commercial, but in the translation the heart of the songs had been lost. Peter spoke for the group when he complained about the production polish: 'Music should reach out to people ... I think that anything that reaches out and touches people emotionally is doing a service whether people understand why it's moving them or not. We always wanted our music to have heart, you know. That's why we sometimes sound a little weird or cranky 'cause we always try to leave the heart in.'

The musical viewpoint was not the only difficulty, since the band found themselves waiting and waiting for answers to filter down the RCA hierarchy, leaving an impatient R.E.M. unimpressed and looking to cast their net further afield in the hope of finding salvation elsewhere. Peter turned this disappointment into triumph by arguing: 'RCA had courted us ... it was a surprise because we expected small label interest but IRS were the smallest one to approach us. But if we'd been on RCA our album would've come out the same week as a Scotty Baio album. Now I don't have a whole lotta dignity, it's just that I would prefer to have our record sold by people used to selling things like us.'

IRS was a relatively new organization set up by Miles Copeland. An independent, it was still a powerful player in the marketplace by virtue of Copeland's own personality and network of contacts built up during his days as manager with The Police. Miles knew the record industry inside out and he also knew how to get the best out of it; his experience of the preceding decade had shown that taking the long view could be just as successful as compromising for short-term advantage. Miles had been made aware of R.E.M. by his brother Ian, who had passed a tape on to him at Bill's request. Ian remembers, 'Miles made the mistake I would have made. I said these were friends from Macon and I don't think he ever listened to it, just wrote it off as me trying to push some buddies.' He remembers, 'Miles had this all-girl group called The Bangs and I didn't really want to handle them [at FBI] so I did a deal with him, "I'll do The Bangs if you sign R.E.M.." And The Bangs turned out to be The Bangles and R.E.M. were very beneficial for IRS so it was a good deal all round!'

Ian Copeland is staunch in sticking to this story, but others have a different view. Jay Boberg was vice-president of IRS and had been vaguely interested by the promise of the 'Radio Free Europe' single. Keeping tabs on the band over the next few months, he recognized that their music had a tendency to grow on you with repeated playings and felt that this boded well for their artistic and commercial future. Boberg offered to sign R.E.M. to a five album deal, preceded by the release of the demo they'd been hawking around. When he went to Miles Copeland to ratify the deal, Miles was finally forced to accept that both Boberg and Ian might have been right after all and agreed to take on R.E.M.. With the IRS deal in the bag, the group had put the trials and tribulations of Hib-Tone and Dasht Hopes behind them and were on their way.

It has subsequently been suggested that IRS was the only label for the nascent R.E.M., and in hindsight it's clear that it was an ideal match. But it isn't true that IRS were the only label they would have considered. As Buck later professed, had RCA been a little quicker off the mark and actually made them an offer, it's quite possible that they would have put their misgivings aside and taken the chance. It's apparent that dreams of avarice were not the biggest motivator behind R.E.M. but money did play its part – they had to eat, had to be able to record and wanted to put records out. Any company that could have fulfilled those criteria would have merited due consideration. However, the kind of musical interference that goes with a major label deal would not have suited R.E.M., so any such contract might have been short-lived. In the end, IRS was the best place for such a wilful group as Miles Copeland explained: 'R.E.M. were one of the very rare groups who practised what they preached. They never walked into our office and said, "Why aren't you doing this? Why aren't you doing that? Why don't we have more money?" Never once. [They chose] to take it slow, do it under your own steam, break every rule, not worry about image, all that sort of stuff.'

IRS as a label gave them that level of freedom while it also bestowed on them a kudos that an association with RCA could never have given. R.E.M. responded by putting into action all the good advice that Downs and Holt had given them, by being financially responsible and concerning themselves with their music first and foremost. Any bigger label might have brought in the stylists, the video directors and the glamorous backing singers, but IRS let them go about things their own way. 'I wondered about those obscure videos they were doing,' Miles conceded to *Mojo*, 'but they were the only act, apart from Sting, that I can think of that actually said, "We'll pay the price: if it isn't a hit then it isn't a hit and if it's a hit, great" . . . I still think if they had made a few concessions we would have had success earlier.'

'Concessions' wasn't a word in the group's vocabulary at this stage, though. Sure of their ability, courtesy of their bar circuit training, and now secure with a five album deal under their belt, R.E.M. had the time to sit back and let things unfold. There was no sign of any creeping indolence, as they continued to write and play as long and hard as they could, but they were happy that by the end of the five album contract, R.E.M. would have made a mark. At this point, their roles in the public mind were starting to harden. Michael was the serious artist who was the most important part of the package, Peter was the rocker who eschewed compromise in any form, Mike was the studious muso and Bill the down-to-earth drummer who held everything together. Naturally, these roles were no more than Monkees-like cartoons. Certainly Michael's performance was a little off the wall, and eyecatching as a result, but it was grounded in the atmosphere that the others provided for him as musicians and as people. If anything, Bill had to take more credit for hauling the group up to its new status by his hard grafting behind the scenes early on and his contacts with influential people like Ian Copeland.

A striking feature of the young group was the number of people who became fanatical about them. As far as US groups are concerned, R.E.M. were trailblazers of a sort, for very few groups had put themselves through the same apprenticeship. In their wake, it's become a common attitude to take to the road and build a live following but US music had previously been geared to starting a group, playing support shows with big name acts and then getting on to television and radio. R.E.M.'s desire to play for people was a very British approach, following in the footsteps of groups as far back as The Beatles and right through to the punk scene and beyond. The Police must have been influential here too, for they conquered the US by playing anywhere and everywhere in the late '70s, a blueprint that U2 followed in the early '80s. By playing small towns, they were putting a face to the name of R.E.M. and generating mass enthusiasm among people who would normally have to travel miles to see a real rock group. R.E.M. were, to coin a phrase, men of the people, what we might call working-class heroes insofar as they went out to see the people that bought their records and had a close, intimate relationship with them. Reflecting later, Michael remarked, 'In America, I don't think what we've done has ever been done before on the level we've got to.' R.E.M. worked hard and people respected them for that.

With their very human approach which offered a curious mixture of hard-nosed realism and effervescent escapism, R.E.M. struck a chord in an America that was going through the Reagan years. As Michael said when discussing his dreams, 'When I sleep, it's pretty much a clearing house for everything that's come at me. I feel very bombarded by the twentieth century in general and I accept it and I revel in it, but I also often feel like a victim of it. I think that's a very common thing, whether people recognize it or not, or choose to discuss it or not.' Since they were tapping into such concerns, fans held them close to their hearts. Their trust was repaid in August 1982 when *Chronic Town* was released to rapturous reviews.

Chronic Town was, of course, a watershed, getting the group noticed on a wider level, racking up more than 20,000 sales in the year. It gave notice that R.E.M. had a decent range of material and were more than competent performers. It provided a neat contrast to the frantic action of their live set, the songs a little more considered and rounded with the opportunities that a recording studio offered gratefully accepted. The EP opened beautifully with Buck's elegant guitar figure ushering in Michael's vocal on 'Wolves, Lower'. As Mitch Easter later remarked, Michael's vocals were as upfront as any Tom Jones record, but somehow his delivery was indistinct and the lyrics hard to catch. As already intimated, the harmonies were integral to this first song, the gorgeous interplay between Mike and Michael setting the tone for many pieces in the future.

'Wolves, Lower' was an excellent introduction to the band, distilling all their most prominent features into one song – an oddball title, harmony vocals, Peter's nagging guitar, solid but inventive rhythm section and a vocal coming out of the mists. It also provided them with their first attempt at the promotional video, Michael lip-syncing along during a mimed performance before deciding that 'I couldn't hack it'.

Chronic Town was marked by R.E.M.'s willingness to experiment and push the boundaries of the songs further. 'Carnival of Sorts (Box Cars)' began in the style of The Beatles' 'Being For The Benefit Of Mr. Kite!', with its hurdy-gurdy sound, introducing the listener to an assortment of sound effects used throughout the EP. Most striking was the generosity of the musicians: each had an opportunity to take a leading role with the other three providing a safety net as one stepped to the forefront.

Listening to the EP over twelve years later, it is striking that the band seem totally unselfconscious and thoroughly conversant with one another's foibles as well as their talents. They do sound like a group that have played a couple of hundred shows together and have an intuitive grasp of what each might do, yet there is no impression of their being tired or jaded as their workload might have implied. *Chronic Town* is refreshingly free of cynicism, bursting with ideas and excitement. More than anything else, it emphasizes that R.E.M. were an indivisible unit, a point Michael echoes: 'What we as a group create is much more exciting than what any of us are as people . . . I have no idea why it works but there is a definite chemistry that works between the four that doesn't when any one of us isn't there.'

Mitch Easter recalled the sessions 'completely fondly because it was so relaxed, and so open to cutting the tape up and putting pieces in backwards and stuff'. Peter accepted that 'we want to try and capture the essence of our live show on record without just sounding like a band thrashing away' and Mike, a little more bluntly, admitted that 'the more you do it, the less spontaneous it becomes and it sounds like you're trying real hard to get it perfect ... if you just go in and knock out the tracks and vocals which is what we do, then you can spend some more of your time playing pool'. 'Stumble' caught that slightly frivolous mood nicely with its faltering introduction. While in keeping with the other four songs, it contained an irresistible chorus, this time it was Mike's bass that framed it rather more than the guitar. In retrospect, it's hard to see quite why people found the record so 'difficult' although admittedly the obscure titles didn't help. Even so, it sounds like a compilation of greatest hits, full of top-class singles that could have done well and been worthy successors to 'Radio Free Europe'; Michael's blurred vocals were the only hindrance in broad commercial terms, yet that elliptical quality was the source of their greatest strength.

The commercial nature of the material in general was lost in the rush of people trying to crawl into Michael's mind and uncover exactly what he was singing about, his frame of reference, his motives, his sanity. He laid the reasons for his vocal style partly at the door of live performance, telling *NME*,

A lot of newer bands go into the studio with a name producer and come out with this amazingly plush and over-produced sound which they then try to recreate on stage and that seems to rob them of any spontaneity ... it seems to me important to start with the live show and then go into the studio ... I think if the band didn't sound the way it does I would probably sing in a different way. The vocal sound came out of there being a necessity for a vocal sound like that.

There was a grain of truth to these assertions but it would be naive to accept Stipe's denial of artifice at face value. The band as a whole were clued in to the machinations of popular music and the way in which groups build. Mystery was important and having inaudible vocals meant that people had to listen more carefully, making a commitment to the group in the process. This has been the keystone in R.E.M.'s evolution, a reciprocal commitment between band and audience, neither taking the other for granted and both putting in a lot of effort. *Chronic Town* was the clearest indication that R.E.M. were actively trying to discourage any mainstream acceptance but instead were looking to build a group in comfortable, manageable steps, taking their fans with them on an interesting journey rather than simply dropping the occasional single on them from afar.

There were occasions when they tried to play down their burgeoning reputation as seers and sages, but on others they positively encouraged it, fostering the impression that these were serious young men whose music demanded some sort of intellectual engagement. Peter, for instance, explained, 'We're certainly not setting out to be deliberately obscure but you have to short-circuit the whole idea that literal language is what things are because literal language is just codes for what happens. Without wanting to sound too arty about it, to by-pass actions and go straight to the results is what we're trying to do, to make people feel moved by something without them even being sure of what we're writing about.' Statements such as this only endeared them to the college crowd that made up a sizeable and exponentially increasing section of their audience. Their lyrical ambiguity was sometimes a little too calculated for some tastes, but it served its purpose in attracting those that wanted to think about music rather than merely experiencing it as an adrenalin rush. The great thing about R.E.M. was that they were able to build both components into one song.

Bill defended Michael's performance in *Melody Maker*: 'Michael gets criticized because people say they can't understand what it is he's singing but I wouldn't want him to sing any other way.' Stipe was in more defiant mood, arguing that

> too much, too often, these days is simply handed to an audience. MTV is a good example, television generally is a good example. There's no room for imagination, no room for improvisation, for interpretation. Everything is rehearsed. No-one's able to find out anything for themselves. It's all become a little too easy. People need to think for themselves again, use their imaginations and not necessarily in an intellectual way 'cause we're not an intellectual band, we're not any of that shit ... we're just asking people to stretch themselves a little and put some of their own experience into the songs or take out of the songs what they recognize. If that means there's some philosophy that they dig out of the songs that's gonna change their lives, that's fine – but if they listen to those same songs and they make you wanna dance your damned ass off, then that's fine too. It might even be better.

Pretty clearly there was no hope of a lyric sheet appearing with future records. 'That would be like going to the movies and getting the script of the film with your ticket,' protested Berry. Michael stood firm too, adding, 'The words to the songs are just as much a part of it as the bass and there's no reason to separate the two.' Peter suggested, 'You should just listen to the songs and intuitively feel what they're about, get your own impressions of them.'

An attractive feature of R.E.M. is that it's often hard to tell whether or not they're being entirely serious. That reciprocal arrangement with their fans mentioned earlier meant that the group insisted that the hard-core element of the audience should put as much thought into their songs as the band themselves had done. At the same time, they also ensured that casual listeners had something to take from the records, be it the harmony vocals or a glistening guitar line. R.E.M. certainly were not an exclusive group, and had no time for the cliquishness that had disfigured the Athens scene, but they were simultaneously laying down just enough obstacles to prevent themselves becoming a household name. Everyone was welcome as long as they passed the entrance exam.

This determination not to 'sell out' is a trait that young bands hold to with great determination, but with R.E.M. it approached obsessive proportions, as if they had a point to prove. Indeed, they did want to make a point, as Mike later said, 'If anyone wants to respect us for anything apart from the music, I think the way we've achieved things has been important. You don't need all those haircuts and clothes and videos and stuff. You can just carry on on your own terms and get there in the end.' It's important to note that R.E.M. were not completely unworldly in their approach to the industry: the difference is they took the long view, accepting that 'hit' status would come later rather than sooner, finally arriving in the shape of 1987's 'Document'.

Maybe it was just that by 1987, R.E.M. had been knocking on the door of public consciousness for long enough to knock it down. They had also been a model of financial probity from the time they signed to IRS. As Miles Copeland admitted,

I didn't have to pay out huge sums of money or anything . . . so this was a profitable group from day one for everyone . . . they were not spending fortunes in the studio and were making money on the road because they didn't have expensive habits. So they were a good tight little business. They lived within their means and cut the cloth based on what they were going to generate which is how you're supposed to run a business.

As a band, with the help of Jefferson and Bertis, R.E.M. realized early on that financial independence was the fastest route to artistic freedom, an attribute they shared with The Cure who have followed a similar path to them in many respects. Perhaps R.E.M. were as uninterested in the material aspects of their lives as they liked to suggest, for they certainly could have made far more money than they have had they wanted to play the game. But they were not naive kids who got lucky; they made certain they weren't ripped off and had good business instincts, Bill in particular. So let's bury that unearthly reputation once and for all. Music and money are very different matters.

Back on the music front, *Chronic Town* had made its mark on the national scene, bearing out the band's wisdom in insisting on its release. It served as a useful trailer for their forthcoming album as well as getting more people into their live shows. By the end of 1982 however, that debut album required planning, with an April 1983 release date looming large.

4

SAY WHAT?

The more cynical observers suggested that *Chronic Town* represented the last independent hurrah from a group that, having made their statement, would now get down to the all-important task of conforming to music industry norms. This assertion gained a little further credence when, just prior to Christmas 1982, R.E.M. agreed to go into the studio with Stephen Hague at IRS's behest. Although the group made it clear that they would rather work with Mitch Easter, with whom they were both comfortable and confident, they quickly fell into line with IRS's wishes. Many took this as a signal that all their fine words about doing things their own way would lead to naught and that, as the record company cracked the financial whip, R.E.M. would jump. Hague's production talents were proven with The Human League's mainstream international success; his recruitment was seen as the abandonment of the incomprehensible in favour of a more obvious production centring around musical hooks and blatant call signs.

Whether R.E.M. were simply humouring the company, discharging an onerous obligation given IRS's generous decision to produce and promote *Chronic Town*, or whether they were genuinely interested in working with a more commercial producer is unclear, though the former seems probable, since they insisted that IRS bankroll a similar test session with Mitch Easter. The Hague sessions degenerated into musical fiasco − Hague's previous and, indeed, future clients, such as The Pet Shop Boys and New Order, were basically studio groups that relied on technology to construct their sound. In diametric opposition, R.E.M. were almost Luddite in approach and would resort to primitive effects to colour songs that were already fully formed after extensive road testing. Naturally enough, Hague simply followed his own methods of recording, working on the basis that he was being employed because of his track record and should stick to what he knew. He'd had a great deal of freedom in the past, working almost as an auteur and he came to these Boston-based trials with some very strong ideas of his own – even overdubbing synth parts on to 'Catapult'.

Electronic music and highly disciplined studio behaviour was not something to which R.E.M. took naturally in 1983. Don Dixon, who was to co-produce their first two albums with Mitch Easter, recalled, '[Hague] did the typical thing of making them do 390 takes and saying Berry sucked and trying to get them to change all their parts and everything – and they hated it.' With Hague's own input completely at odds with the sounds they were looking for, he clearly had no future with the band; insulting one of their number simply served to alienate them still further.

It was a foregone conclusion that they would make their album with Easter as far as they were concerned but the formality of a test session had to be endured first. Easter felt that IRS were liable to edge him out of the process, as they wanted to protect their investment by seeking the insurance of a name producer rather than a musician who ran his own studio and was a friend of the group. Never ones to avoid nepotism when a troublesome brother or nephew needs a job, record companies frown on incestuous behaviour from their artists. Fully aware that, although R.E.M. might be fighting his corner, his Drive-In studio would not meet IRS's more exacting standards, Easter suggested that they should record at Reflection in Charlotte, North Carolina which had a twenty-four-track set up. To further bolster his credibility, he recruited Don Dixon as co-producer. Dixon was an old school friend of Easter's and knew his way around a studio. Totally sympathetic with R.E.M.'s attitude, he and Easter made a formidable pairing.

Together they went through 'Pilgrimage' to present as evidence to IRS, although Dixon recalled working on several other songs. Faced with little alternative, IRS acceded to R.E.M.'s demand and the die was cast; indeed the recording of 'Pilgrimage' was so good that it went on to the album unchanged. With the benefit of hindsight it's hard to imagine that there was ever any doubt, for Dixon and Easter made an ideal pairing. 'The material was very prepared,' recalled Dixon. 'They were very limited musicians technically in some ways but the vision was very, very acute and that's what I'm always looking for.' With their communal distaste for commercially prepared music, the six fitted together exceptionally well, R.E.M. appreciating the producers' desire 'to leave as little imprint as possible. We felt like our job was to, as cheaply as possible, reproduce what appeared to be them just playing live,' as Dixon told *Mojo*.

Mitch Easter felt that the group had lost confidence over the Hague session and that he and Dixon had to rebuild their belief in themselves prior to recording anything. This was a relatively straightforward process, the internal relationships being so strong, and everyone heading in broadly the same direction. It is not beyond the realms of possibility that it was the determination of Easter and Dixon to help R.E.M. make an interesting record, ignoring the need to 'shift units', that finally gave the band its firmest vision of the future. Although they've regularly proclaimed that they dance to their own tune, there had been examples of weakened determination when IRS and RCA had become involved. Easter and Dixon as seasoned studio performers helped R.E.M. make a record that was honest to themselves, making it clear in the process that they need have no reservations about sticking to their guns. The reaffirmation that the two gave, insisting that R.E.M.'s principles and values were worth preserving, was of incalculable value to the band. In the wake of this, Peter was able to say:

Murmur was meant to be a textural-type record. Without really thinking about it we knew we didn't want to make the traditional first album which usually involves merely laying down the live act. We wanted to try something a bit different and the songs seemed to call for a textural approach so we used a lot of twelve-string guitar, piano and even some strings. Without it taking a firm approach, we wanted the album to be coherent in a way that meant you couldn't pick it up and say, 'I like this and I like this but I hate that bit.' It had to be something that fired you or else left you totally cold.

Later he was to add, '*Murmur* is more about warmth and things being together. It's not the kind of record where you sit and admire the pristine clarity of the separation. I mean, there's about twenty acoustic guitars on some tracks, it's supposed to be a mush. We worked really hard to get it to be a mush.'

Work on the album was begun in January and continued into the following month, though they didn't remain in the studio for that whole period because of outstanding concert commitments. The album's title, *Murmur*, was ideal on a number of levels, conjuring up the mumbled style of Michael's delivery and the indistinct, slightly out-of-focus sense of the music. Fighting shy of mysticism for once, Stipe noted, '*Murmur* is one of the six easiest words in the English language to say, I think it comes right after mama which is probably why it was picked. It's got nice implications I guess.' The sleeve was also picked as a metaphor of sorts, the kudzu apparently covering some solid construction, but without stripping the vine away, thereby depriving the scene of its beauty, it was impossible to tell just what was there.

As an album, *Murmur* carried that kind of deceptive simplicity that Stipe was suggesting, but the sound was remarkably rich and solidly constructed. When there was talk about getting the live R.E.M. down on to tape, Dixon had clearly been referring to the essence of the group, its ethics and values rather than a straight translation from the stage. As such, recording took a considerable period of time, but there was a great sense of enjoyment to the proceedings. Closeted away in North Carolina, the group were removed from all preconceptions and were free to compile exactly the record that they wanted. Having got the producers they'd hoped for, there would be no-one to blame but themselves if things went awry.

There seems to have been little chance of that happening, for the group approached recording in a very professional manner with a clear idea of the impression each song should create. There were some obvious cornerstones to the album: 'Radio Free Europe', of course, which would have to open the album; 'Talk About The Passion' was a strong piece, too; and they had a real ace in the hole in the shape of 'Perfect Circle', a song which is still as powerful as anything in their canon. The recording of 'Perfect Circle' was an excellent example of the open-minded manner in which the sessions progressed, as Don Dixon recalled in *Mojo*: 'Obviously we knew it couldn't be just them playing live because that would not be interesting enough. We played little things, parts here and there, I think [on "Perfect Circle"] where both Mike and Bill were playing keyboards, I'm playing bass on that and Mitch played a guitar part.' The way in which R.E.M. allowed Easter and Dixon to play on their album, the debut which must have been very close to their hearts, does bear out the fact that they are a strangely egoless group, willing to share the glory with other musicians, providing they approach the music in the requisite spirit.

'Perfect Circle' was an evocative piece, illustrating superbly the mesh of sound which R.E.M. could create. The song seems to mean nothing tangible in conventional songwriting terms, but has a singular poignancy about it, and is deeply moving. Talking about their work in general, Mike put his finger on the attraction of songs like this one: 'You don't have to understand all the words to get a good feeling or some kind of emotion from the songs. It's just the whole thing that affects you in the back of your mind and you can't explain why this song moves you or what exact sentence is so important, it's just the overall effect.' 'Perfect Circle' is emotionally charged, certainly, but this is a raw feeling rather than a wallow in shallow sentimentality. Like so many of R.E.M.'s strongest songs there's a warmth about the vocal, a compassion about the playing that envelops the listener; this song in particular would not have been out of place on *Automatic For The People*, although it has none of the directness of that album.

With 'Perfect Circle' there is no difficulty with Michael's diction: the words are clear and yet they refuse to lodge in the brain, as if mere semantics are incapable of carrying the emotional weight. Even within the group there was confusion – Michael stated that it was a song about an ex-girlfriend while Peter felt it detailed an experience of his own when he was transported by the sight of some children playing baseball. Outsiders had no chance of giving it a precise meaning, which was exactly the effect after which the band were striving. If R.E.M. had never written another song, 'Perfect Circle' would have justified their existence and marked them as a special talent. Peter's pride was thoroughly understandable: 'The first thing that really moved me was "Perfect Circle", that was the first time I thought we were a real band.'

With such a strong song as the beating heart of the album it was tribute to R.E.M.'s fund of material that the other tracks weren't swamped. *Murmur* is coherent, it consistently evokes mood and atmosphere, and has quirky humour and open passion. Everyone involved maintained the experimental attitude but they were smart enough to keep that in check, avoiding the trap of putting works-in-progress on tape. '9-9' was a track that was totally different from 'Perfect Circle'; this time the vocals were deliberately obscured to make a point, as Michael elaborated later: '"9-9" is a song about talking, about conversation and fear of conversation – it's not supposed to be understood; the only thing you can pick up on it is "conversation fear".' In other hands, this might have proved leaden, but such was their ease with the material, it came across as a mixture of bleak humour and social observation. Michael confessed, 'I watch people a lot. Three-quarters of my lyrics probably come from overheard conversations, though it's getting harder to steal because I can't go to parties without people wanting to talk about the band.'

A number of people picked up on the theme of travel and movement on *Murmur*, which Stipe professed not to have been aware of. However, he did admit: 'People have pointed out that many of the songs are about particular times in the life of the band. It's kind of nice to have a set of words which are so intensely personal that they become universal at the same time.' Having spent so much of his life as an itinerant, both as a child and now as a musician, it was little wonder that the idea of motion and travelling played on Michael's mind, though again there were no direct references. *Murmur* was a restless kind of record, not in any negative 'I'm so bored' way: rather it raced to the thrill of discovery, the urge to experience and to learn.

That was the magic of this first album. R.E.M. were learning about themselves, about their music and about their country; in the process, they held a mirror up to their audience and invited them to share the ride and see if they could use any of what R.E.M. had to say in their own lives. There were no instructions, no shouting, no orders, no pontificating; just a sequence of events that might or might not lead to a wider understanding of yourself. Unlike any other group of their time, R.E.M. were happy to let you take whatever you needed from them, determined that you should draw your own conclusions. This gave *Murmur*, and the albums that followed, a peculiarly timeless feel; when the dust settles on the routine promotional campaign for an album and the band has told you how to interpret their work, there's very rarely any need to listen to the record again. With *Murmur*, every time you hear it you can look for some nuance that you might have missed, some little clue as to a song's fuller purpose, a secondary emotion that the melody or the harmonies might trigger. As Dixon put it, 'Our job was to get the sound dense and interesting.'

'Pilgrimage' was definitely that. To begin with, it sounded like a Charlie Brown soundtrack but the lyric took it somewhere else,

Michael's apparent references to freaks of nature and the pilgrimage of the title hinting at superstitious acts of atonement, while the 'speaking in tongues' line presumably dealt with religious fervour. Given the folky treatment of the song – the harmonies featuring Bill and Mike are glorious – it suggested that Michael was looking into the folklore of the South, its mythology and superstition, ground that was to be especially fertile over the years. 'I draw a lot from religion – this is the very belt buckle of the Bible Belt. But it's fascinating in the same way as I find geology is fascinating. It's easier here to go watch people worship than it is to go look at rocks. It's fascinating from an outsider's point of view. But I have a sort of insider's point of view,' Michael added, alluding to his grandfather.

Religion *per se* seemed to be a subject that troubled Michael quite considerably, with songs like 'Talk About The Passion' and 'Moral Kiosk' dwelling on the hypocrisy of religious organizations and their leaders. He later argued that, 'I actually wrote a lot of political songs early on, but nobody knew it. "Talk About The Passion" was a song about hunger but the lyrics weren't clear enough.' In fairness to him, the 'empty prayer' and 'empty mouths' duality was reasonably clear if you gave it some thought, an attack on those that profess to care about the starving millions, who give at the office but who don't give another thought to the situation and its causes. Stipe objected to the mealy-mouthed who talk and talk about how committed they are to their religion and yet support political and other administrations which prop up an economic system that encourages divisions between rich and poor. U2's Bono later commented, 'To me, faith that is not aligned to social justice, that is not aligned with the poor, it's nothing,' a statement that Michael seemed to endorse with 'Talk About The Passion'.

Even so, there was an element of compassion in his castigation: the admission that individuals can't change the world single-handed apparently undermines the rest of the song and yet simultaneously suggests a way ahead – religious organizations that are already united and have a coherent voice might be able to set a different agenda by using that voice on important issues. On the other hand, the phrase 'weight of the world' might simply have been Michael's attempt at wriggling free of the 'spokesman for a generation' noose that is always looking for a suitable neck; in early 1983, he had plenty of evidence of its power as the press homed in on U2. This wasn't a destiny he wanted for R.E.M., but it was a pressure that led to the inclusion of songs such as 'We Walk' on the album. The nursery-rhyme approach in this song worked well whichever way you looked at it; it was plainly a piece of studio nonsense, as Michael's affecting closing vocal amply illustrates, but it acted as a false trail for those always looking for hidden meanings within the songs. 'We Walk' meant precisely what it said – nothing at all – but that didn't stop it being analysed to death, to their shared amusement.

Michael was always in an invidious position at the forefront of the group, as his lyrics would inevitably be dissected with the assumption that they had some autobiographical reference. Perhaps this was the reason for the way in which the vocals were recorded, as he admitted later: 'To be fair, I did insist on mixing the vocal down and not having big disco drums like every other band that was coming out in 1982. I just didn't really know what I was doing, the earliest records were us kinda learning how to write songs and throw the tantrums in amongst ourselves. I was a little shy and uncertain of myself around then.' Peter, a little mischievously perhaps, said, 'I kinda like the idea of people with one hand cupped to their ear and going, "What's that they're saying?"' Michael's reticence was borne out by his decision to record some of his vocals in a darkened stairwell away from prying eyes, but his problems were exacerbated by his responsibility as the most obvious representative of the group to the outside world; he therefore had an obligation to the other three musicians. 'With the band I kind of have to keep myself in check because a lot of weight is put on the words at times and I'm representing four people and not just myself so if I have a particular viewpoint, political or what have you, religious, colloquial, that the other guys don't share, it's really unfair.'

'Talk About The Passion' and 'Moral Kiosk' framed a desire within the band to go beyond simple pop fare and to observe and comment on issues that transcended the merely personal. Peter's thoughts on religious faith were as blunt as ever, informing *Melody Maker*:

This whole faith thing is something that goes through American culture like a knife. It has done for years. At the turn of the century I guess it was a big thing ... they're all crooks, there's this American evangelical huxterism, America's full of religious nuts, they all came here for that reason. They got kicked out of their own countries. My family came over from Sweden because they were agnostics and atheists, they came here to get away from that.

R.E.M. were to take up this tack again in the future when faced with the Southern censorship zealots, and Tipper Gore, who favoured censoring rock music, in particular (see Chapter Eleven).

Most of the songs on *Murmur* have a very personal meaning, hence the album's obliqueness for outside observers, but it was simply something that grew from the songwriting process, as Mike explained: 'Writing songs is a very organic process for us. Either Michael listens to the songs and then makes up the lyrics or else he goes to his backlog of lyrics and finds the ones that seem to fit ... they're really all intensely personal, all personal experiences he's been through.' Peter embroidered further by adding, 'The imagery is pretty strange sometimes but that's just the way it is, there are a million ways to tell stories and there's no law that says you have to be straightforward about it. If you're writing personal stuff, sometimes it's gonna be kinda obscure.'

It is inevitable that reviewers and interviewers concentrate on the lyricist and singer – after all, the lyrics represent at least one facet of a band's outlook on the world around them and they're far easier to write about than such visceral matters as guitar lines or rhythm sections. This is unfortunate, and means that down the years Mike, Bill and, to a lesser extent, Peter haven't really received the credit they deserve for R.E.M.'s artistic vision. Yet without their collective ear for a song, their subtle restraint, Michael would have had no material with which to work – given the offbeat nature of some of his other work, such as the performance noise of Tanzplagen, Michael might never have had any real impact on the world of music beyond a small coterie of like minds if left to his own devices. By the same token, without Stipe's ability to take simple ideas and twist them into the apparently enigmatic or, if you prefer, poetic language that he has used over the years, a Mike, Bill and Peter band might not have been accorded the critical acclaim that R.E.M. has won. The diverse elements that the four bring to the party means that they have been commercially successful on their own terms while stretching the definition of mainstream music to the benefit of the wider public. R.E.M., among others, set the scene for groups such as Nirvana and Pearl Jam, as Mike accepts: 'I think maybe what we did was give people a touchstone. As an alternative to the synthesizer-dominated electronic music that was being made we were the most visible sign that something else was going on. Perhaps we were the most accessible and the most visible.'

Murmur was quickly hailed as one of the great debut albums of all time and it's hard not to agree with that assessment. Even then, there are a couple of weaker moments on the collection in the shape of 'Catapult' and 'We Walk', though these serve to lighten the atmosphere, providing a little breathing space before the album picks up the pace again. Michael's voice, clear or not, is undeniably emotive throughout, and deeply affecting at times. Peter was marking out a territory – along with U2's The Edge – as a tasteful and talented guitarist for a new decade. It's certainly not a coincidence that neither was a hotshot technical player, but were instead more concerned with songwriting, giving their playing a quality that was ideally suited to the song format and dispensing with the need for irrelevant solos. Mike and Bill played crucial roles on two levels. As a rhythm section they were remarkably innovative in classical rock'n'roll terms, never indulging in the straight-ahead beat beloved of the form, but instead trying out new ideas and treatments for each song. Mike provided the technical musicality that gave the group roots, but he and Bill proved to be so completely in tune that their work was always lively. That empathy spilled over into the beautiful harmonies for which they were broadly responsible. 'The neat thing about us is our harmonies,' Mike agreed. 'We have three people who can not only sing but make up their own ideas about what to sing, instead of building a song on one-three-five harmonies.'

Murmur was a very fine record – named by *Rolling Stone* as 'Album Of The Year' – but it was as much what it represented as what it sounded like that made it resonate. In 1983, music was dominated by synthesizers and highly arranged, mannered, polished production which had neutered rock'n'roll. R.E.M.'s sound was not startlingly original, but, rather than dealing with the fashion of the time, they had drawn inspiration from the finest music of the past, had stirred in their own ideas, experiences and influences and emerged with a record that was quite literally out of its time. Buck later said, 'It was an old-fashioned record that didn't sound too much like what you heard on the radio. We were expecting the record company to say, "Sorry, this isn't even a demo tape. Go back and do it again."' Having digested the lessons of the past, the album couldn't have come at a better time, coinciding with an

increasing maturity in rock criticism which was starting to shake off
the shackles of fashion and was instead returning to a set of values
that reflected the quality of the music.

The quality of *Murmur*, its classical and subtle references,
couldn't be faulted. Its appearance sowed the seeds for a radical
change of agenda within American music that was to see college
radio take an increasingly important part in shaping the future.
R.E.M. became the patron saints of that movement whether they
liked it or not, and it is here that *Murmur* is of lasting significance.
As the figureheads of this new movement that soon encompassed
other groups like Husker Dü, R.E.M. came to represent the
aspirations of a disenfranchised section of young America who felt
that their voices were being ignored by the White House – which of
course they were. R.E.M. offered hope for the growth of a new
counter-culture of sorts that might transform the latter part of the
decade.

IRS quickly realized just what they had on their hands once
Murmur was released to ecstatic reviews in the US in April 1983.
Those reviews filtered across to Europe, David Fricke writing in
Melody Maker, 'To those who complain that they don't make
records like they used to, I point to *Murmur* and say, "No, they
make them better."' The European release didn't come until
August, reviews again unanimously affirmative, with Richard
Grabel in *NME* calling R.E.M. 'one of the most evocative pop
practitioners around'. Such worldwide exposure gave the group
their first taste of international touring when they visited Holland,
France and England in November 1983, having spent the months
since *Murmur*'s American release on the road. It's easy to see how
Michael won his reputation for eccentricity in those days, but there
was considerable method in his madness as Peter recalls: 'When we
used to fly economy, Michael wouldn't shave or change his clothes
for about four days beforehand and then right before we got on the
plane he'd get chocolate ice cream and eat it and leave some around
his mouth. Then he'd lay in his seat and twitch, so that when people
came by they'd refuse to sit next to him and he'd get two seats to
himself.'

The world was already beginning to close in on R.E.M. by this
time; they'd played their first television shows back home, including
the Letterman show, where they played a new song, 'So. Central
Rain', then so new it didn't have a name. 'We did all the things that
are ridiculous and numbing and embarrassing, all the weird little

TV shows,' Buck admitted later. 'We did kiddie shows with an audience of children. Three of the kids, incidentally, were The Beastie Boys, these cute little child actors.' Live concerts, however, were still their forte and they approached the challenge of new territories with characteristic gusto. *Melody Maker*'s Allan Jones saw the Dingwalls show in Camden and he noted that 'Buck was a kinetic exhibition', praised 'the continental shift of Bill Berry's drumming' and still had time to mention Michael Stipe who 'looked like an asylum inmate, [with] a face that was a twitching landscape of nervous tics'.

Fans and critics on this side of the Atlantic might conceivably have been upset by the live R.E.M., for their shows had little of the majesty of the album. Instead they replaced that with a passionate drive towards good-time rock'n'roll with a theatrical edge that Michael provided. By the time they left the European scene with a promise to return in the following spring, R.E.M. had made enough impact to suggest that they had a future as an international rather than a strictly indigenous American phenomenon.

And phenomenon wasn't too strong a word, for *Murmur* had become a major success story in the States. Within a year, they had sold 200,000 copies and had reached number thirty-six in the Billboard album charts, thereby surpassing anything that any 'college radio' act could have thought possible. Peter was genuinely surprised: 'We'd finished the album and thought it was OK, that it would sell its forty, maybe fifty thousand copies and keep us in relative obscurity. But then the college radio stations started to play it continuously until even the commercial stations picked up on it. One day in LA we heard our music in between tracks by Neil Young and Def Leppard!' Bill's version of success was proof positive that here was a band with their feet firmly on the floor, one that wouldn't get carried away by album sales: 'Success was when we put *Murmur* out, we were pretty proud of it and we started to think there was something there.'

As their acceptance of a children's TV appearance amply illustrates, R.E.M. recognized that IRS was doing everything that it could to sell their records – even cutting the price to $6.98 as opposed to the standard $8.98 – but, given the record label's small-scale operation by American standards, R.E.M. accepted that they would need to help out, hence the small degree of compromise. One further concession was made when they finally agreed to do a support tour with The Police, having already turned down U2, The

Clash and even the B52s. With their close business relationship with Miles Copeland at IRS and Ian Copeland at their agency, FBI, and given the number of occasions Bill had sought favours from Ian, R.E.M. could hardly reject the idea of The Police tour. Even had they wanted to turn the chance down, it's hard to see how they could have done without upsetting some important people, particularly the Copeland brothers, which might in turn have done their promising career no good – the offer of $10,000 for the outdoor gigs might also have changed some minds. It was ironic, though, that they wound up supporting a band who had cracked the US on the back of a policy of never supporting anyone.

The band ended up playing five shows in August 1983, including two outdoors at Shea Stadium and JFK Stadium in Philadelphia. At the outdoor shows they only had to do twenty-minute sets as they were third on the bill behind Joan Jett. Since The Beatles had made Shea Stadium famous in rock'n'roll terms, R.E.M. got a vicarious thrill from playing there, but that aside, they simply detested the whole process of playing second fiddle to such a major league group as The Police on such a big stage. Bill dismissed it as 'the most wretched and abysmal experience of our lives . . . it was a joke. The record company tried every means of coercion to get us to do it and finally we said, "Okay, we'll do it, we're curious, maybe we will sell records and maybe people will respond." But it was hopeless. We shoulda stayed home and got drunk for all the fucken good it did us.' And Peter stressed, 'We hated every minute of them, they were really boring,' while for Michael the highlight of it all was the rain at Shea Stadium while they were on stage. 'Watching all those umbrellas going up and realizing that the audience loved it – the rain that is – it was real strange.'

Bill was particularly angry about the whole thing: 'We shoulda done what we believed to be right. Just because we're hooked up with this vast business machine doesn't mean we have to go along with everything it says. Our intuition has been more valuable to us than any of the great words of wisdom passed on to us by the damned record company.' In fairness to IRS, Bill's vehemence suggested that he was just as upset at the idea that, had he continued with school, he might have turned into one of these advising executives himself, and was as disgusted with that scenario as he was with the business itself. Peter summed up the group feeling best when he told *Sounds*, 'It was the first time we took the advice of anyone outside the group and it just proved we're always right. The Police are a good band, but I don't wanna open for anyone.' So there would be no more compromise – at least not until the summer of 1985, when R.E.M. supported U2 at its outdoor shows in Dublin and Milton Keynes. The only other question left is why do R.E.M. take support groups out on the road and inflict the same torture on them?

After an exhausting year, a year that had put R.E.M. into a far healthier financial and commercial position than they could have imagined, 1984 would give them the chance to go straight into the studio and begin work on their second album. This album would indicate whether or not R.E.M. were a nine-day wonder or a far more substantial band that could go the full nine yards.

5

NOT BOUND TO FOLLOW SUIT

By all normal criteria, R.E.M. should have approached the second album with some trepidation. After all, the public's eyes were now on them, a distinct shift from the minimal expectations that had preceded *Murmur*. Happily, although R.E.M. had been hurled into the same whirl of promotional and touring activity that besets most groups when they gain a measure of success, the good musical habits that the group had forced themselves into stood them in good stead. Continuing to write new songs in soundchecks and on the road, the band succeeded in compiling more material than they needed for their second album. Consequently, they avoided the perennial trap of gathering together scraps of discarded ideas in order to meet a record company deadline.

With *Murmur* having registered such great success, IRS were willing to leave the band to their own devices this time around, working on the principle that they knew what they were doing after all. Mitch Easter and Don Dixon were assigned to production duties again and the studio at Reflection was booked for about a month either side of Christmas 1983. Dixon remembers the recording and mixing taking twenty-five days, and Easter thinks it might have been twenty. For some reason, R.E.M. themselves have taken to looking on the recording of *Reckoning* as some kind of macho contest, suggesting that it took a mere eleven or twelve days to make. Peter was especially keen to show and tell:

> We'd planned to take a month recording it but after three days we had seven songs recorded. We tried to slow down but we still had it finished in under two weeks. That's why it came out

69

real rackety but it was decided not to do them again. So 'Little America' has the cheesiest guitar ever. I wanted to clean it up but the rest of the band wouldn't let me, so it stayed, mistakes and all.

It's understandable that Peter thought the record was made so quickly since, as he has regularly professed to have absolutely no interest in the mixing stage at all, it's likely that he would not have counted that part of the process. Michael's assertions were a little more difficult to explain, given his interest in the whole idea of recording. 'It was kinda intense. That was a twelve-day drunken party. No sleep, just staying up and staying drunk or whatever.' The only theory that stands any kind of examination is one of fear of failing to follow *Murmur* with an equally impressive album. R.E.M. seemed to fall back on the conversations that go on outside examination halls around the world – 'I haven't done any work, I'll never pass.' By telling the world they'd worked at breakneck pace, or rather, by pretending they'd worked even faster than the still pretty slick three weeks they actually took, it might be that R.E.M. were trying to insulate themselves against criticism, along the lines of, 'No wonder it isn't as good as *Murmur*, we didn't have the time to do it properly.'

It's equally plausible to suggest that given the growth of the hard-core scene in the US, with groups like Black Flag rising to prominence, the band were feeling a little threatened, concerned their territory was being invaded. By embracing similar production values and a greater level of aggression in the playing as a result, R.E.M. might have been trying to make a point. Certainly Peter had worried earlier that 'most of the bands I like are a little more threatening. R.E.M. is the wimpiest band that I like and I'm not sure that I like us yet.'

There was a very definite line taken by the group going into the *Reckoning* sessions; they didn't want to go over old ground and simply reprise *Murmur* to ensure commercial success. This was an admirable artistic decision on the part of the group, for consolidation would certainly have been advised by the industry as a whole. Instead, they stripped away the layers of sound that had made *Murmur* so appealing and intriguing, turned the volume up to eleven in most places and tried to sound like a live group. Each song was to have its own distinct character so that it could be isolated from the album without suffering – something that couldn't be said of some of the tracks on *Murmur*.

Peter's view was, 'We wanted *Reckoning* to be an album of songs, so we were far more interested in getting them down as naturally as possible. We had all of them written before we went in and we'd been hammering them out live for a month or two, so when we came to record them it was just a question of putting the bass, guitar and drums down in one or two take and then overdubbing more guitars and adding vocals.' Michael noted that the real title for *Reckoning* should be *File Under Water*, a recurrent theme on the record which suggested passage and movement, though perhaps it was also a little dig at those who had tried to categorize R.E.M. on the basis of their debut. However, movement was prevalent in the way they attacked the songs with such vigour, *Reckoning* eventually becoming their most guitar-fuelled album until *Document* came out three albums later. The atmosphere of the tracks caught their kinetic lifestyle very accurately, creating a vivid image of this little combo hurtling across the US from one gig to another, playing wild shows to passionate audiences and getting completely wrecked as a consequence.

The theme of passage came through in a more sombre tone too. Carol Levy, who had been a friend of the group for many years and who had taken the rear cover photograph for the Hib-Tone single, was killed in a car crash in the spring of 1983. The group's tribute to her came in the form of 'Camera', although several other tracks were tinged with regret and a wistful nostalgia at the passing of time. Merely listening to 'Camera', the outsider would have no idea what the song was about but, as with 'Perfect Circle' before it, the underlying emotion of the song was transmitted with such disarming clarity by the instrumentation and by Michael's choked vocal that it would be hard not to be moved by its mournful, melancholy flavour. It bore out Michael's fascination with the concept of memory and his increasing need to document things in song to help him remember.

Michael confessed his compulsion to *Select*:

In *The Year Of Living Dangerously* . . . there's this character in it – I think his name is Billy – who keeps all these cabinets with files of everyone he knows in them. I really identify with that character . . . it's just that the idea of the almost desperate need to document a piece of time or history – to get something down in some way – that's intrinsic to the human spirit. And because of the technology we've brought about in the last 100 years or so it's possible through film and recordings to grab all of these moments.

This train of thought, more than any other, explains the impenetrable nature of his earliest lyrics when he was almost always dealing with the personal. In that sense, his lyrics were purely selfish memos, diary entries not intended to mean anything to anyone else, though he was prepared to let people take impressions of their own from the work. It wasn't until later in the band's progression when wider issues were tackled that his lyrics became a little easier to follow.

'I'm really intrigued by memory,' Stipe expanded in *Melody Maker*. 'It can take the real and the unreal and combine them so that you really can't remember if you went to church without your pants on or if you dreamed or thought or imagined it ... photography has come into the world and altered that a little bit because we now have documented ways of proving, "Yes, I was in church without my pants on," or "No, I wasn't." Or, "Yes my mother put me in the cedar chest when I was bad," or "No, she says she didn't."'

For 'Camera', it is Michael himself who is functioning in that way, capturing the evidence for posterity. 'If I'm to be a camera' must be alluding to that responsibility, his mission to keep Carol's name alive, to ensure that she will be remembered, to prove to himself and to everyone else that she did actually exist. It's a touching piece that says much about Stipe's compassion, as well as that of the rest of the band, who provide such a beautifully pitched soundtrack.

From a historical viewpoint, the interesting thing is the way in which Michael and the other members of the group deal with the idea of death and of passage on *Reckoning* compared with the treatment the subject receives at some length on *Automatic For The People*. On that later album, there is a powerful wash of regret but also a sense of resolution: that life does go on and you have to draw strength from loss – 'Everybody Hurts' is a particular example of that philosophy. Where *Automatic For The People* provides an adult perspective on loss, with the subsequent album, *Monster*, taking that rationale a stage further with its life-affirming celebration, *Reckoning* and, to an extent, *Murmur* before it try to cope with the shock by, if not ignoring it, retreating into a world when life was not disfigured by tragedy and complexity. 'Catapult', for instance, looks back to when we were little children, while 'Reckoning' is filled with a desire to return to a childhood world where there were certainties and you were insulated from the harsh realities of life and death by the protective blanket of your parents and family. 'Camera' again looks at a time when 'it was simple', evidence perhaps that Stipe and R.E.M. were so shaken by the loss that they wanted almost to ignore or avoid the reality of it by running away. Carol Levy's death may have been the first loss that was sufficiently close to home to affect them all very deeply, and their reaction may simply have betrayed an inability to cope with the finality of it; if that was the case then it was all the more to their credit that they put 'Camera' on record.

There is a sadness in some of the tracks, but R.E.M. were deliberately out to stretch themselves stylistically on this second album and there are definite injections of a humour that was broader than that used on *Murmur*. Michael's Elvis impersonation prior to '(Don't Go Back To) Rockville' – a song that Mike had written back in 1980 – is reminiscent of the clowning that preceded 'Stumble' on *Chronic Town*. 'Little America' has a black comedic quality to it, including a dig at their manager/driver/navigator Jefferson Holt – 'I think we're lost' – but it maintains the theme of change in its role as observational travelogue featuring a band on the run across the US. *Reckoning* is an important milestone in that it is the first broad comment on R.E.M.'s collective view of their homeland seen through the windows of a tour bus. Reagan's vision of the US was to become a central theme in R.E.M.'s work in the coming years so this example of disquiet was particularly interesting.

The confusion that the band were picking up on during their travels, as well as the internal effects of their hectic schedule, is summed up by the sleeve to *Reckoning* which features a painting of a two-headed snake, though it could just as easily be a winding river, to tie in with the recurrent water motif. The outline was Michael's and he then passed it to the Reverend Howard Finster to complete. Finster was something of an Athenian character, as Michael explained: 'He's a Southern minister, he had a church for forty years or so. He painted bicycles on the side and one day he got paint on his thumb and saw in it the Virgin Mary saying, "Howard, paint sacred art!" You don't even have to go to school to be a preacher, you just "get the call". He got the call when he was fifteen . . . you just get up and preach hellfire and damnation.'

Peter elaborated a little more:

> He's a visionary, not really a painter or sculptor. He has visions from God, who I don't believe in, but somebody's sure talking to him. He's trying to bring together the fragmented heart of the world by essentially taking junk and making art out of it. It's really other-worldly. He did the cover to *Little Creatures* by Talking Heads. He originally did the cover to the title *Peeping Heads* . . . he had this idea that the Peeping Heads were angels looking down but not talking.

Finster's primitive art intrigued Michael's visual sense and the opportunity to work together on *Reckoning* was something of an ambition fulfilled.

Musically, the record certainly fulfilled many of the criteria that the band had set out in advance. On its release, Peter enthused, 'I like it a lot better than the first album, I think because the songwriting's better, the songs are a little more emotionally open and it's more diverse, consciously. We went out of our way to make a record that didn't sound like the first one. It's not like we're trying to touch all the bases or anything but there are a whole lotta sides to us that people don't really see.' This urge to experiment with different forms and to expand their repertoire was not done with any commercial motives in mind for, if anything, songs like 'Pretty Persuasion', 'Second Guessing' and 'Letter Never Sent' were even more wilfully uncommercial than those on *Murmur* had been.

'Second Guessing' is something of an oddity. It has the clearest lyric on the record with a seemingly irascible Stipe complaining about people trying to interpret the band from the outside while the band whips up a storm behind him. It sounds like a drunken tantrum slammed on to tape at the end of a session, Bill's drums threatening to bring the roof down. If the song is about the press concentration on Stipe's enigma variations of the previous year – and the fuck you 'here we are' line seems to scream 'just enjoy the songs without an autopsy' – it also takes a swipe at the media penchant for following fashion at the expense of any work of substance. As a defiant statement of intent and a promise of longevity it works, but the apparent speed with which it was put together militated against it; playing the album repeatedly over the years, 'Second Guessing' reveals itself to be one of those rare R.E.M. songs that is all surface and no depth.

Love songs make their presence felt on the record in a way that isn't true of *Murmur*, whatever 'Perfect Circle' is really about. 'So. Central Rain', probably the best song on the album, is an atypical ballad, ushered in by a lovely guitar refrain of Peter's that Mike then takes up as Peter plays rhythm. Michael's plaintive vocal is laced with regret, further evidence of change and loss, a physical dislocation presumably rooted in the band's hectic lifestyle and their continual absence from home through touring duties. The waiting for a call section has Michael, or the character he has adopted, on the receiving end of a communication breakdown, the 'rivers of suggestion' of which he then sings apparently putting the relationship under stress through a mutual lack of trust when apart. 'Letter Never Sent' with its reference to Athens seems even closer to home but again it may merely be a metaphor for homesickness rather than being directed at a specific person – the band were having to endure dense passages of touring after all, and Michael, having finally adopted a place where he felt at home, might have felt the strain of touring more keenly, a suggestion that he confirmed later in the wake of the *Green* tour.

'Time After Time (Annelise)' steps straight out of the Velvet Underground song book, Bill's primitive drumming being the perfect backdrop to Peter's incandescent guitar. Again, the music implies disconnection rather more cogently than the lyric does but by now, people were starting to get to grips with the R.E.M. method of working. There was far less analysis of *Reckoning* compared with *Murmur*, as people were willing to let the record wash over them and try to take it in on a subconscious level. '(Don't Go Back To) Rockville', yet another song of potential separation, though one which is more hopeful of a satisfactory resolution, defies that kind of approach with its gloriously catchy chorus and off-kilter allusions to Country and Western. Mike's song had been around for nearly three years now and it's likely it would have stayed in the vaults had it not been for its thematic connection to the rest of *Reckoning*, though some sources suggest that it was recorded as a favour to Bertis Downs, who loved the song. Showing excellent commercial instincts if that was the case, Downs rescued a gem from obscurity, as it is undeniably the most conventionally enjoyable song on the record and ultimately gained a single release and substantial airplay.

The rest of the record is especially inscrutable. 'Harborcoat' is allegedly 'about Nazi Germany, a rewrite of *The Anne Frank*

Diaries' according to Michael, though whether or not this is an example of his American dry humour is up to you. 'Seven Chinese Brothers' draws on the old folk tale and maintains the tradition of childlike simplicity that 'We Walk' had introduced on the first album. Finally, 'Pretty Persuasion' is a potent rock track but, as Michael says, 'There's a tradition of lyrics that aren't words – "Pretty Persuasion" is not words, parts of "Radio Free Europe" and "9-9" are words but they don't necessarily go together to make exact sense.' Yes . . .

Unsurprisingly, *Reckoning* took its share of good reviews once again, even if it lacked the impact of *Murmur*. Collective opinion held that R.E.M. had come through the ordeal and established themselves as a very fine band indeed. In *NME*, Mat Snow called it 'another classic . . . when I get to heaven the angels will be playing not harps but Rickenbackers. And they will be playing songs by R.E.M.' *Melody Maker*'s Ian Pye was a little more reserved in his judgment, but was perfectly correct in his assessment of where the band were going: 'R.E.M. have used the great American myths to enhance the depth and roots of their music while exposing the empty vessel at the end of Disneyland's rainbow. This is an album made by Americans, but Americans who are unsure about America – it's fascinating.' That fascination would increase over subsequent years.

With those rave reviews repeated around the world, R.E.M. were assured of a warm welcome wherever they went. Not that they were going to allow complacency to set in; a huge tour was booked to run virtually non-stop from April through to Christmas 1984. Although the group's stock had risen such that travelling was now easier and more comfortable, the success of *Murmur* meant that they now had to tour the world rather than simply concentrating on the US. Even in their home country, there was still a lot of work to be done to carry the message to the rock'n'roll hinterland, so they had no way out of the treadmill – not that they were complaining. They still loved to play live, for they all felt this was the best representation of the group and to be paid well for doing it was a real bonus. With nine months of solid work stretching before them, the idea was to take a few breaks through February and March to get themselves prepared for the job ahead. Yet so locked into the music were they, Peter, Bill and Mike went straight back into the studio with Warren Zevon to help him record some demos as he sought a new recording contract. Simultaneously, they recorded a single as The Hindu Love Gods, 'Gonna Have A Good Time Tonight', with singer Bryan Cook.

That was not the only project undertaken during this brief lull. Promotional videos were required for potential singles such as 'So. Central Rain'. Having given little thought to the genre in connection with *Murmur*, the band knew that this time there was a little more interest abroad, particularly in Michael, who now fully assumed the role as the group's visual co-ordinator. 'So. Central Rain' used the theme of separation and placed Peter, Bill and Mike behind screens while Michael gave a passionate, deceptively simple vocal performance. Refusing to lip-sync any longer as he had on 'Wolves, Lower', Stipe actually sang on the video and the effect was to give the clip a greater integrity.

The film project came about back in Athens, though it was filmed in nearby Gainesville. Peter was typically dismissive of the whole thing, never having had any interest in appearing on screen: 'We did a twenty-minute film with a guy called Jim Herbert, a weird image thing that doesn't have us playing instruments or anything but it has a side of *Reckoning* as the music. It didn't do our careers loads of good because it didn't have any naked women in it.' *Left Of Reckoning*, as it was titled, got little publicity until it appeared on the *Succumbs* video compilation several years later. Michael was pleased to have the opportunity of working with his one-time lecturer Herbert, who was installed as the director of the piece. Picking up the non-linear style of both the music and the video of 'Radio Free Europe', *Left Of Reckoning* was rich in imagery, but, as Buck had intimated, short on the kind of action to keep MTV viewers glued to the screen.

Taking the first five songs from *Reckoning* – the left side – as its soundtrack, the film itself had a nice grainy quality and a particular atmosphere of its own, the layers of film reflecting the multilayered feel of the band's work. However, it added little to the songs themselves and appears to have been purely an exercise to document a part of the landscape and a period of time that was important to the group – the film was shot in primitive sculptor R. A. Miller's whirligig gardens. As selfish in that sense as the songs themselves, the film was too inaccessible for a general audience. For those people, *Left Of Reckoning*'s greatest virtue was as an experiment – it provided a learning process for both Herbert and, especially, Michael, and there were little ideas that ran through the film which were capitalized on in later productions, such as 'Finest Worksong'.

Work was the order of the day in 1984. The band had signed up for dense passages of touring, playing for weeks on end with barely a day's rest and, while it was fun to cover new places and see interest growing around them, it was a debilitating experience too. Tired of the celebrity spotlight that had been turned on the group since the advent of *Murmur*, Michael added lighting design to his extensive CV, leaving the group to perform in semi-darkness for much of the time. The punishing schedule they had committed themselves to meant that for the first time, cracks began to appear in the R.E.M. camaraderie, ultimately having an impact on the live shows. In *Melody Maker* in November, Tom Morton reviewed the Edinburgh show by saying 'bar bands are ten a penny', indicating that the subtlety of approach which was their most potent weapon had been bludgeoned into submission by the sheer grind of road work. To be fair, other reviews at the same time were less caustic. Reviewing a Dublin show in December, Helen Fitzgerald said, 'R.E.M. are the vanguard of a breed who have only their heritage to keep them from the brink of extinction. Long may their colours fly.'

It's apparent that things were starting to go awry as the band were growing exhausted by the sheer pace they were maintaining. From the band's launch in 1981, they had scarcely taken a break, their exuberant lifestyle of those early years in particular beginning to catch up with them. No matter how close the friendships were between the band – and there is nothing to suggest that they didn't remain more committed to one another than to the group – a way of life which throws you together in close confinement for almost twenty-four hours of an exhausting day for months on end is going to impose a serious strain. Once the novelty of life on the road had begun to wear away, the reality of travelling huge distances in tour buses without the opportunity to escape for a little solitude started to take on more and more importance in the lives of the four men: travelling at the best of times can be a very wearing business, but when finances are tight and accommodation has to be skimped on, it can be unbearable.

By the end of 1984, R.E.M. needed time to step back, reassess and spend some time at home; the separation images used in 'So. Central Rain' and 'Letter Never Sent' suggest difficulties dating back as far as the end of 1983. It was particularly unfortunate then that the run of almost unbroken good fortune they had enjoyed since April 1980 came to an abrupt end. There would be no time at home; there was another record to make and, thanks to irreconcilable logistics, it had to be made in England.

6

STILL A WAYS AWAY

It would have been nice for R.E.M. to have taken stock of their first four-and-a-half years' worth of achievement as 1984 came to a close. They'd helped to change the whole perception of US rock in tandem with a host of like-minded groups, had played concerts across the globe to almost unanimous acclaim and had produced two of the decade's finest albums to that point. Given the speed at which they'd been working, that was a pretty remarkable feat, for the quality of their work certainly hadn't shown any noticeable dip. A brief period of recharging the creative batteries would have set them up for the second half of the 1980s.

Unfortunately it wasn't merely the boring routine of touring that was starting to fray their collective nerves. By 1985, they were beginning to discover that they couldn't avoid all the music industry traps after all. Their workload was excessive but, to some extent, they brought that upon themselves with their willingness to tour and their desire to have a new album out each year. External pressures were being brought to bear to do more and more televisions shows, increase the number of press and radio interviews and generally be more accessible to the public. By generating this publicity, IRS felt that record sales would naturally increase. In addition, IRS were also pushing the group to change their image a little, to produce video performances that could be shown on MTV. Mike's reaction to the relatively gentle coercion that IRS tried on them was one of horror. 'I think the business side is appalling, it's chauvinistic, repressive, disgusting all the way round. All we can do is manipulate it so we get to do what we want and how we want but that is fighting against the current. We would rather do our own style and not sell as many records than capitulate to somebody else's idea of what you should do.' Michael was a little more succinct. 'We're a commodity as a band, a face, an image. You have to overcome that.'

As far as IRS were concerned, they were facing the age-old problem of independent labels everywhere. They were quick to spot new talent, but once that music found its way into the mainstream, the major label vultures began to circle. R.E.M. had a five album deal with IRS, and by now they were at the halfway stage. IRS were, understandably enough, looking for R.E.M. to start making money sooner rather than later. If R.E.M. broke through at the fifth album point, IRS would lose out in a big way should the group choose to change labels. A rueful Miles Copeland later admitted, 'We could have used the sales earlier for our company.'

The effort expended on fighting off outsiders giving well-intentioned advice drained some of the ebullience from the band, leaving them tired before they had reached the studio, but other difficulties were self-inflicted. Given their refusal to accept IRS's offers of substantial advances, allied to the fact that royalties take an age to come through, they weren't reaping the financial rewards in the early years, although they were selling records. To maintain their cashflow, R.E.M. had to stay on the road for as long as possible, making the best use of specific touring periods – college shows in spring and autumn, for instance. As a kind of security blanket, tours were always booked well in advance to guarantee an income for the year ahead so that the band could stay liquid; although this was essential for their financial well-being, it did mean that once committed they couldn't back out of shows that they were really too tired to play. As 1985 dawned, R.E.M. had a full twelve months of work stretching before them. They also had a whole new album to write.

Only a few of the songs that would reach that album had been played live, such had been the chaotic nature of the year of *Reckoning*. 'Driver 8', 'Wendell Gee', 'Old Man Kensey' and 'Auctioneer (Another Engine)' had been tried and tested but that left the group desperately short of songs. Peter recalls them writing fifteen new songs in eight days – which, if it's true, is a pretty astounding feat. By the same token, it also means that the songs were not as thoroughly crafted and corrected as earlier material had been, in turn meaning that the band were going into the recording studio lacking confidence in their material. They had also decided to change producers, having worked twice with Easter and Dixon. To gain a fresh perspective on the studio and on recording in general, now seemed like a good time for a change.

Michael had a very definite idea of what he wanted from this new record in lyrical terms.

A lot of what I was listening to was cassettes recorded in Tennessee, in the mountains, Appalachian folk songs, field recordings, literally someone with their tape recorder recording an old man with a fiddle with a woman in the background with her hand on the stove. That sort of image I think really infected the way I wanted it to sound . . . old men sitting around the fire passing on these legends and fables to the grandchildren . . . each song had a specific voice.

Van Dyke Parks was a potential producer, especially since he had recently released an album of his own based around the Uncle Remus stories, stories to which Stipe was particularly attracted. Stipe was aspiring to this style, and arguing for the acoustic format since 'when the songs are quieter, I can less get away with just bellowing a lot which I love to do. You kinda have to sing and it helps if there's words so my folk songs are more concise,' though given the continued lyrical obfuscation, this seemed a hollow claim. Sadly, the idea of using Parks never came to fruition, while a potentially explosive combination of R.E.M. and Elvis Costello fell through, due to communication difficulties between Miles Copeland and Jake Riviera, Costello's manager.

Peter's view was that Joe Boyd would be a sympathetic choice because of his grounding in the folk rock tradition. Boyd had worked with Pink Floyd when Syd Barrett was with them, adding Nick Drake, John Martyn, Fairport Convention and Richard Thompson to his impressive list of credits. Given Buck's boundless admiration for Thompson in particular, his enthusiasm for Joe Boyd was not too surprising, and that affected the rest of the group. This third record was rapidly turning into a nightmare to organize – they were already down to a window of four possible weeks of recording before having to go on tour again – and things didn't improve when Boyd had to decline their offer because of prior commitments.

Flying to Canada to work with Mary Margaret O'Hara, Boyd arrived to find that she needed to rearrange her own schedule. At a loose end at last, but with a 10,000 Maniacs project looming in April, Boyd 'called Jefferson and said, "Could we do it by March?" And he said, "Come on down!"' This was in mid-February and, given the very necessary sense of urgency that all had to show, Peter's recollection seems to be spot on for once: 'We just gave him a call' – okay, nearly spot on – 'and he said, "Yeah, I'll be in the area and I've got some free time, let's do a demo." We did something like sixteen songs with him in one day. He was in town on the Monday, he saw us play on the Tuesday. I think on the Wednesday we said, "Let's do the album." We flew to England that Friday.' Later Peter was to embroider that story further by suggesting that there had always been a master plan that would take them to England: 'Charlotte is not one of the major glamour spots of the West and everything closes at six. The only good thing about Charlotte other than the studio is there's a Salvation Army shop where you can get great polyester clothes and that isn't really much of a recommendation so we thought we'd go to London instead.'

IRS were uncertain about this change on the basis of one day's work, particularly since the group were off to record in England at considerable expense. Allegedly, the band crossed this particular bridge by saying they were merely going to record further demos, though once their hand was declared, IRS were pushing for singles from the collaboration. Boyd remained unsure of just who he was working for throughout the process – was it IRS or R.E.M.?

When Michael's preoccupation with folklore and storytelling was coupled with the band's desire to stretch themselves in a more musical direction, away from the raw edge of *Reckoning*, R.E.M. should have been aiming to compile an almost pastoral, acoustic sort of record. *Fables Of The Reconstruction* – or, to give its full cyclical title, *Fables Of The Reconstruction Of The Fables* – really should have been recorded in Georgia or at Reflection Studios once more. By all sensible criteria, R.E.M. should have been at home in the environment they were addressing. Instead, for the first time they found themselves recording in a big city. R.E.M. were not hillbilly hicks by any means, but living and working in London or any capital city is very different to just passing through.

Ironically, it was this tension that made *Fables Of The Reconstruction* such a great album. As soon as Peter opens proceedings with a cathartic guitar intro on 'Feeling Gravity's Pull', the songs pull the listener in every possible direction. It lacks a coherent musical direction, but there is a disturbingly unbalanced edge to the songs, a darkness that tells you everything about the group's state of mind, as Mike explained: 'A lot of things were catching up with us. We didn't realize we were going to be asked to do certain commercial kinds of things and we thought, "Is this what we really want to do?" It was maybe a crisis period, just an overall feeling of unease … that was a miserable time, but it was interesting all the same. It's quite a dour record but I still kinda like some of it.'

The problems that surrounded the recording were not just matters of tension between band and company. Exhaustion had set in to go with their disgust at the commercialism they had encountered. Michael recalls that he was in a particularly poor state: 'I had a breakdown when we were making that record. It was a very dark period and I had this breakdown. It wasn't too gorgeous a time … we almost broke up.' How much of this is myth-making in hindsight is hard to tell – the tortured artist struggling through bravely despite his handicap is a compelling portrait – though Stipe isn't usually given to dramatizing the recording process, and prefers to reduce it to the level of mundanity it deserves. However, Joe Boyd remembers that 'he [Stipe] quite enjoyed London', making the most of its museums and amenities. At one point Stipe went to a surrealist exhibition which inspired the cover artwork as well as finding its way into lyrics such as the 'Man Ray sky' of 'Feeling Gravity's Pull'.

It's likely that the group did not confide in Boyd to the same extent they had with Dixon and Easter, who had been confederates for a number of years. Instead they carried their burden in private as the difficulties built up around them. Even the weather seemed to be laughing at their expense: Peter's memory, which might be indulging his love of hyperbole, is that 'it rained every single day it wasn't snowing'. For a band used to living in the South with its warm climate, this was yet another problem with which to wrestle. Peter's mood wasn't improved when, on arriving in London, he discovered he had to travel by tube because they couldn't afford a car. According to his story, their flat was a mile from the nearest station while at the other end of the journey they had to walk another mile to the studio which, in the snow, did little to improve their humour.

Exhaustion was the keynote, it appears; reflecting on the years leading up to *Fables Of The Reconstruction*, Peter said, 'We were sleeping on people's floors and not eating. Y'know when I was twenty-two I didn't really need to sleep, I could sleep curled up on a couch with someone's dog and after two hours I'd wake up and feel refreshed. Things don't stay like that, you get grouchy, I like to sleep and I have trouble sleeping on the road so someone snoring in the same room, it really drives me insane ... it's just hard to be away.' Four years of living on the road had taken its physical toll and it was testament to the strength of the bond between the four that they survived with sanity and group intact, Boyd seeing that unified front in action: 'They were after the blend. They saw themselves as an ensemble from which no one part stuck out. They're incredibly smart and it works.'

For Peter, things reached a crisis during recording, as he later admitted.

> We were at the point where we could feel ourselves getting sucked into the business. I was pretty much a wreck for most of that time ... you think, 'Do I want to be in a rock'n'roll band?' ... I think we were thinking, 'Why can't we just be hippies and say fuck the record? We don't want to do it, we're going home.' In the end we worked through it ... I do like that record, I'm not saying it was a failure. I mean rock'n'roll isn't showbiz, we don't have to be happy. Fuck it. As weird as that album is, that's how I felt every day.

Fables Of The Reconstruction was a weird record in many ways, carrying their folk preoccupation through to its natural conclusion, with Boyd probably the best producer for the job. 'They liked my approach,' he told *Mojo*. 'I don't try to put hands on the music, I try to create the right atmosphere for the artist to do what they want. I'm not going to spend three days getting a drum sound.' However, in other aspects of the recording process, Boyd was painstaking in the extreme, as Michael ruefully recalled: 'He's a very meticulous producer especially when it comes to mixes. He has this idea that there is The Perfect Mix for each song and he'll work and work to get that mix ... and it drove me up the fucking wall! But in the end I'm really glad he was so meticulous.' Michael wasn't the only one with problems though, as Boyd suggested: 'With R.E.M. everyone wanted it quieter. It made it difficult for me to get a vivid image in my mind, an ideal mix as I kept getting knocked sideways by "Don't turn up the voice! Don't turn up the guitar!"'

With so many difficulties, that *Fables* was made at all was a triumph; that it should be so good is a minor miracle, although it's still an oddball in the R.E.M. canon – people either champion it as their finest hour or dismiss it as their lowest ebb.

Whichever side you were on, its quality proved that R.E.M. were now in the upper echelons of rock's aristocracy. As Michael had noted, the sense of storytelling was absolutely central to the construction of the record, though in some respects it was an extension of his concerns on *Reckoning*. 'So. Central Rain', for example, had touched on the pain of separation and of dislocation, and some of *Fables Of The Reconstruction* also followed that line. 'Auctioneer (Another Engine)' for instance was, according to Michael, 'pretty much about shifting from one place to another very quickly. In order to stay sane I talk home a lot on the telephone.' This time the theme ran far deeper, as R.E.M. as a group were ransacking America's mythology in a compulsive search for cultural roots. Michael noted, 'The cyclical title to me really defined the whole entity that the band was taking on at that time ... *Fables* brings up the whole thing about storytelling and that kinda ties in with lost heritage, the tradition of a story being passed on.' With its comment on R.E.M.'s position, Stipe might have been referring to the tour/record/tour cycle they were locked into, but he might equally have been aiming a satirical swipe at himself, commenting on the way in which their original ideas were being corrupted by the industry. R.E.M. had aimed to reconstruct the music business but now found themselves in the belly of the beast having, temporarily at least, lost their way.

Michael also took a personal struggle and turned it inside out for a change:

I think I'm probably searching for some kind of background that is there, but still kind of buried. That's typical of the last century in America. There's no sense of ancestry here – for a good reason; they wiped out all the Indians. No-one wants to remember that. If you're not like second or third generation Swedish, you really don't have much idea where you come from. Unlike Europe there's no long-standing tradition or heritage ... there's a lack of history here which would be the American version of Catholic guilt. I think that's a big flaw in the American dream. You're not taught about the annihilation of the entire culture of the Indians whose land this was.

On the next album, *Lifes Rich Pageant*, 'Cuyahoga' appears to be offering a naive alternative with its desire to start up a new country of the mind, taking the best parts from existing lands, contrasting that with the face of the US's indigenous people.

R.E.M. took the political point further on 'Green Grow The Rushes' although the lyric was so opaque that few picked up on it at the time. 'I think what America is doing in Central America is nothing short of genocide,' Michael revealed later, adding, '"Green Grow The Rushes" was a song about guestworkers, particularly Hispanic and Mexican guestworkers in America. In fact, the song brings in pieces of the whole history of guestworking in our country but it wasn't obvious enough and people never really caught on to it.' Their concern with US domestic and foreign policy was something which began to assume an increasing importance in their lives, though the group had yet to articulate this properly.

The slightly eccentric title of *Fables* was central to the album and to R.E.M.'s faltering steps towards a different role for their music in the future. 'Little America' had hinted at a growing political motivation, the band having seen the good and the bad in their homeland during their extensive travels. Fighting shy of manifestos at this stage, *Fables* represents a halfway house between the introspection of *Murmur* and the political attack of *Document*. In that sense, Michael accepted that 'a lot of people have picked up on the reconstruction politics thing, after the civil war and that was not unintentional. The whole reconstruction politics thing was a pack of shit and it's kinda like politics today.' Peter expanded on the theme in *Melody Maker* saying, 'It's a period when the South was rebuilt in the image of the way the North would like it to be. Y'know, it was a thing of promises made and not kept and a time when a place's heritage was kind of suppressed 'cause they're on the wrong end of it all. The South was wrong in slavery and on leaving the Union, but things went the other way after reconstruction.'

R.E.M. were taking up the cudgels once again on behalf of their beloved South. Mike felt that the thread of the record was 'just a sense of the South and a sense of the past, that's what I feel because having grown up down there, we have a sense of it that no-one else has. You can't get the mentality unless you live there; that pervades the record.' Peter accepted that 'this record has more of an atmosphere of a time, a place and a culture than the other two'. Perhaps this was the upshot of their relief at returning home from the road but then having to write the songs so quickly – all else was bypassed and their emotions of the moment were placed on record.

Wallowing in nostalgia for the South can't have made their stay in London any more pleasurable either. As they had admitted to homesickness in various forms, going into the studio and playing tracks that were meant to evoke Georgia was torturous and added to the miserable feeling that surrounded the sessions. Joe Boyd, however, remembers the band getting on as well as any other he'd worked with, though that may have been their Southern politeness preventing them creating a scene in front of outsiders. The sessions were the longest they endured, going right through March, which for avowed studiophobes like Buck and Berry was a nightmare come true. Bill in particular suffered during the recording of *Fables Of The Reconstruction*, beginning a long cycle of personal problems, as he told *Hot Press*.

I'm certainly in the right job to justify the kind of abuse that I was directing against myself. If you're an insurance salesman, you can't really drink on the job but it's okay for rock stars to abuse themselves ... a lot of it was that I had never had a chance to grow up and have any perspective of being other than the least important member of R.E.M.. My problem was that I took that home with me after the touring stopped. I was drinking very, very heavily. I've never really taken drugs. I've certainly never done heroin. I did cocaine for a while but that wasn't a problem because I didn't like it that much. Alcohol was a problem. It doesn't really screw things up on the road because having a hangover all the time is sort of your natural state but when I got home I realized that this wasn't right.

It wasn't until R.E.M. came off the road in 1989 that Bill finally sorted things out:

I stopped drinking long enough to learn that I don't really need it. Things started coming into focus. My marriage improved. I've been married since 1985 but it wasn't really a marriage until I got off the road and realized that I have other attributes apart from being a reasonably okay drummer with a very good group. I started respecting myself more and things just took care of themselves.

It's a measure of the poor state the rest of the band were in that they didn't spot the genesis of Bill's problems back in 1985; and of course it's nonsense for him to suggest that he is the least important member of the group, for if any group in the world can claim to be comprised of equals, R.E.M. can. Berry's songwriting has been inspirational at times, beginning 'Hairshirt', 'Everybody Hurts' and 'Perfect Circle' to name but three, and the R.E.M. songwriting process ensures that everyone stamps something of his personality on to each song by the time it's finished. Berry's drumming provides more than just a solid backbone for their music; it has an impressive improvisational quality that can completely alter the colour and shape of a song. It's unthinkable that the others failed to appreciate Berry's talents given their closeness, so one can only put things down to them having problems of their own. Peter owned up to that, remembering, vaguely, 'We weren't being very nice to each other around '85. We were just mean to each other. We didn't really talk. I seem to remember seeing most of that year from the bottom of a glass. If I had to go back and change something, I think I'd make us see a group therapist.'

March 1985 is not a month they remember with great fondness. 'Four weeks was a long time for us to be in a studio,' Peter complained at the time. 'We spent the usual amount of time actually recording but we just spent a lot of time mixing. Joe likes to do that, especially the final mixes, because that's where you can make it or lose it in a short time. We felt we'd mixed some of the others too quickly so we wanted to spend a little extra time on them. We mixed the tracks three or four times instead of once and I think they're better for it. It can be a real pain actually doing it that way but Joe was really great at that, so we thought we should use him to do it right.' *Fables* did sound like a more fully realized album in comparison with the 'bang 'em out' feel of *Reckoning* and it indicated a change in R.E.M.'s attitude to the studio, a change that would see them spending increasing lengths of time on writing and recording over the years.

Peter revealed, to no-one's great astonishment, that Michael was 'a great fan of those Library of Congress records, old guys in the hills banging away on pots and pans ... it's pretty much related directly to English folk music. Where it's recorded the people have been hidden away in the hills for so long they still speak with eighteenth-century English dialects. These songs have been done for thousands of years and that's where Michael gets his inspiration for a lot of things.' Michael admitted as much on 'Can't Get There From Here'; when in need of inspiration, he'd go to Philomath:

'The Reverend Ruth has a little K-Mart organ on his kitchen table
... [he and his wife] sing gospel songs. It's about the most amazing
thing you've ever heard ... it really brings you down to earth when
you think of digital recording and all that stuff and you realize that
these people are so much better ... the kind of thing where your
eyes are so much better than cameras.'

Michael's interest in folk history goes a long way to explaining
his use of language and the apparent complexity of his lyrics. His
conversation is peppered with archaic phrases and sentence
construction, a mode of speech that he has adopted – consciously or
subconsciously – from these backwood people. The friction caused
by this mode of speech, its combination with modern phraseology
and the electricity that powers the music is central to the band; it
helps them achieve a forward-looking nostalgia, another example of
their oxymoronic muse. To add to the confusion, Michael's
appearance – he sported a monkish crop and beard at this point –
and obvious fondness for this past lent him a kind of Amish aspect
at odds with his avowed lack of religious belief, but in keeping with
his work as a writer.

The Stipe conundrum went further than that, though his
fascination with the folk roots of the US played a very important
role in people's perception of it. On the face of it, to be a rock star
of sorts in a reasonably successful rock band must imply a desire for
celebrity, but R.E.M. genuinely seem to find it an annoying adjunct
to their main goal, which is to create an impressive body of work.
For Michael, the glare of publicity is even greater since not only is
he the singer, but he has become an enigma which people want to
dissect. If Stipe is such an enigma – and this seems grossly over-
exaggerated – it must be the source of his songwriting ability. To
strip him of mystery, then, would be an act guaranteed to destroy
that talent, so why continue to hound him?

Michael understandably enjoys solitude at times, finds it an
essential part of the creative process and is happy to shy away from
mainstream life. Doing this, he feels that he won't be picking up
influences that would turn his work away from its focus and
towards mainstream culture. In a report on Athens in *Vox*, Martin
Townsend suggests: 'Stipe isn't frightened by the usual invasions of
privacy: the photographing of his home; the discussions about his
sexuality; the publication of his annual earnings. What he does fear
is the invasion of his mind; the despoilation of his thought
processes. In silence and solitude almost anything can come
knocking at the door.'

Equally hard to explain is his fascination with film and photography, given their role in capturing and demystifying moments. As a compulsive documenter, it's essentially a prop that helps him capture a moment in time, yet he is fully aware that he isn't catching the reality and complains that you look at situations differently through a viewfinder, a technical requirement overcoming a visceral desire. If Stipe doesn't go so far as to subscribe to the primitive view that having your picture taken equates to the theft of your soul, around the time of *Fables* he was aware of a delicate balance between surface and mystery which had to be cultivated.

It was folk culture that redeemed the US for R.E.M., the idea that the country was still so vast that you could escape into it from the modern world. 'I'm real saddened by what's happened to this century, to the world. Specifically, America's become like a dumping ground, its culture is dying and when the cultures dies so does the country ... somehow that has to be preserved.' With *Fables*, Michael felt that he was nailing his colours to the mast, but he was also realistic enough to accept that he was toying with 'a romanticism ... that is somehow associated with that mythological America that never really existed except in people's minds'.

That romantic bent was often represented by train imagery on *Fables*. The railroads have an enormous importance in American history, since it was the laying of tracks across the land that paved the way for the colonization of the whole nation. The pioneering spirit has an undeniably romantic appeal. Mike admitted, 'It's very nostalgic. Who can listen to a train go by in the night and not cast your memory back a few years? They're a part of American heritage: to me it is essentially American, building the West with the Iron Horse and all that. Michael gets a real romantic feel from just looking and listening to trains, which is why it's all over *Fables*.' Peter had a comment to top that, as you'll have come to expect: 'I think everyone lives a stone's throw from the rail tracks, they would rattle me outta bed sometimes.'

'Auctioneer (Another Engine)' dealt with the idea and pace of travelling while 'Driver 8' had a similar feel. Mike explained: 'Driver wheels are the big wheels of a train, they've got them in big configurations and if there's eight, they call this "driver 8". But it's also about the number eight driver, the number eight engineer on this particular shift.' The song's lyric, which implores driver eight to take some time off, sounds like a comment on R.E.M. themselves, given their intensive schedule. That the band were finding life tough was reflected musically, too, as that shifted towards a darker texture, 'Feeling Gravity's Pull' in particular striking a malevolent tone throughout, based around Peter's discordant guitar. For Buck, 'It's really a twisted dreamscape which suits it perfectly ... our songs usually have a bridge to widen it out, make it airier, but this one we wanted to be really claustrophobic so we cut away at the excess stuff to get this weird crushed-in feeling which is where the strings come in. We put cello and violin on to add an air of doominess.'

As a comment on the state of the group, 'Feeling Gravity's Pull' was a little disturbing for observers, generating an atmosphere of disenchantment that plainly caught a band going through some internal crisis. The tone of the record as a whole was tired, perhaps even disappointed at times, but this song was almost violent in its frustration. The theme was picked up by the polarized 'Life And How To Live It'. Corresponding with fans on the Internet recently, Michael elucidated the thinking behind the song: 'Mr Mekis of "Life And How To Live It" had actually divided his house into two apartments, each outfitted different than the other on Meigs Street in Tinytown. I made it two houses for hyperbolic clarity.' The song mirrors R.E.M.'s need to adopt both private and public personae at different times, but also smacked of Stipe telling a waiting world that everyone has a multifaceted character and he is not alone in that.

Locked into a touring tunnel, it's little wonder that they tried to come up with a song to lighten the load, and that came in the shape of 'Can't Get There From Here', though it made listeners ask whether they were deliberately aiming for a hit single. 'Peter "almost funky" Buck! Let's face it, we're honkies, right?' Peter admitted. 'But we grew up with that soul stuff. This is the tongue-in-cheek poke at ourselves, you have to admit it's pretty silly for us to be in a soul group and silly for a lot of people to pretend to be soul men when they're not, so it's a light-hearted thing.' The Stax-style horns topped the song off nicely and it gave R.E.M. a chance to come up with a promotional video later that finally caught the humour in the group. It was a low budget romp that helped get them on to MTV at last, and started to change a few preconceptions of the group as serious and doom laden.

The final piece on the album was 'Wendell Gee', perhaps the most attractive song, and a peaceful conclusion to a record that had rarely approached tranquillity. The vocal conjured up images of the South, while the banjo which, according to Peter 'comes in like a chicken from hell', added to the flavour, taking it to another level. The harmonies were understated, but were touchingly nostalgic and admirably suited to the camp-fire feel of the track. The name was taken from a used car lot in Gainsville where, Peter says, the Gee family 'own the town'.

Fables Of The Reconstruction lacked a little of the spark that had characterized *Reckoning*. It didn't have as many songs that stood up in isolation, but as a seamless piece it eclipsed its predecessor. It would always be viewed as flawed, but it caught a moment where R.E.M. were no longer sure quite what they wanted or what they were. They were at a point when they were outgrowing their underground status and at a time where they were looking to shed their oblique image. For those reasons, it's an album that is a little tangled, askew and confused. But then, so was *Revolver*, and while not even R.E.M. themselves would suggest that *Fables* ever approaches the level of *Revolver*, it served as the same kind of clearing process, a shaking off of ideas that were no longer relevant, trying out new clothes and presenting a vivid image of a group in turmoil. *Fables Of The Reconstruction* closed the first phase of R.E.M.'s evolution. The more pressing question by now was whether they'd still be around to start phase two.

7

FORSIGHT HAS AN E

In 1985, having written and recorded an album within around six weeks, R.E.M. went straight into rehearsals and then back on the road. Starting at the end of April, they worked through to the end of August without a break. Using September as a holiday, they then continued to tour from 1 October to 20 December, with their few days off mostly taken up by travelling. Over those weeks and months, they covered the United States in its entirety, played two substantial tours of the UK and Ireland, visited Belgium (twice), Canada, the Netherlands, West Germany, France and Switzerland. This sounds like a nice, if hectic, package tour. The problem was, they'd done precisely the same thing in the wake of *Reckoning* and, prior to that, they'd not been off the road since the group had started in earnest back in 1981. Peter's view was stark, but realistic: 'We'd been on the road for five-and-a-half years and it was kind of tense. Everyone was tired of being away from home and broke and always in each other's company. We were staying at cheapo motels and sometimes you'd get a quart of beer and sit on your own in the parking lot. That would be the only time you could be alone for a week. It reached a point where we were ambivalent about going on.' Peter rejected the idea of breaking up, though, for there were still goals for which to aim: 'All I want to do is make great records and be a great band and play great live. I think it's within us to make one of those top twenty all-time rock'n'roll great records ... sometimes inspiration hits and you hope it hits when you're awake and you have a guitar in your hands.'

Bill was plainly worried that the touring process was taking its toll on the group musically, as well as turning R.E.M. into a job rather than a hobby. Speaking about *Fables* later, he claimed, 'The material was OK but the record we weren't happy with at all. We decided it wasn't the money we were in it for, it was the love of the records.' The dichotomy they faced was simple: to keep the band alive they needed money, but the drive towards getting it was killing the band. In many respects R.E.M. suffered the same industry pressures that beset Nirvana, the demand to keep working, recording, writing, touring and making videos, though R.E.M. were fortunate in that they were not in the public eye to quite the extent that Nirvana were later.

Returning to Athens from London once *Fables Of The Reconstruction* was completed, the group were struck by the horrifying knowledge that they had around a week to unwind and would then be gone until Christmas, eight months away. If they'd felt like throwing in the towel when they were recording, this really brought things home to them. The pace at which they were working was fraying nerve ends and disturbing their general health – the frenzied activity would do little for them musically either, as production-line values threatened to swamp musical ideals. There was a very real chance that they would cancel the first round of concerts at least, which would mean the album coming out without any promotion. In effect, this would have meant sacrificing the work they'd done in London so that they could rest and recuperate for a while.

In the end they decided to go back on the road for a variety of reasons, the most important being the quality of *Fables*. They were pretty proud of the album, which challenged the traditional Rickenbacker sound they'd perfected on the first two albums, and felt obliged to give it a fair shot, which meant touring it on release. Financial considerations entered the equation, too – cancelling gigs is a very expensive business, does your reputation no good and throws future work into question. Ambition was another motivating force, as Jefferson pointed out to them. Failure to tour would harm the record and their future. The choice was: remaining on the college circuit for life, making enough money to live but never reaching the wider audience beyond the already converted congregation; or touring, building up the audience, getting a higher chart placing for the album, and so engineering a breathing space for the following year, to be devoted largely to writing and recording.

Won over by this common-sense argument, R.E.M. fulfilled all their obligations – ironically, the work ethic which had almost driven them into submission became their saving grace as they submerged themselves and some of their anxieties into eight months of solid toil. An acceptance of their fate came by way of the bleak humour in their tour brochure – 'R.E.M. Ponders Perpetual Motion'. In fact, it was that humour and camaraderie that kept the group together, Buck agreeing that 'we reconcile pretty easily, that's one thing we figured we had to learn. You can't hold grudges and carry on – our friendship is more important than anything else we do.'

There were flare-ups of various kinds on tour; Peter was pretty candid about some of the problems that beset them when looking back several years later.

Nowadays if I don't go home in months I can get my clothes cleaned and eat real food. In the old days if I was gone for a year it meant I ate nothing but cheese sandwiches or the deli tray and slept on the floor of someone's house or in the van or shared a room, or even worse, a bed with Mike Mills. The one time you were alone was in the shower and maybe not then; there'd be someone shaving. Five years of that and everyone was really worn out. The lack of privacy was mind-boggling.

Living on top of each other was the greatest source of dissatisfaction, as firm friends found themselves occasionally at one another's throats. Bill remembered that 'Mike and Michael had some pretty bad friction going there for a while'. Michael's problems seemed especially severe, and some reports seemed concerned at his mental state during the course of a year in which he cultivated hairstyles ranging from the monkish, through a shaven head (including eyebrows) and a punky crop that he dyed yellow, apparently adding mustard each day to maintain the peroxide style. By the end of the tour he was kitted out in Salvation Army hobo chic and had taken to writing 'DOG' across his forehead, the ink running down his face as he began to sweat under the spotlights. There was a rational explanation, of course, as he told *Melody Maker*: 'I was so sick . . . I hadn't eaten anything but potatoes for a week 'cos the food is so bad in England. All I could eat was a sprig of parsley before I went onstage and I was vomiting and shitting. It was just awful. I felt like a dog so I took a felt tip and wrote it on my face.' For one as attracted by solitude and thinking alone as

Michael, spending so much time around others must have been particularly tiring – it certainly explains why he chose to ride in a separate tour bus as the group made its way up the ladder later in their career, a simple question of taste rather than the evidence of some bloody feud.

There were arguments within the group, but as a band their friendships were secure enough to be able to fight and then allow things to blow over. There were a number of occasions on tour when they were forced to close ranks and adopt the 'us against the world' stance that had been so strong a force in getting the band off the ground. Playing at Milton Keynes Bowl as support to U2 in June 1985, having agreed never to do these outdoor shows again, they had an especially torrid time from both the audience and the elements. Mike recalled 'having a conversation with this guy who was trying to hit me the entire time with a plastic bottle. I kept going, "Ah, not quite that time, try again," and I'd kick the bottle back and he'd try again. It was good fun,' he concluded unconvincingly. Ultimately, though, they accepted that they had chosen to set their face against internecine strife and had simply to reach Christmas intact, when they could reassess their situation.

That reassessment when it came was to change the way R.E.M. looked at everything that surrounded them. Although IRS had not been as heavy-handed as a major label might have been in pushing the band to work harder, tour more, write singles and make good-looking videos, pressure had been exerted. From the band's point of view at the end of 1985, they had worked non-stop for more than three years under the auspices of IRS and had relatively little to show. Certainly each album had sold more copies than the last, but *Fables* had only just made the top thirty, which was a relatively minor jump from the number thirty-six that *Murmur* had achieved. Even less encouraging were the reports coming from beyond the USA, where IRS did not have the machinery to push a group that were not blatantly commercial; in Europe, R.E.M. were a cult group but nothing more.

To be fair to IRS, R.E.M. didn't really provide the raw material for singles success. If the songs were strong enough – '(Don't Go Back To) Rockville' should have been a hit – the only promo that was vaguely suitable for MTV use was 'Can't Get There From Here' and that was not really 'posterboy' fare. In the long run, their unwillingness to make artistic compromise worked extremely well for them, lending an artistic gravitas and integrity that many

Michael Stipe on stage during the 1984 Reckoning tour.

Mike Mills, Lifes Rich Pageant, 1986.

Peter Buck in 1986.

Left to right: Michael Stipe, Bill Berry, Mike Mills and Peter Buck during their 1987 Document tour.

Berry and Stipe, Out of Time, 1991.

Peter Holsapple and Peter Buck on stage together, Out of Time, 1991.

Stipe during The Green Tour

At the MTV music awards, September 1993.

Stipe and Mills with Adam Clayton and Larry Mullen of U2 at
Bill Clinton's inauguration party, 1993.

Michael Stipe, Monster, 1994.

contemporaries lacked, but that way of working also meant that it would be a long haul before they reached their commercial peak.

Were R.E.M. seduced by money? This is a hard question to answer – had money been their prime motivator, they could have done so much more to get it without any additional work. By the same token, they felt that the work they were doing deserved a better level of reward and, given the touring schedule outlined above, it's hard not to sympathize with them. To that extent, *Fables* and the ensuing tour were a turning point. R.E.M. clearly felt that they were undervalued at this stage and vowed collectively not to allow that to happen to them again.

In retrospect, the *Fables Of The Reconstruction* album and tour can be seen as the beginning of the end for R.E.M. and IRS. Miles Copeland admitted as much later when he revealed to *Mojo*:

> They were getting to be a hot group and we went back to re-negotiate and said, 'We'd like to give you a lot of money right now and get two more records out of you,' which is a traditional thing you do in this business. And they said, 'Well, no, we're happy. We don't need to re-negotiate, we don't need the money. We'll go through the contract and when we've delivered all the records we'll go to the open market and obviously we'll consider IRS and we'll take it from there.'

If money wasn't the be-all and end-all for R.E.M., they had at least come to grasp the complexities of trying to make a career out of the group and the need to look at implications far wider than simply being able to do a concert on a Saturday night for a bunch of friends. The band had all had college aspirations at one stage, and Michael had been marked out as a particularly promising student. Having given up a number of years to R.E.M. it was perfectly understandable that they wanted it to go on and become a real success financially as well as artistically, though their expectations were not excessive; they simply wanted to engineer a comfortable lifestyle for themselves that would facilitate songwriting and recording.

Ironically, it was the very fact that R.E.M. were more concerned about making good records than becoming multi-millionaires that was to eventually lead them out of the independent sector. Since IRS were comparatively small and had a correspondingly small promotion and distribution network, a band had to work twice as hard to make the same impact that a major label could generate. When they went to Warners in 1988, all the machinery was in place to turn their records into international hits; the band had to maintain the quality of the work, but since they were virtually guaranteed better sales they had more time in which to create and work on new material. Warners gave them the creative freedom which IRS could never have delivered.

It's difficult to be sure that it was a conscious decision, but from the beginning of 1986, R.E.M. were very definitely looking forward three or four years, rather than just to the next record. With two more studio records required to complete the IRS contract, their attitude shifted subtly. Realizing that IRS could not offer any hope of real advancement in Europe, the band basically ignored the continent for the next two years with a few sporadic dates here and there reminding the hard-core fans that they still existed.

Peter spelled out the problem they had with IRS. 'IRS was distributed by MCA. I remember being told by MCA's Head of Promotion at the time of *Lifes Rich Pageant*, "We're not going to promote this record because there aren't any hit singles." I mean, he's sitting there telling me this. In Europe they assigned us the lowliest guy to do our promotion. He loved us, but he was like one step up from the guy making the tea.' Perversely though, Peter then suggested another reason to avoid Europe – embarrassment at being representatives of the US: 'We've got this horrible ding-dong of a president who none of us likes and it's almost as if we're supposed to be like ambassadors for America. I don't wanna be. I wanna come over here and say, "I don't want the cruise missiles in England either! I don't want it in my backyard. I don't want Reagan as President!"' Michael made the point at a live show recorded for German television by wearing a 'No Cruise' sticker on the back of his jacket.

1986 and 1987 were, therefore, devoted to keeping the USA happy, making records that were directly related to their home country and playing substantial tours to maintain their profile. The business logic was simple – if they could show a major label that they were a hit in the US once the IRS deal was finished, the offers would begin to stack up; the US is, after all, the biggest market in the world. By effectively restricting tours to the US only, they continued to improve their standing at home, while simultaneously avoiding the long periods on the road. This in turn meant an improvement in personal relationships in the band as well as giving time to make the records properly.

Whether it was a function of the greater time allowed to write and record or whether it was a deliberate commercial ploy, R.E.M. seemed to be getting a handle on writing singles – 'Fall On Me' on *Lifes Rich Pageant* and 'The One I Love' on *Document* were in the R.E.M. tradition, but were a little more obvious in style compared with previous offerings such as 'So. Central Rain' or 'Driver 8'. Peter Buck understandably bridled at such accusations, insisting, 'I'll set my job up against anyone else's any day and say that I make less concessions to what people tell me to do than anyone else around.' Of course he's right, but he has a job where people expect an unrealistically heroic devotion to the romantic 'starving in a garret' deal. When the videos that accompanied R.E.M.'s records became a little more MTV-friendly, increasing the audience for the band in their homeland all the time, questions were raised. Unfairly maybe, given that 'Fall On Me' still stuck out like a sore thumb, but they were raised all the same.

Although they had chosen to take some time off at the beginning of 1986, they were far from idle. Working on the dictum that absence makes the heart grow fonder, they each took to their own means of relaxation: Bill spent time fishing; Mike produced the Waxing Poetics' *Hermitage* album; and Peter produced albums for The Feelies and Dreams So Real, another excellent Athens band that worked in the R.E.M. guitar idiom; in addition, he went back to working at the Wuxtry record store, taking his wages in vinyl.

Their main work was with Warren Zevon, however. Mike, Bill and Peter backed Zevon on his *Sentimental Hygiene* album, Michael adding backing vocals on one track. While they were working on that project, they took one evening off to run through a bunch of old blues songs at Zevon's suggestion. Bill explained that 'it took about as long to do as it takes to listen to it', Mike adding, '[He said] we'll call it Monkey Wash, Donkey Rinse. We said fine and we all got drunk and cut this bunch of blues covers and "Raspberry Beret". We never thought it would be a real record – we didn't think anyone would have the balls to put it out.'

The record did surface in 1990 under The Hindu Love Gods moniker, though the R.E.M. participants weren't entirely delighted with its release. Mike pointed out that 'we didn't think about it for another three years and then all of a sudden his manager decided he wanted to make a record out of it'. Bill had no axe to grind with Zevon, saying, 'He kind of borrowed The Hindu Love Gods, took it for what he could – and I don't blame him. He's a great guy, good luck to him. I'm not so fond of his management though. It got a bit ridiculous – they were making demands on us, wanted us to do videos and stuff and we were saying, "Come on, this was done as a drunken thing!" Now they're saying we're sabotaging his career by not co-operating at this point!' In fact, given Zevon's commercial ill fortune, the album seemed to be more a case of capitalizing on the involvement of the ascendent R.E.M. to raise interest in a faltering career.

Michael also took time out to become more involved in production work, taking the helm for Hugo Largo's *Drum* which they recorded at John Keane's one-storey house in Athens, the site for many of R.E.M.'s own rehearsals and demo sessions. 'I have some sense of what you can and can't do in the studio and as far as I'm concerned you can do anything you want to do,' Stipe argued. 'The most important thing is to make sure that an atmosphere is created where everybody's comfortable and feels a real strong current of creativity. We did most of [*Drum*] on the front porch. You could hear the cars passing and people walking by on the sidewalk. At one point you can hear the screen door slamming shut. Somebody had walked out while Mimi Goese was singing. We just kept it in there. That's the kind of way I like doing things; it just seems real natural.'

Work also continued on making their Athens nerve centre a reflection of the group's philosophy. Michael admitted:

A giant influence on us was the Midnight Oil office in Sydney and also the National Resource Defence Council – we read about their office in New York where somehow, in that collapsing city, they're able to solar heat their office and get in carpeting made out of recycled tyres, use all recycled paper and all their light is natural. If they can pull something like that off in Manhattan, we had to ask ourselves, 'Why can't we do that here?' So we did.

R.E.M. have always been a very savvy group when it comes to business dealings, a reflection of the natural business acumen that Bill in particular brought to the table, plus the expertise of Jefferson Holt and Bertis Downs. Peter was able to say, quite sincerely, 'You can't believe how many people are really into that thing of making money. As if it means anything.' R.E.M. certainly were on the verge of making substantial sums of money, but the difference was that it was the by-product of artistic endeavour, a direction which they would have been following as a hobby anyway. Where R.E.M. made their fortune was by driving hard bargains to ensure that as much of the money generated by the group ended in their pockets rather than flowing into corporate coffers. Peter pays due homage to the Gang of Four who provided a basis from which R.E.M. could learn: 'We had opened for them and got to look at the way they worked and ideologically they were pretty great and musically they influenced us but I just felt so strong that they could do it on that level, signed to a major label but were able to keep a moral edge which I didn't see very much in rock'n'roll in the early '80s.'

Refreshed by their break, R.E.M. were ready to reconvene. They'd set the tone for the group year early on when they met at John Keane's studio to work on 'Fall On Me', using the time to try out a new producer, Don Gehman, who had most recently been working with John Cougar Mellencamp. They recorded in the spring at Mellencamp's studio in Indiana, which Gehman had helped build. Consciously looking for a harder sound in reaction to the folky instrumentation at the fore on *Fables Of The Reconstruction*, Gehman was a fairly obvious choice. Mike went on record in *Melody Maker* saying, 'Who else is there? We wanted someone who would make us sound like a band, really clearly and crisply and he did that.' Gehman said he 'felt that R.E.M. were great songwriters and had a great mystique, but a lot of the power was lost – they weren't able to get things across in a real direct manner. That was the essence ... my idea of how to make something direct and their idea about the fact that things weren't really supposed to be that way.'

This time around, they wanted to recapture the spirit of the exuberant live shows they'd played in the early days. Maybe the album was constructed deliberately for radio play – Gehman's record in that regard was certainly promising – or perhaps it was merely a case of R.E.M. wanting to play some real rock'n'roll to dispel the gloom and doom of the *Fables* tour. The outcome was their most mainstream record yet, a fact that was reflected in it becoming their first US gold record for sales in excess of 500,000. The only link with *Fables* came in the form of the folk ballad 'Swan Swan H', a swooning croonalong, the lyrics inspired by a book concerning post-civil war slave hymns. A lovely song, it provoked a slight note of dissent from Mike: 'The only thing Michael did this time that I can't stand was ... [the title] "Swan Swan H". I didn't know he was going to do that. I hate it. He does things to be different, that's great it makes us different from other bands and I like that. But that's just a little too much. Too far towards pretension.'

The most obvious shift from their previous output was Michael's voice, which was considerably clearer than it had ever been before – this may have been Gehman's influence, simply natural evolution, or a realization that if they were seeking bigger audiences they would have to be a little more obvious. If the latter is the case, they were less than convinced of the wisdom of the approach, including a number of tricksy tracks that could only dumbfound the mainstream, such as 'Underneath The Bunker'. Mike admitted that both that song and the cover of The Clique's 'Superman' (on which he took the lead vocal) were songs thrown in to the mix to lighten the load and to prevent the album from being taken too seriously, for by now R.E.M. were beginning to take a stand on issues rather than being purely introspective. It is this new conviction that seems to have pushed Michael over the edge towards a clearer lyrical and vocal performance, though the creation of a mystique and a wilful perversity were still the main tools of his trade. Mike pointed out, 'I think a lot of the humour in R.E.M. goes unnoticed but it's definitely there, there's a good amount of comedy. There has to be humour even in the most dire situations.'

A number of the songs on *Lifes Rich Pageant* were directly political, while others were more whimsical. The title of the record came originally from a line in a *Pink Panther* film, where Peter Sellars as Inspector Clouseau, undergoing yet another disaster, picks himself up, dusts himself off and pronounces these pitfalls to be all part of life's rich pageant. The album contains that kind of defiance as well as a comic element. 'These Days' encompasses both, with a breakneck backing track that established R.E.M. as political spokesmen voicing their concern, while simultaneously laughing at the absurdity of a rock band telling the rest of the world how to behave.

On the Internet, Stipe admitted, 'I made Mike sing this part at the end, "Take away the scattered bones of my meal." Oh, Lord, hope you're not disappointed with me there.' Michael had already made an apparent, though inevitably oblique reference to his burgeoning messiah status among rock's younger generation on the opening song, 'Begin The Begin'. He told his fans that looking to him for answers and reasons was unfair, that he was just a normal guy asking the same questions as everyone else. Berating apathy and the silent majority in the same song, Michael pointedly told his most fervent followers, the self-styled 'distiples' to get a life and start thinking for themselves.

Given the way in which R.E.M. were gradually becoming more and more feted as great soothsayers by the press across the world, they, and Michael in particular, were loath to add to the myth or to increase the degree of celebrity they had to endure. Unwilling to rush headlong into the mainstream with their new rock attack, the get-out clauses such as 'Superman', which proved they could still be a dumb pop band if they chose, were central to the record's construction. It was inevitable, however, that this was ignored amid apparent anthems such as 'These Days'. Mike conceded, 'He's being more topical than he has been, though for Michael being topical is like, so what? Who can tell y'know? Some of the songs are more distinctly about something than others but he still couches these ideas in such oblique phrases you have to be really lucky to stumble on where he's coming from.' On the other hand, as Don Gehman noted, 'I wasn't really interested in the music being perfect, I was more interested in providing a little bit more clarity to Michael's voice ... they were probably ready for it.' Michael must have agreed with Gehman's questioning of both his vocal style and his lyrics, since this time he sent a lyric sheet to some reviewers.

There are many moments of clarity on the record, especially with 'Cuyahoga', a gorgeous melody laced with beautiful harmonies that made a compelling contrast with the lyrical subject matter, looking at a past and future United States. Michael explained,

Americans are searching for a history that doesn't exist. In a really big way. That intrigues me. We're a restless people, however much we try and placate our spirit. We're still pilgrims. In Europe you can walk around in the sense of history, you feel a great sense of place. In America that sense of place is essentially a myth. Especially in the deep South. We destroyed a culture to build ours – that's what 'Cuyahoga' is about in a consciously naive way.

In that sense it was a leftover from *Fables Of The Reconstruction* in its nostalgic melancholy, but it was rather more savage, indicting previous generations with massacring the Indian people, and then the White history books for erasing the same people. Instead of the blissful America of a Rockwell painting, Stipe saw his country's history in the chaos of Pollock.

It was an American arrogance that he noted in the world round him too.

> It really is sickening to see people of my age walking around spewing this really right-wing, closed-mind, I'm number one . . . one of the great things about America is that there are so many things and places that if you've got any want to carry out an idea, you're probably more able to carry it out there than anywhere else. But when it gets to the point where people are stomping over everybody then I don't like it all. I'm not at home there.

'The Flowers Of Guatemala' continued in this vein, an apparently pastoral piece that borrowed heavily from The Velvet Underground in tone and which addressed itself to US foreign policy in Central America. Peter aligned the group with Michael's work when he said, 'We're living in a time of moral chaos – forty people go missing in Guatemala every week, why do we support that?' 'Hyena' carried a message of a country and a world gone mad a little further.

That drive for greater and greater wealth was reflected on 'Fall On Me', a deceptive song which carried an essentially ecological message, both about the dangers of acid rain and the corporate world which would buy and sell any commodity to improve its profitability. It dwelt on the dangers of ecological disaster as industrial corners were cut to make money: by the *Green* tour of 1989, it had come to sound prophetic when each night the song was directed at the Exxon Corporation (Esso), responsible for the spillage of twelve million gallons of crude oil into Prince William Sound in Alaska, and failing to clear up the mess promptly. 'Fall On Me' was perhaps the most coherent statement of the green politics with which R.E.M. were occupied and which would characterize their stance through the rest of the decade.

It also provided them with a route into the heavy rotation of MTV, the Stipe-directed video causing a stir with its ground-breaking style. Jim McKay, who worked on some of R.E.M.'s videos and who later formed the film company C-00 with Michael, commented, 'He works a lot with mistakes . . . take the video for "Fall On Me". He shot all this industrial footage and used every bit of it, colour bars and all. Then he played it upside down. And then he added the lyrics which no one was doing at the time. It was awesomely powerful. "Fall On Me" was also great because here you have a video that's being played on MTV, yet it has no girls, no cars and no band footage.'

Musically, *Lifes Rich Pageant* broke the R.E.M. mould. In the past, with Michael's voice taking a back seat, the music had as great a responsibility to convey a song's meaning as the lyric had; this time there was a subtle shift as Michael took a more conventional centre-stage role. As a consequence, the music had to change its focus, too. The layers of sound were pared back as the playing returned to an economy last seen on *Chronic Town*. This didn't necessarily make it a better record than any that had gone before, but it did help to make it more popular, reaching number twenty-one on the *Billboard* charts. The critics were unanimously in favour of a record that was easier to listen to than *Fables*, *Melody Maker*'s Mat Smith drawing the conclusion that it was 'R.E.M.'s greatest LP to date . . . a public baring of the collective soul'. *Sounds*' Edwin Pouncey was equally impressed, stating that R.E.M. 'have trodden wisely by cutting their own path through terrain that still enthralls them', and Andy Gill of *NME* noted that 'the sticker on the shrinkwrap bears the deadpan legend "Mammoth Huge Colossal Understated". That ain't the half of it . . . one of '86's benchmark offerings.'

Viewed from this distance, *Lifes Rich Pageant* seems the least substantial of R.E.M.'s albums and a slightly superficial reaction to the murk of *Fables Of The Reconstruction*, a record which has stood the test of time far better. There are certainly a number of very good songs on *Lifes Rich Pageant*, 'Fall On Me' and, in particular, 'Cuyahoga' matching anything else in the canon and 'These Days' emerging as an excellent rocker, but there are too many that feel like fillers, such as 'Just A Touch' and 'What If We Give It Away?'. In smoothing out the edges, R.E.M. and Gehman lost a little of the band's unique quality. While they didn't sound like an AOR rock band, it was an album that suggested a group heading in that direction. The legacy of the album was that it gave R.E.M. a new methodology, a willingness to question their work as a whole and as individuals and to avoid falling into the traps of complacency and repetition. It also indicated that they shouldn't give too much away. *Lifes Rich Pageant* is a record that seemed a little confused, as though they were uncertain of whether to reveal themselves to the mainstream or to continue along their chosen path. The answer was obvious, for as Michael noted at the time, albeit with his tongue firmly in his cheek, 'I don't think radio deserves me yet.'

8

NO SENSE OF DECENCY

Determined to maintain their wilful reputation and reluctant to do anything by the book, R.E.M. followed their most successful album to date by releasing a budget price compilation of B-sides and out-takes under the title *Dead Letter Office* in April 1987. It offered glimpses of their sources of inspiration with covers of The Velvet Underground and fellow Athenians Pylon, along with the more surprising Aerosmith; it also provided newer fans with a chance to pick up on the band's humour and their method of letting off steam in the midst of recording sessions by playing a drunken improvisation. As an insight into their working practices, *Dead Letter Office* was interesting but as a record to be played over and over, its saving grace came with the CD release, when the tracks from *Chronic Town* were added as bonus tracks. As the moving force behind the compilation, Peter accepted that it was an oddity for the fans – that was the rationale behind it, after all: 'We didn't have too many illusions that it would sell two million, it's a summertime album . . . I was gonna leave out some of the ones that were more embarrassing, but fuck it!' *Melody Maker* noted that 'the best of this suggests that even what the group have discarded over the years is more intriguing than the official catalogues of most of their contemporaries'.

Dead Letter Office made it clear that R.E.M. and IRS were soon to go their separate ways, as Peter suggested: 'If we put it out now, we can have control over what's on it as well as the packaging. If we were to change record companies we wouldn't have that control.' That admission set the tone for the year that followed. The indications were that R.E.M. had had quite enough of being a cult

107

band living on the road and wanted to make the move towards greater commercial success. Viewed in that light, *Dead Letter Office* was a kind of farewell to their ramshackle days, a clearing of the cupboards before they moved on to more traditional methods of work. The video compilation *Succumbs* was released in the US at the same time, replacing Bon Jovi at the top of the music video charts.

To reach a huge audience, you do not have to compromise your music to the point where it becomes muzak, but presentational and promotional concessions are required. A band has to raise its profile, has to be visible on television and played on radio. Within that though, there are a number of ways in which a band can subvert the typical rock star genre and do something original and provocative. This was R.E.M.'s modus operandi for 1987. The group realized that this would be their final year with IRS, although their public stance was that they would talk to anyone, including IRS, at the conclusion of the contract. For them, 1988 and 1989 were to be key years, a point when, having taken on the support of a major label, they would have to play the game a little more fully to take advantage of the corporate machinery offered by them. The album that would accompany the move into the big league would need to be toured extensively around the world, preferably with material that had a global flavour.

That being so, R.E.M. allowed themselves the luxury of concentrating on the US for a second year, choosing to play just a handful of foreign dates to maintain their profile. This had repercussions for their material, as their next album took American themes, notably in the realm of politics. This had two benefits; first it provided the opportunity to attack subjects that were dear to their hearts, as *Fables* and *Lifes Rich Pageant* had started to show. Secondly, there was every chance that home sales would flourish, improving their position vis-à-vis a new company.

Everyone has their own interpretation of R.E.M.'s music and motivations; that, after all, is part of their appeal. With *Lifes Rich Pageant* established as their most successful record to date, making a sequel would have been the obvious move, so R.E.M. did something else. Buck said, '*Lifes Rich Pageant* was like the Bryan Adams records – I really liked the record but it was very direct in a lot of ways. This time we wanted to make a loose, weird, semi-live in the studio album.' They did not take a leap into the avant-garde but they did develop the more aggressive aspects of their muse. In so doing they created a different kind of album, but one which was still direct and accessible to the public. If not a mainstream offering, it wasn't a retreat to the underground, either.

Political activism was the subject for much of this new album, *Document*, which was a bold move for a band wanting to attract a major label, although U2's success with *The Joshua Tree* earlier in the year and the *Conspiracy Of Hope* the previous year had shown that a sizeable proportion of young Americans were not put off by politics. In the aftermath, the major labels began looking at politics as a 'lifestyle choice' that they could exploit. Even so, R.E.M.'s outspoken attacks on the US and its politics might have made a few executives a little nervous.

Musically they caught the mood of the times, as Peter explained: 'The buzzwords for this album were "crunchy" and "angular" . . . anything jangly or comfortable was out. We wanted to make a noisy record rather than a commercial follow-up, which is the accepted practice. It was America in 1987, a feel of a big chaotic time, like standing in the centre of a whirlwind.' Michael took the reference further, whimsically remarking that 'there's a blind dumbness to this record that's real male to me'.

R.E.M. had often spoken about getting their live sound down on tape in the studio in the past, but had rarely been able to do so. However, since *Lifes Rich Pageant* had been their most direct collection so far, it made sense to continue working with Don Gehman in the hope that increased familiarity with one another might lead to the desired effect. With that in mind, the band had decided to record an old song, 'Romance', with Gehman in the winter of 1986 for the low-budget film *Made In Heaven*, before getting down to the next album in the new year. When the band were able to make the time available during their touring schedule, Gehman was already locked into other work and was unable or unwilling to spare them the time. His suggestion was that they get together with Scott Litt, who had been establishing a reputation for himself as the house engineer at The Power Station in New York where he had struck up a particularly good relationship with Nile Rodgers of Chic, the man who had produced records such as 'Let's Dance' for Bowie.

Litt's work with Rodgers meant that he was technically excellent – his work with orchestral sounds would prove to be vital to R.E.M.'s future – while his roots went back to working with The dB's on 1981's 'Repercussions'. Given the friendship between Peter

Holsapple of The dB's and the rest of R.E.M. – Holsapple had supported them alone in 1982 and would tour with them again as part of The dB's in 1987 – Litt had much to commend him. On a personal level, the five hit it off immediately in much the same way that they had with Mitch Easter five years earlier, and plans were swiftly laid to work on the next album.

Oddly, the album was recorded in Nashville's Sound Emporium Studio, a location almost totally at odds with the kind of music they were producing. Mike described it as an 'all-out attack' which was pretty close to the mark. *Document* saw them taking some of the lessons they'd absorbed on *Lifes Rich Pageant* and applying them in a more alternative fashion rather than the mainstream rock sensibility Don Gehman had encouraged. *Document* was more spit, less polish, but with the added prominence of Michael's voice and the more straightforward lyrical content with which he was toying, it was clear that it could only increase the audience.

Even so, R.E.M. should be commended rather than condemned for this record, since its increased popularity was a function of natural development rather than forced commercialism. If *Lifes Rich Pageant* had seemed to make a compromise towards a big rock sound, *Document* was a step back in many ways. It recaptured the essential R.E.M. spirit, it emulated the power of their live sound and, in its attack, it provoked debate on the state of America. It could so easily have been the first record in a descent towards easy-listening rock pap, but instead it was the first instalment in a golden period of productivity for R.E.M., a prolific run of form that has not yet come to a close. *Document* was the step that transformed R.E.M. from a brilliant, if sometimes wayward troupe that could be coerced into musical concessions into a powerful, adult rock'n'roll band that would rely wholly on their intuition and do things their own way from now on.

Musically there was change in the air as the group's foundations continued to shift. Mike's role was especially fluid as he took on increasing responsibility in the studio and as an arranger, leading to a minor split in the ranks between him and Michael on one side and Bill and Peter on the other. While this did not seriously threaten the band, there was nonetheless an increasing difference in opinion as to how they should make records. 'Bill and I prefer quicker, spontaneous and rougher recordings and Mike and Michael wanna work on things a bit more,' admitted Peter. 'The dichotomy between those factions is really good. I'd probably release demos if it was up to me and they'd spend two years doing a record and that tension is really a great thing, but not necessarily during the making of a record. It drives me nuts.' Scott Litt added that the change really began with this record: '*Document* started off as just that – a document of how R.E.M. play live off the floor in an ensemble situation. But on the mixing of that album I began to experiment a little until we reached a point where we'd found a consistent character in the band's studio sound. Up to that time they'd believed in simply knocking things out.'

Michael had come increasingly under the spotlight in the aftermath of *Lifes Rich Pageant* through the band's greater commercial success as well as the political aspects of his work. Choosing to keep to the political theme, with an eye on the presidential elections just over a year away, *Document* was filled with references to the state of the nation and the unsavoury nature of many of its leading lights. The central track was 'Exhuming McCarthy', referring to Senator Joe McCarthy who had organized the anti-communist witch-hunts of the 1950s. Peter noted in despair:

> Reagan is going to get us all in these little bush fires, little fights because he's scared of communists. It doesn't make any sense at all. It's all coming back – commie hunting I'm sure will return ... sometimes you just look around with disgust ... 'Exhuming McCarthy' is about exactly what it sounds like – it's the '80s and McCarthy's coming back, so why not dig him up?

Using McCarthyism as a metaphor for the ills afflicting the US, R.E.M. attacked the jingoistic noises emanating from the White House, the 'buy American' campaign, the protectionist lobby that was gaining ground and the government's determination to involve itself in foreign wars that would lead, they felt, to a wave of popular support on the back of some spurious patriotism – the 'Falklands Factor' as it's known in Britain. The Gulf War was the bloody culmination of the foreign policy initiatives that R.E.M. were pointing to on *Document*, and the stimulating work of groups such as R.E.M., and their pleas to fans to stop and think about the consequences of US policy, had its effect.

At the time of the Gulf War, Stipe noted the disturbing tide of disinformation propagated by the press and the way facts could be suppressed to present the government in a better light: 'It's significant to say that the biggest anti-war protest in the history of the States occurred in front of the White House and was not even reported in the Washington Post, a newspaper that's less than a block away.' He also accepted that he had an obligation to use his position in the public eye: 'Straightforward media reports don't motivate people anymore. News items don't stick, they come through and they're gone, horrors are regurgitated and sanitized in twenty-four hours. Especially in America which is so massive and decentralized . . . pop culture is still the one way in which someone who is without power can attain it and bring change.'

The band were not slow to illustrate the beneficial aspects that that war had on the US economy, castigating the vested interests and those loyal to the Bank rather than the ideal of the United States. As Peter expressed it, 'I personally despair of our president, his foreign policy and everything he stands for . . . the people [that run the US] are at best without taste and at worst a bunch of criminals.'

'Exhuming McCarthy' is a chaotic experience, the sugar-sweet harmonies rubbing against a caustic vocal performance, and the disorientating musical mix achieving the required atmosphere. It embodies the new confidence the band shows on *Document* compared with its predecessors. *Lifes Rich Pageant* had cloaked some of their political leanings in enigma and effects, but this time their intentions were rendered crystal clear by Litt's production and Michael Stipe's determinedly precise vocal. Peter explained, 'With the first record we definitely wanted to make a mystery record. I feel that on this new album, the songwriting is best served by having lyrics that are fairly understandable . . . it's a bit more harsh, more angular in some ways. It makes sense therefore to have the lyrics play a part in that, to be more upfront.' Michael didn't make any comment on the matter but it's apparent that he felt the time had come to be politically engaged and to nail his colours to the mast.

It would be overstating matters to say that R.E.M. were a group with a manifesto, but they now felt it was necessary to start pointing the finger at the culpable and asking pertinent questions. The band didn't try to become spokesmen for their generation, but simply felt that it was the responsibility of a big rock'n'roll group to use the opportunity for free speech that was presented to them. They weren't shy of accusing their countrymen of apathy or ignorance either, as Michael went on to the attack: 'People see

Kennedy as a beacon of liberalism. They forget the other things he was involved in – Vietnam, the Bay of Pigs. History seems to have been rewritten around him because he was assassinated, he was immediately set up as a martyr, a legend. He became an American myth and America loves myths. America is more comfortable with myths than the truth.'

In trying to put the case for change, R.E.M. were merely hoping to provoke debate, suggesting that their audience should become more involved in their own lives and should get more information on the world around them. Their own opinions did, of course, permeate the songs though; Peter felt the record was 'a sideways look at the world and us. It has a kind of Orwellian wry humour. It's not that we're making light of America, it's just that I can't look at it the way Bruce Springsteen does. To me, America in 1987 is Disneyworld.'

'Finest Worksong' followed in that vein, with its insistent, driving rhythm that was effectively a call to arms. R.E.M. made no secret of their desire to rearrange the nation's behaviour. They wanted the American people to be allowed to return to their best, most decent instincts and to create a society that cared as much about its homeless as it did about its captains of industry.

A shameless evocation of the work ethic is set against a backdrop of mass unemployment. In Peter's words, 'America's pretty much the fat selfish man of the Western world. We put nuclear weapons in Europe, we invade central America, we don't pay attention to the homeless and hungry in our own country. What's to be happy about?' Buck's swooping guitar on 'Finest Worksong' sets the astringent tone for *Document*, and his guitar-playing is the focus of the sound this time around: 'It seemed that on the last record there was very little room for guitars because of all the keyboard parts. This time I got a bit greedy!' It was a move that suited the material admirably, giving Stipe's words the aggressive backdrop required. Even so, Peter had to reassess the songwriting process under some duress from his colleagues. 'I'm the one who has to have a chorus in each song,' he confirmed, adding, 'there are three or four songs on this LP which just don't have a chorus in the accepted sense, which is neat.' Much of this was a result of Mike's handle on the arranging side of group activities, as he insisted, 'It's all about chaos and the absence of control. It was done very much in a state of confusion which is what we all are in . . . a lot of our songs now are starting to be written in a different manner. Rather than sitting down with one guitar to write, everybody's been writing as they play noise – the big band theory of songwriting.' It was that new method that gave rise to the album title, according to Peter: 'I like it because it's dry and straightforward and the record is not. The word that I've taken to using to describe this record is "chaos" – it's a bit more chaotic. I kind of like that contradiction, because the record is noisy and strange ... it's exploding outwards, more free-form ... it's so obviously not linear.'

'It's The End Of The World As We Know It (And I Feel Fine)' does include a chorus, but it is definitely not linear. More importantly, it gives light relief to an album that is serious in tone; without such songs, *Document* could seem portentous and pompous, but this track, which had its origin in one of Michael's dreams, pricks that particular balloon.

There's a part in 'It's The End Of The World As We Know It' that came from a dream where I was at Lester Bangs' birthday party and I was the only person there whose initials weren't LB ... it's like a collection of streams of consciousness ... I wrote the words as I sang it. When they showed me that song in the studio I just said it's the end of the world as we know it and I feel fine. I wanted it to be the most bombastic vocal that I could possibly muster.

Decidedly humorous in content, it also maintains the theme of disaffection with the US's foreign policy, the SDI (Star Wars) project and the attendant risks which that carried for world peace. The apocalyptic theme of that song is echoed throughout the album by the recurrent theme of fire. In the same way that *Reckoning* had been called 'File Under Water', *Document* was subtitled 'File Under Fire'. The incendiary imagery is not coincidental in a record that details conflagratory times.

Peter was forthright about the state that his country was in and the way in which people were being discouraged from thinking for themselves. 'Though I like Bruce Springsteen, sometimes his songs get misrepresented as Ya Hoo American stuff. That's so disgusting to see a crowd of people waving flags and thinking your country's great when in fact we're going through a dangerous period.' The only way to respond was with the vitriolic fervour that some of these pieces carry. 'Welcome To The Occupation' covers Central America, a perennial preoccupation, as Michael conceded:

'Essentially "Occupation" is a rewriting of three songs that went before it. Mainly it's revisiting "Green Grow The Rushes" [and "Flowers Of Guatemala"] – a song about Central America. I do that a lot.' Its companion piece of sorts is 'Disturbance At The Heron House', a song of which Michael was particularly proud, though he was to be disappointed with the reaction. 'I think "Disturbance At The Heron House" is the most political song I've ever written and yet a lot of people never got it. Metaphorically speaking I might still be a little too obtuse. It's a failed revolution, that song – Orwellian.'

The tone of *Document* is cynical, a departure for a group that had previously tried to uncover optimism in their work. In retrospect, there was a tinge of regret that their record had been so bitter without offering any kind of hope in return. R.E.M. had never been a brutal group, but on *Document* they changed that with a vengeance. It was, as the cliché goes, a record of two sides, the political on one and the more personal on the other. Inevitably, there are personal ramifications coming from the political and so it was with 'The One I Love', the song that finally provided R.E.M. with a hit single in the US and promptly secured their future, though Peter jokingly suggested there might not be one: 'I always thought the day we had a hit single it would be one of the seven signs of the world ending.'

'The One I Love' was widely misinterpreted, riding to success on the back of that misunderstanding in the same way that Springsteen's 'Born In The USA' had. This caused some concern in the camp, with Peter asking, 'I wonder if people listen to the records and really know what's going on musically and lyrically, that's what you worry about with success: a huge audience that don't really care.' Michael later professed to being happy with the misapprehension, given that the song is so violent; taken as a standard love song by the public at large, it is actually a sadistic, vicious put-down of a lover used as a way of marking time – Michael's dispassionate vocal has just the right air of detachment to make the skin crawl. 'The One I Love' appears to be the final outcome awaiting a nation which R.E.M. felt had been desensitized by television and media manipulation, a people who could only respond to situations and to others in a selfish, wholly callous fashion. Stipe claimed, 'We're essentially a brutal race and we're gonna continue to fight with one another but you do what you can.'

The rest of *Document* harks back to previous glories, though

'Oddfellows Local 151' is not an affectionate memory. By now, US legends angered the group rather than attracted them, for they could see the seeds of the nation's current problems in its desire to mythologize. 'Oddfellows' is an attempt 'to debunk *Fables Of The Reconstruction*', according to Michael, creating a new story for new times. Peter went further, remarking that it is about 'these winos who used to live down the street from us, they used to live in cars . . . and drink all the time'. For these people, the American dream means little or nothing and the group wanted to capture that aspect of modern America: 'the home of the brave as the home of the mad' as *Melody Maker*'s Allan Jones termed it. On the other hand, R.E.M. were still a mischievous bunch as 'Lightnin' Hopkins' shows. Peter clarified the song: 'It's not a tribute, Michael told me to say that it doesn't mean anything, that it's utter bullshit.'

Document is a tribute to R.E.M.'s strength of purpose and clarity of vision. It represents the culmination of seven years of hard work, a record that finally placed them firmly within mainstream popular culture. They had reached that plateau on their own terms, or as close to that ideal as most bands you could name. It was a time for a little celebration, but also for reflection. Peter was in ruminative mood, though he surely had an eye on the future too, for by now a major record deal was a racing certainty: 'You know, people say we don't play the game, but I don't know. To a certain degree we do things that are unpleasant to us, photo sessions and the like. It's just that we don't do things that we feel are deplorable or are against our ideals. They'd like us to have a glitzy video where we all sing and look sincere and there's a pretty girl and we have to say, "Wait a minute. If we did that we'd look such pricks."' Keeping his options open for the future and girding his loins against the inevitable cries of 'sell out', Buck's honesty was admirable because R.E.M. have, like anyone in a multi-million dollar business, had to compromise. Their lasting monument is that they've done less of it than most.

Document was again well received, though *Q* mourned the passing of their glaring eccentricity, Mark Cooper finding 'the band employing an acerbic cutting edge . . . this is their most forthright LP yet, perhaps a trifle less loveable as a consequence.' David Quantick told *Sounds* readers that *Document* was 'loaded with Stipe's hilariously black version of the world and music like hellfire . . . after four albums of weirdness, R.E.M. went off and decided to make a sensible record. It's brilliant.' Allan Jones of *Melody Maker* noted that R.E.M. are 'bleak not cheerless, rage mitigated by a black, laconic humour', adding that *Document* is like being hit by an avalanche. It's bruisingly direct, explicit, stripped of ornamental diversions.'

The live shows that accompanied it achieved a similar power, although R.E.M. chose to play for a mere two months this time, an indication that they were taking things easy in preparation for their crack at world domination under the auspices of Warner Brothers. However, the *Work* tour, as it was titled, drew press comment of another kind. Since R.E.M. had now entered the stadium league as a rock band, they had a large crew on the road with them, necessitating a second bus to carry the extra people. Michael soon began to travel in one bus, with Mike, Peter and Bill in the other. This inevitably led to stories of factions appearing in the R.E.M. ranks and an imminent breakdown. This was exacerbated by the fact that Natalie Merchant from 10,000 Maniacs, the support act on part of the tour, was travelling with Michael. The fact that they were obvious admirers of each other's work allowed the press to jump to conclusions as to the intimacy of their relationship. Both stories were unfounded, Michael refusing to comment on the Merchant gossip except to say, 'I'd like to quash that story.' As to the travel arrangements, he was more voluble. 'We need two buses because of the number of people and so we use one for quiet and one for everything else. Travelling on the bus is often the only chance I get to have a meeting with someone or just think and things can get pretty rowdy on the other bus sometimes. I also like fresh air a lot and open windows can drive other people crazy.' Another rumour prosaically nailed.

Live, R.E.M. were recognized as a force to be reckoned with, *Melody Maker* saying they were 'what U2 should have been, a stadium rock band that absorbs rather than merely reflects light, churning and regurgitating the most basic of elements into a roaring storm'. However, the move into stadiums was not all that it was cracked up to be: Mike Mills fretted that crowds there lapped up anything that the band did without any kind of questioning or discernment. That led to 'Turn You Inside Out' on the next album, but its most significant legacy was to set their collective face against IRS and towards a big label in the knowledge that this was the only way to free themselves from the touring treadmill, and to give them time to think again about how they wanted to operate in future.

Even if the group had been heading inexorably towards this

decision for the previous three years, it was still something they took seriously. IRS had, after all, given them their chance and they were on good terms with the company, while there were worries that a multinational corporation might not be the best ideological setting for a band such as R.E.M.. In the end, the options a bigger label offered were highly seductive. Peter complained bitterly that

> It's embarrassing that Elvis Costello and Husker Dü turn out so many albums. We could turn out records at that rate if we were at home. As it is we have to cram songwriting into three weeks. Also, as we get older we have a bit less patience with hotel rooms and crummy food ... every now and again you find yourself in Iowa at two in the morning and you haven't eaten for two days and all that's on TV is *Gilligan's Island* and you think, 'Why am I doing this?'

To emphasize the point, Peter turned up in the news pages during the UK visit to promote *Document*; he appeared on the roof of the Mayfair Holiday Inn, stripped to the waist and in a 'tired and emotional' state. Returning to his room, he walked out the fire escape and ended up locked out and on the roof. He attracted the attention of passers by dropping his clothes on to them from a height of 200 feet before he was rescued. Buck had clearly had enough of the road and was looking to make some more records, a view that was true of all four.

In fairness to the group, they made no excuses or apologies for the move and did not try to pretend that the money had nothing to do with the deal, sensible PR given that the contract they finally signed with Warner Brothers was rumoured to be worth around $6,000,000. Peter conceded, 'We've always wanted to be successful. It's just the trappings that leave us a little ambivalent – the stadium dates, the MTV awards, the interviews and endorsements ... you don't survive in this business without an ego. We never entered this for a career but now we're here we want to give as many people as we can the chance to hear us.' Michael gave him support on this point telling all and sundry, 'IRS's distribution had gone as far as it could and it was time to move on to someone who could get the records out worldwide.'

As a farewell gesture, R.E.M. helped compile the collection *Eponymous* which was released in October 1988, contributing sleeve notes to the package as Peter had done with *Dead Letter*

Office. Sounds commented that it 'reminds us that the decade's most consistently excellent rock band have kept us entranced by their dreams since 1981. Let's hope they don't wake up just yet.' *Melody Maker*, on the other hand, saw a cheap cash-in: '[The cover] says "File Under Grain" – "Gain" would have been more appropriate.' *NME*'s Edwin Pouncey came closest, writing, 'There is a note of finality about this record, the sound of a door being firmly closed behind them.'

Michael understood IRS's financial reasoning behind the record, but was dismissive of the track selection:

> I don't think I would ever listen to it. There are only two songs I like on it ['Finest Worksong' and 'Fall On Me']. My greatest hits of the last five years would be very different from that and would probably be incredibly boring . . . IRS gave us this list of songs they wanted to go on the record and we said, 'Well, let's not put on 'Radio Free Europe' from *Murmur*, let's put on the original.

Michael was also responsible for the sleeve art; the angelic portrait was 'my high school graduation picture. I felt like after eleven years I get to redeem myself for that photograph because my mother refuses to take it off the shelf. It's something that everyone in America can completely connect to because you get your picture taken when you leave school and they take it to their labs and take off all your pimples and give you blue eyes'.

But R.E.M. were not willing to continue as a parochial American band any longer and, in order to make the transition to international status, they needed a corporate machine behind them. Mike accepted that there were many dangers to be confronted once they'd taken Warners' money: 'There are a lot of qualms about moving to a large record company like that. There are a lot of possible disasters that could happen. I feel like we've pretty much taken care of the contingencies though.' Warners' reputation as an 'artists label' stood them in good stead with R.E.M. when they entered the ring as a potential company, and their head Larry Waronker himself was a record producer of some note, though Michael suggested they signed with Warner Brothers since it's 'the home of Bugs Bunny'.

The band went through some soul searching before inking the contract, though surprisingly this was more over whether or not they should continue with the group rather than over the move to Warners. Michael described the process he underwent:

> I had to reassess the last seven years and decide whether or not I wanted to take that big of a leap . . . and it is a huge, really colossal leap for us as a band and as a business and as everything else that we are . . . as friends. Having assessed that, I decided yeah I wanna keep doing this and I wanna work with these people and I really admire and love them. I felt like we had a couple more records inside of us that were really great.

Going further, he confirmed that the band's chemistry was the source of its momentum, but declined to enlarge on that, arguing, 'I think to pick it apart like a frog on an operating table would maybe destroy it.'

Ultimately, the musical credibility of R.E.M. in the future was the decisive factor that pushed Stipe into continuing; once they decided to carry on, there was never any question that Warners would help them achieve the next rung on the ladder of ambition. They were a little worried that fans and media alike might take this move in the wrong spirit and accuse them of selling their collective soul for money, so to counter those accusations, Michael went out of his way to stipulate that 'nothing has changed except that the move from one company to another has excited the band all over again . . . we were very specific about our contract. We have absolute control over everything. We give them the record and the cover art and say "Here's our album?" That's the way we've always done it.'

It's interesting that Michael used the phrase 'excited the band all over again'. The feeling of renewal and of regeneration is very important to R.E.M., for whom repetition is anathema, hence their growing distaste for the regimented kind of touring a band of their size has to endure. The last couple of records with IRS and the realization that they could only ever present themselves to an American crowd was a demotivational factor to them, putting a ceiling on their ambitions. Additionally, they had nothing to prove to IRS – they were the biggest band on the label and could have stayed with them forever without being challenged. A move to Warners meant that they had to convince a new company and their employees that here was a group worth backing. The increased exposure compelled them to produce new songs that would move a vast new audience that had yet to hear them since the multinational set up ensured that they were approaching new territories and new perspectives where there were no preconceptions about the group. In the small underground pool where R.E.M. was a very large fish indeed, there were no new hurdles to surmount, nothing to push them on to greater glories. With Warners, they faced the biggest test of all – to infiltrate and conquer mainstream music opinion without diluting their musical vision in the process.

9

WITH FEATHERS

With negotiations between R.E.M. and Warner Brothers out of the way, the group returned to Athens and set aside a couple of months to write new material for their debut Warners record. Writing ran from February 1988 through to April, a substantial increase on the time they'd previously allowed themselves. Scott Litt picked up on the attitude the band had as soon as recording began at Ardent Studios in Memphis in May: 'We booked eleven weeks which is an incredibly long time. They were very aware of the importance of the album . . . they were happy to take the time to experiment.' With the might of Warners behind them, they could finally afford to pay for this additional studio time, a luxury they used rather than abused. Indeed, this was the greatest benefit that the band derived from Warners' money, Michael claiming, 'Money doesn't wig me out. I tend to ignore it and I'm not concerned with the ramifications of being rich or poor. Of course if you can't afford to eat, that's a problem and you have to deal with it but having extra money is just a luxury.'

In spite of the weight of expectation this new project carried, they did take some time out at the beginning of the year to work on individual projects so that they could return to the band with fresh ideas. Michael co-wrote a song with Athens duo Indigo Girls, 'I'll Give You My Skin' which turned up on the 1991 PETA benefit album *Tame Yourself*. The whole group subsequently contributed to Indigo Girls' eponymous debut record. Michael received 'an offer to play Lord Byron in a Frankenstein movie but Michael Hutchence beat me out of it', so turned to producing the Hetch Hetchy album, *Make Djibouti*, which featured his sister Lynda. At the same time

Peter played some gigs with Robyn Hitchcock, appeared on his *Globe Of Frogs* album and went into the studio with The Primates and The Ladidas; more importantly he found the time to get married. His wife Barrie was the co-owner of the 40 Watt Club in Athens where Peter had spent much of the previous decade. Bill refreshed the creative faculties by recording a solo single ('My Bible Is The Latest TV Guide'/'Things I'd Like To Say') for release on Jefferson's Dog-Gone label. This burst of creativity made it perfectly clear that everyone in R.E.M. had their own musical agenda to follow, the results adding something to the overall mix of their albums.

The main business of the year was to compile their sixth studio album which would be called *Green*, for reasons Peter made clear. 'Green is everything that you want – youth, maturity, growth, strength and also it's money and the other kinda nasty, grubby things.' They approached accusations of obscene wealth with a jaunty humour, such as suggesting that the filthy lucre had been delivered to their door in a large van, and defused those comments by making them appear ludicrous. Behind the scenes in songwriting rehearsals, they were ready to approach everything about themselves anew, to rip up any R.E.M. rule book and start all over again. Michael was particularly taken by this iconoclastic attitude: 'I feel that *Green* is pretty much *Murmur* revisited. I went back there pretty intentionally and the rest did too, though it wasn't a spoken thing ... that irony is not lost on me. A similar cover. Material that carries different interpretations, kinda internal and knocks you down at the same time and makes you ask, "What's this about?"'

The internal dynamic may have been similar to that on *Murmur*, which had the same urge to create a 'mystery record' of sorts, a level of excitement at a new departure and the determination to produce their very best work, but from the fan's perspective the two records have little in common musically or lyrically. The most obvious thread between the two is that element of mystery; recognizing that they were about to be exposed to a vast new audience, R.E.M. had absolutely no intention of playing to the lowest common denominator and making the songs and their content blatantly apparent. Instead, they made it clear that people would have to put in some work of their own to get the full benefit of the new record, introducing the new supporters to the R.E.M. way of doing things.

Green was not only a reaction to their new status as 'major label recording artists' but to *Document*. They all felt very strongly that *Document* had been a little too brutal at times. Given that 1988 was an election year and that all the indications pointed to George Bush sweeping the polls, the collective feeling was that people would need some encouragement to get through the difficult times ahead. Peter accepted that 'hope was a nice quality to have on the record this year ... *Green* is probably the album that reaches out most positively. *Document* was cynical and Michael said he didn't want us to write another set of angry songs ... that's not necessarily a bad thing in 1988.' Michael, for his part, chimed in with 'hope is important, it's an intrinsic human emotion to think there is some light at the end of the tunnel'. For the liberal sections of the community who had been savagely attacked and increasingly marginalized by the myopic right-wing government and media, it was a source of strength that a group as successful as R.E.M. lent their support to alternative ideas and ideals.

Avoiding angry outbursts was difficult for concerned Americans and Peter finally exploded in a *Melody Maker* interview prior to the election. 'We're pigs! Americans are pigs! I think I'm gonna be a pig that owns a gun. I'm so fucking furious I feel like shooting people – George Bush first then the people who vote for him ... if Adolf Hitler came back and said, "I won't raise taxes," he'd win in a landslide.' Mike the diplomat balanced the rant by telling people not to shoot Bush on the grounds that Dan Quayle would then become president.

R.E.M. were not planning to desert the political arena just yet, but they did begin to layer their music with a possibly unrealistic hope. On balance, their retreat was probably justified; certainly further vociferous musical protest would have done them few favours as a band embarking on a new phase of its career, but the real justification for their subtle shift in emphasis was far more deep-seated than selfish financial considerations. The '80s had already seen the likes of Sting, U2 and Peter Gabriel flying the political flag with varying degrees of success; among those Gabriel was the archetype. By dipping in and out of the political maelstrom, he had never sacrificed his role as an entertainer first and as a writer with political leanings second. Sting and U2 had both become so submerged in their roles as ambassadors for the rain forests or as political mavericks that fans who did not agree with their politics had begun to ignore them. Gabriel's approach had been more insidious, hooking people with 'Sledgehammer' and then getting them to listen to 'Biko' too.

This was the way in which R.E.M. chose to work, Michael confessing, 'I'm kinda going against a lot of the things I said earlier on. I felt like music and politics do not mix too well. I have been attempting though to combine those two elements in a way that does work, that is not didactic, not preachy, not messianic in its approach and delivery.'

A very large, die-hard section of R.E.M.'s fans understood that R.E.M. was not the only thing in the lives of the four individuals and that they had an interest in Amnesty International, Greenpeace and many, many other organizations. R.E.M. were therefore in a position to influence their fans politically. Peter told Q about their extracurricular activities: 'We go to city council meetings, we give money to certain candidates, we vote, we sign petitions, we've done benefits for local food banks and AIDS organizations.' Back in 1987, for instance, Michael had recorded a message for Senator Wyche Fowler that went out on local radio; the admiration was reciprocated a couple of years later when Fowler held a fundraising reception in honour of R.E.M., later giving a speech in praise of the band's 'stewardship of our planet's resources' in the House of Representatives.

Their local activity extended to supporting a candidate for Mayor, the sublimely named Gwen O'Looney. 'She's a wonderful woman,' Peter told *Sounds*.

She's forty-two and has spent more or less her whole life helping others – she served in the Red Cross in Vietnam, for example. Then these real estate developers who were standing against her accused her of being a dope addict and all these hippy-free-love-sex clichés. Because we'd all quietly given money to her campaign they started talking about all this stupid Satanist rock crap – if I had a tape of it I'd sue for libel. If they want to see an uneven race we could quite easily play a show at the Coliseum, bring in 50,000 people and slap a few hundred thousand dollars into the campaign fund ... we didn't do that because I don't think it's our job but if they're gonna call us Satanists because we each gave her $800, there's a whole new level we could take it to. In the end the fat, red-faced old men lost ... they said Gwen got the hippy, conservationist, women, minority, college student vote. Who does that leave out? She got everyone's vote except the real estate developers!

Political engagement was an integral part of their personal lives, bearing out their 'think global – act local' approach, the chain reaction theory in action once more.

Michael illustrated his commitment to a number of causes in and around the *Green* process with his film company C-00. As the band's supporters would have come to expect, the company did not indulge in the production of mindless entertainment, but instead looked at ways in which it might stretch people's minds. Using his own personal power as a 'media celebrity', Michael told the world, 'I just had no idea how lacking our population is in public figures who speak common sense.' US law had provided an opportunity to address that shortfall by insisting that television channels air a certain number of Public Service Announcements (PSAs), 'usually to the effect that we ought to be more kind to dogs', according to Michael but this piece of legislation was revoked by the Reagan administration. Trading hard on Michael's celebrity status, C-00 were able to get their films shown as he explained in *Hot Press*:

> We're going to make seven and they'll range from women's rights to organic farming to AIDS information to racism to why the military should be put to use cleaning the environment . . . we've also made one hour-long documentary. It's called *The Duplex Plan* and it's essentially interviews with these old men in a nursing home in New York state about their opinions, memories and values. It's pretty funny but it's kinda sad.

The point about employing the defence forces to clean the environment was well made, for environmental concern was to be the theme of the *Green* year. Even so, the group could not resist one final political act, ensuring that *Green* came out on the day of the presidential elections, 8 November 1988, the day George Bush was elected the forty-first president of the United States. The advertising for the album was initially intended to show a picture of the album alongside a picture of Bush's opponent Michael Dukakis, with the slogan 'There are two things you need to do today', but it proved impractical.

Michael had already made the point in college newspapers in

Georgia and California by taking out adverts which read 'STIPE SAYS/DON'T GET BUSHWACKED/GET OUT & VOTE/VOTE SMART/VOTE DUKAKIS', the 'Bushwacked' pun later turning up on 'Drive' from *Automatic For The People*. He took a lot of flak for this approach, the press accusing him of abusing his influential position. Given that the mainstream press in the US is fairly right-wing and was right behind Bush, this is something of a hollow claim, as the advertisement was merely his small attempt at redressing the balance. It was interesting that he chose to place an advert in California, given his disparaging views on the state: 'I have this theory that people in California, they're the people that just went and went until they couldn't go any further unless they fell into the ocean. So they set up a lemming camp and that became Los Angeles.'

The level of application R.E.M. demanded from listeners was matched by their own reappraisal of how they should write and record. When the band had started, much of the musical friction and originality had resulted from Mike and Bill's experience and ability colliding with the naivety of Peter and Michael, who would never have called themselves accomplished musicians. However, having played guitar night after night for eight years, Peter now felt, 'I've gotten kinda competent on guitar and I can write R.E.M. songs in my sleep, but on mandolin or dulcimer I stumble around in the dark, I don't know what I'm playing.' Peter had experimented with a mandolin during the *Work* tour, which led into an early idea the group had for *Green* – making one side acoustic music, the other 'bubblegum heavy metal', as Peter termed it. That plan fell by the wayside, though its influence was to be found in a number of the songs, but it was the use of new instruments that really brought a new life and dimension to R.E.M. in songs like 'Hairshirt', 'You Are The Everything' and 'The Wrong Child'.

Six albums down the line, they were questioning their own validity and certainly their methods. Scott Litt, who was becoming more central to their recording, told *Melody Maker* that *Green* was a difficult record to write in the light of this ongoing assessment. 'At the time they were still very much in two camps. Peter, Bill and Mike would present virtually finished songs to Michael and he'd say, "I'm not so keen on this." Then he'd hear one of them messing around on a mandolin drone or something and say, "That's great. What is that?" So we started building songs around soundscapes rather than chord sequences.'

'Hairshirt' is a perfect example of this new musical style, with its spontaneity making it one of the very best songs on the record. It is based on a mandolin riff that Bill hit upon, bringing to mind his childhood days as a ukulele player. Peter – who actually played mandolin on the record as Bill played bass and Mike accordion – admitted, 'When we were doing demos "Hairshirt" was one minute ten seconds long and we only played it one time at a soundcheck. When we did the album, Michael said, "Play that for six minutes." He filled up every second and I didn't even see it coming.' One of the more melancholy moments on the album, 'Hairshirt' might have been construed as autobiographical with the same sense of self-doubt and futility that had been included in earlier material, but it could just as easily be interpreted as an acceptance of the solitary nature of modern life. As promised, Stipe was not going to allow himself to be pigeon-holed this time around, and the layers of mystery slowly built up around him.

This is in sharp contrast to the centrepiece of the album, 'World Leader Pretend', the lyric of which is printed on the album sleeve. This song stirred up considerable personal difficulty for Michael as the 'I' was immediately assumed to be Stipe himself. He was adamant that this was not the case: 'That song is the voice of Everyman or Everywoman desperately trying to better their finest enemy which is, of course, yourself. I feel that my voice and the direction of thought in the band is very much presenting the confusion that is inherent in our society in this century . . . we're just questioning . . . it summed up the whole idea behind *Green*.' With that in mind, it becomes clear that 'World Leader Pretend' is a companion piece to 'Hairshirt', taking the theme that the building of an alienated society is the result of every one of us putting up walls to keep the outside world away, rather than taking advantage of all the beneficial aspects of a communal approach. Stipe's assertion that, on a personal level, many of our problems are self-inflicted rang true with listeners across the world.

In its most simplistic sense, the song is a 'people in glasshouses shouldn't throw stones' parable, arguing that each individual needed to look long and hard at their own behaviour before blaming anyone else for their plight. Stipe admitted in *Sounds* that it was about 'personal liberation . . . people are just incredibly cynical and it's not inherent. It's completely manufactured and I wanted to offset some of that . . . I consider this to be a deeply galvanizing record.' As such, 'World Leader Pretend' is a song that looks to the future, a hope for an improvement that will start within each individual. Even so, Michael had to address himself to the controversy at each concert by saying, 'This is a song about you,' in a vain attempt to defuse allegations that he was setting himself up as some kind of youth leader.

Equally addressed to the audience was the frivolous pop of 'Stand', another call for the audience to become a little more aware of their environment and the world around them. Peter explained it as 'a really fun song, really dumb . . . you can do a little dance to it and if you're twelve and it makes you think that you should take control of your life a little more, that's great too.' 'Stand' became the theme tune to a situation comedy, *Get A Life*, so it was only fair that it should provide one of the funnier musical moments on the record. Buck confessed, 'I really am the worst guitar soloist in the world, but "Stand" needed a solo so I went out and bought a wah-wah pedal and worked with it for ten minutes and did the solo when everyone was at lunch. They all came in and started laughing and I said, "That's it then."' However it came about, 'Stand' was another hit single for the band in the US, helped to prominence by a fairly absurd video featuring some ludicrous sequence dancing by a specially hired group of extras. 'Since none of us can dance,' Peter graciously conceded, 'we had to hire someone else. I couldn't do that to save my life, but this is like some kind of Dick Clark special. I guess they must have told the people to bring some silly footwear.'

Given the group's collective repugnance over MTV fodder, it was odd to see them becoming a staple act on the video channel. For Peter there are no redeeming features: 'MTV? I'm sorry I don't like songs about twelve-year-old girls, I mean especially with guys my age, that's starting to get into paedophilia, the whole thing is dumbfounding to me.' R.E.M.'s fresh approach to music video meant that they attracted a new audience who were stimulated, provoked or amused by their very different slant on the whole genre. Along with groups such as The Cure, R.E.M. proved that it was possible to do something interesting with the pop video format rather than simply trotting out variations on live performances or what Michael refers to as 'gratuitous tits and ass'. This is where 'Pop Song 89' comes in.

Taking the 'girl in video' idea to its logical conclusion, Michael danced topless with three girls as an attack on the 'whole phenomenon of gang rape', a censored version being required before a television airing. Here the chests of all four protagonists were covered with censor bars because, as Stipe explained, 'a nipple is a nipple'. It was typical of the band to invert an existing stereotype by pushing it to its boundaries, forcing people to question the usual logic of television censors, which says four topless people dancing and clearly having a great time together is unacceptable, while girls dressed in flimsy clothing and threatened with violence is acceptable. The video was paired with a classic dumb pop tune which Peter treated as 'a cliché pop song that's poking fun at itself. I love those kind of things, it's a good little dumb song. I reserve the right to be dumb.' Michael admitted, 'It's a piss-take. I guess it's the prototype and hopefully the end of the pop song ... I think it describes where a lot of pop music stands right now.' With its bland questioning in the lyric, it looks at artificial provocation and stimulation, conversational devices that mean nothing, and makes a dig at the superficiality of the modern world.

The hope that Stipe had alluded to came in a number of forms; 'World Leader Pretend' was the crux of the album, but other songs, such as 'You Are The Everything', gained strength from their expression of the warmth and tenderness of human relationships which persist despite the dangers lurking beyond that security blanket. Michael admitted, '"You Are The Everything" was written from a very personal point of view. I have had so many people come up to me and say they've been waiting all their lives for a song that mentioned riding in the back of your car with your parents driving and the feeling of trust that you have as a child with your parents just looking up through the windows and watching the sky go by.' The song is reminiscent of the filmic quality of Robbie Robertson's 'Somewhere Down The Crazy River', although it does not take the short-story form in which Robertson excels.

By this stage, it's readily apparent that as a group, R.E.M. had found a new palette of sounds and styles with which to work, the delicacy of the mandolin transforming the traditional R.E.M. jangle into an understated but nonetheless visceral mix suited to Stipe's fractured narratives. 'The Wrong Child' is very much in that vein, Michael again asserting that there was 'an incident in my own childhood that inspired it but it does apply to virtually any outsider and at various times in everyone's lives we all consider ourselves outside the norm. I set that song in childhood because it's a real potent time of life and one that is always very much coloured by memory. The adult version of childhood is something that is very fantastic − it doesn't exist.' If the song was so autobiographical, perhaps Stipe is addressing a childhood where he was always on the outside, unable to make friends because of his father's transient lifestyle.

Many of the songs point to the same kind of smoky, wistful regret that had coloured *Murmur* half a decade earlier, a concern with the passing of time and a world that was not as simple as it had once appeared − although 'The Wrong Child' is stoic in its resolution to make the best of life. As R.E.M. took themselves on to the world stage with *Green* there was a hint of regret that they could no longer be small-town nobodies observing the world as it went by, a suggestion of foreboding now that they would be the centre of attention. With so much of Michael's material coming from his keen observational qualities, for him to become the watched rather than the watcher was disconcerting and could have been artistically suffocating.

The rest of *Green* is not so pastoral however. 'Turn You Inside Out' with its electronic thwack of drums and percussion is a very different animal that appeared to have grown out of the *Work* tour and R.E.M.'s response to playing stadiums. Where Mike had been worried about the Pavlovian reactions of the crowd, Michael in his central role was particularly aware of his ability to carry an audience with him in whatever direction he might choose.

Stadium rock now resembles nothing more than the Nuremburg rallies, with thousands of people whipped up into a feverish state of excitement by a range of subliminal devices such as lighting cues and song selection. While the gigs are obviously entertaining and fun for the audience, they seem to have become an excuse for a massive game of 'Simon Says'. U2 exploited this audience reaction to make a political point in the Zoo TV shows: the climax came in 'Bullet The Blue Sky', a song concerning US imperialism in Central America, where the vidiwalls were aflame with burning crosses and swastikas as Bono screamed, 'Never let it happen again', referring to Germany under Hitler. Before the end of that song, he had the crowd with their hands in the air clapping in time simply because he'd told them to. The point was well made, though it escaped many in the sweat-drenched atmosphere of the performance, as fans were too interested in keeping time to think about what they were doing. During the *Green* shows, R.E.M. tried to make the point with a little humour, flashing up slogans on the backdrop to engineer some 'audience participation'.

'Turn You Inside Out' proves that Stipe was in on the act, that he could twist an audience around his little finger if he had a mind to do so. It's fortunate that most rock stars have been relatively benign in intent, such is the hold they have on their audience; R.E.M. warned an audience against docile acceptance of whatever the band might have to say, alerting people to the potential dangers. 'Orange Crush' is in the same vein, a huge crunching sound obviously designed for the heavy metal section of the record, while lyrically it also dwells on people's propensity to follow any authority figure to the bitter end. It had come together originally on the *Work* tour as Peter explained, 'We wrote it in a soundcheck but we were trying to figure out what to do in the bridge and we kinda thought it would be great to have things that aren't music in there. I think that's totally valid to use sounds as opposed to writing a different chorus.'

The musical chaos of 'Orange Crush' leads it into political territory, with Michael contributing a lyric on the US's role in Vietnam and the dropping of the defoliant Agent Orange on to the Vietnamese people. A selective weed-killer, its intention was to deprive the communists of the extensive ground cover which they used for protection. It was subsequently proved to contain the poison dioxin; thousand of US troops who handled it developed cancer or fathered deformed children, while its effect on the Vietnamese people is incalculable. As Michael's father had been in the air force and had flown missions into Vietnam, many naturally thought the song dealt specifically with that part of his life. Peter was at pains to say, 'As Michael will tell you, he didn't write it about his father. His father was in the helicopter corps – I'm not sure if he actually dropped the stuff but he was around it. Even so the song's not about his father's life, though his father sometimes thinks it is.'

Whatever the case, the concept of Agent Orange serves as a powerful metaphor on a record called *Green*. Not only is it a particularly harrowing story of the impact of war on both sides, it also indicates the way in which our technology is being channelled. 'Orange Crush' makes the point that if we can channel so much money into defence spending in the race to kill more people more efficiently, then the resources exist to turn that reasoning on its head. The idea beyond the song is: spend the money on ways of saving the environment and improving the quality of people's lives.

The follow/don't follow chorus is another example of Stipe's devil's advocate approach to lyric writing, asking whether you should serve your country when your country might be wrong. In its way 'Orange Crush' was a throwback to the question of folk memory from 'Cuyahoga' and *Fables Of The Reconstruction*. The massacre of the Native Americans was joined in the twentieth century by the murder of America's own young people as well as the Vietnamese as a stain on the nation's collective conscience. Peter Buck argued, 'It's this one skeleton in the closet that keeps rattling its chains. Everything that's gone wrong in America is due to the drawback in faith in the government after the war ... people are running scared, only afraid that what they have is gonna be taken so they vote for whoever lowers taxes.'

'Orange Crush' points to the way successive American governments hoodwinked the population over participation in Vietnam. 'Get Up' looks in turn at the thin line between dreams and reality, Michael explaining it to *Melody Maker* by referring to a story about Ronald Reagan.

Y'know he was a movie star? There was a study done showing anecdotes that he would tell earlier in his ... reign ... where he would talk about this character he played and say that this character would do something in this film. And later on it became not a character but him. There's actual television broadcasts that bump these one by one and you watch this story become completely hyperbolized to where, y'know, a character from *Bonzo Goes To Washington* becomes him and Nancy in 1985.

R.E.M.'s songwriting eccentricity comes to the fore on this track, Bill confessing to 'a dream that we needed twelve music boxes all going at once for the bridge, so we got all the people in the studio to call up their grandmothers and put out the call to get these boxes. It worked pretty good too.'

Green was received as the finest album of the year by many, with Andy Gill from *Q* in rhetorical mood: 'Are R.E.M. the best band in the world? I reckon so.' *NME* described them as 'the most inventive voice in contemporary rock and roll ... the world's last great literate rock group'. *Melody Maker*'s David Cavanagh eulogized further: 'They sound unlike any other band, including the four intelligent-looking young men who made *Murmur* ... we all know exactly how great they are,' and *Sounds* was content to tell its readership that 'R.E.M.'s puzzle box remains a fine way to pass the time'. Peter's own assessment was perhaps closest to the mark: 'It reminds me of a Led Zeppelin record because it touches a lot of different ground; there's the big rockers, there's long, slow, weird psychedelic ones, there's a folk song, there's kind of mantra-ish stuff on it. Perhaps we're closet dinosaurs.' In hindsight, *Green* represents the first steps towards a new way of working for R.E.M., an album that only half-realized the potential that their new recording contract offered them, a transitional record that was stimulating, but also a little too familiar in parts.

Although calling the album *Green* was a clear indication of where their environmental sympathies lay, only general allusions to the subject were included in the content of the record. It wasn't until R.E.M. started to promote the album that they got their teeth into the issue, Peter saying they were interested in it because 'it's one of the few things we can save in America'. Michael was a little more erudite, explaining to *NME* why he had taken to wearing a disposable razor around his neck:

I was in an aircraft having a shave and it suddenly struck me. This razor is like junk culture. If you take a single disposable razor and you throw it in the trashcan you don't think about it. But if you think how many disposable razors have been thrown away since 1971 and imagine them all in one place and how many mountains of disposable razors you might have, well that's kinda frightening.

Bill's argument was easily the strongest:

You don't have anything if you don't have your health and if the Earth isn't going to support us because of negligence, we're in a lot of trouble. I'm getting of an age now when my wife really wants to have a child and I'm not so sure. I don't want to because we don't know what the future will bring. And I'm starting to realize that I'm thinking in those terms then it's getting real bad. I'm afraid to have a child, it's that simple.

The group's response was to give financial assistance to organizations such as Greenpeace as well as smaller, local pressure groups, but mainly to try to raise people's awareness of the severity of the situation. The Exxon boycott whereby Michael encouraged audiences on the Green tour to boycott Exxon products because of their appalling environmental record has already been touched on, but they chose to take other action too, taking certain organizations on the road with them, continuing a long-standing R.E.M. tradition. 'Greenpeace have been with us for five or six tours,' Peter explained. 'It wasn't a big altruistic thing, it didn't cost us very much at all to have these people with us in the lobby. And it was a cause that we've all been supporters and members of for a long time. We decided it would be a nice thing to do, to expose the audience to something other than sex and drugs and rock'n'roll, which are all fine in their place.'

Their place is usually the massive arenas of the world, the next stop for the band. As good as their word to Warners, they spent most of 1989 touring, thereby ensuring the highest possible profile for their new material, and appearing on television and radio with alarming regularity. Stadium rock was not something to which R.E.M. took naturally, although it did have its compensations as far as Michael was concerned: 'There's a lot more freedom for me in terms of going off on tangents, speaking or singing whatever in bigger places. But we have played venues especially in America that were just too big.' A lot of thought had gone into the presentation of the *Green* tour; the stark set fed off the way in which U2 had toured *The Joshua Tree*, but, in its turn, the radical nature of R.E.M.'s show provided some of the inspiration for Zoo TV.

The tour was one of the best received in recent memory, eliciting rapturous reviews. Probably their greatest achievement was to create a feeling of spontaneity within shows that had to be governed by specific lighting cues. Bill made the point that 'we changed the set a lot but we still weren't able to be as flexible as we wanted to be . . . that made it feel like going through the motions sometimes'. Peter Holsapple, who played on the tour, confirmed that 'as loath as they were to have to do a set-list, Peter Buck would sit there every night two hours before and figure out the order'. In that way, it had a similar feeling to the *Work* tour; what the four didn't put into the equation was the fact that a below-par R.E.M. performance was still superior to the huge majority of acts on the live circuit.

The tour was presented as a deconstruction of the concert form, although it didn't go as far as Talking Heads had done with *Stop Making Sense*. Nevertheless they stripped the stage to its barest essentials, the lighting was stark and minimal and the use of backdrop films were integrated so as to be moving, absurd or both, depending on the song. There was never any point at which the audience could have been unaware that they were witnessing a piece of theatre, artifice incarnate, from the liner under Stipe's eyes through to Buck's Townshendian windmilling. R.E.M. took the time to be shambolic with the Velvet Underground cover 'After Hours', chilling on 'Turn You Inside Out', humorous on 'It's The End Of The World As We Know It', frantic with 'Get Up' and compelling on 'Perfect Circle'. The anti-fascist interpretation of *Green* gained further ground with Stipe's ambiguous use of the Nazi salute on 'Disturbance At The Heron House', something he refused to do in West Germany, for obvious reasons. The show was always trying to provoke questions, to force the audience to step back for a moment and consider their response. If Michael gave the salute from the stage, should you salute back in the same way you'd been applauding at his request? Next, he would tell the crowd with game-show sincerity, 'This is a song of great intensity and import and it was written just for you,' as was the next and then the next. Questions, questions.

The obvious question was, 'Why not turn it into a concert film?' which is precisely what they did. Under the generic title *Tourfilm*, Jim McKay and Stipe of C-00 endeavoured to usurp *Stop Making Sense* as *the* concert film and they were at least partially successful, Steve Sutherland writing in *Melody Maker* that 'it's a gas – no, it's all the gases; nerve, napalm and laughing'. The live footage was farmed out to five separate editing teams, and the result was a mishmash of styles that was constantly riveting. *Hot Press* remarked on Stipe's ability to parody 'virtually every rock star shape and inventing a few new ones in the process' and *Q* called it 'an exemplary film of an exemplary tour'. When Michael was asked for his opinions of the film, he was brutally frank: 'It was *Tourfilm*,' Jim McKay adding the sobriquet 'guerrilla filming'.

The *Green* tour was no ordinary rock show by any stretch of the imagination. R.E.M. live, just like R.E.M. on record, demanded as much from the audience as they gave themselves. This time around, aware that a lot of people would be seeing them for the first time, they deliberately played a host of old material, partly to give the newcomers a better idea of the breadth of their muse but also to ensure that they didn't get things handed to them on a plate. These extra elements kept the group engaged and the addition of Peter Holsapple on keyboards and occasional guitar helped them to flesh out the sound a little further so that they were happier than ever before from a musical standpoint. However, by the British dates, halfway through the tour, tempers were beginning to fray. Travelling conditions and accommodation might have improved but there were fewer free days, more travelling, more interviews and more television work to be done.

To escape these rigours they returned to the music as a form of release. Some of the concerts were cathartic, but it was in soundchecks that they felt they were doing something worthwhile, building on their new method of writing together, as Peter affirmed.

> Mike, especially in the early days, was a much better instrumentalist than I was so it was natural he'd come up with the melodies and harmonies and I'd play the chords. We tend to write things differently now. We used to think if it didn't have forty-seven chord changes then it was just a bullshit pop song. I like it now we're writing two and three chord songs. We wrote 'Belong' in a soundcheck, it doesn't strike me as a departure. We seem to be writing with more subtle dynamics and a very few chord changes.

'Belong' would emerge as the cornerstone of the next R.E.M. record, along with 'Low' which also came from a soundcheck.

This new confidence confirmed that the band had made the right move in going to Warners. The greater level of security offered them a platform to experiment and to concern themselves purely with musical matters, rather than worrying about paying the rent. For most of the 1980s, R.E.M. had been locked into the album/tour/album/tour cycle. Warners had provided them with the opportunity to break out of that, though the company wasn't aware of it at the time. After spending 1989 touring solidly, R.E.M. were not planning to take the next album out in any conventional sense. Bill said, 'I'd forgotten that this is the ideal job. From the inside though, it had gotten to seem like a series of chores that I didn't want to do. If we'd done another tour, that would've been it.' In retrospect, Peter accepted that

> the fun was still there but sometimes finding it was a pain in the ass ... I don't want to sell something that I wouldn't give away. And that's what playing is, you're giving that away. And if you're doing it just to make money, then you're selling it and there's something wrong with that ... whatever kind of band we were in the '80s, the '89 tour pretty much capped it,

that was as rock'n'rollish as we'll ever get and I thought we did it very well.

Not touring meant that they could stretch themselves and the studio to the fullest, safe in the knowledge that the songs wouldn't need to conform to the live format. As individuals they were fully aware that now was the time to step away from the insidious nature of the rock machinery; as a band they had to be wary of becoming the lumbering dinosaurs they had so despised. Few were ready for the consequences of that decision.

10

TIMELESS, MATCHLESS, FRETLESS

A year working hard in support of *Green* was extremely tiring, but it was not in vain. It was the finest form of promotion that any band could ask for and had doubled their core following. The size of their fan base ensured that for the next record at least, they could do whatever they wanted and people would buy it. Like The Beatles before them, it wasn't a cue for sloppy writing and recording but a challenge to create a music unlike anything they'd produced hitherto. Having survived the challenges that *Green* had posed them, the hurdles simply got bigger.

The source of their success was, obviously enough, the music they made. Yet this was also the source of their greatest challenge. Although the critics, and, to an extent, the public at large, had lapped up their first six records, there was a slight feeling of disquiet that there was a trademark R.E.M. sound on which they were relying a little too heavily; jangly guitars, call and response harmonies, an impenetrable vocal and vague folkish pretensions. Bill admitted that the group's sound was not as diverse as he and the others would like, accepting that their greatest weakness was a tendency to remain rooted in the same basic musical style.

Six albums into their career, *Green* had illustrated that they were coming to terms with themselves as musicians, learning to draw on their strengths and disguise their weaknesses more effectively than at any other stage. *Green* had also shown an invigorating willingness to stretch the R.E.M. format, the songwriting process moving towards 'soundscapes' and away from the standard chord sequences, as Scott Litt has testified. However, while *Green* was their most crafted record to date, an album over which they had expended considerable intellectual as well as musical effort, it was something of a halfway house. The new instrumentation had extended the sound, steering it into new territories, yet there were still R.E.M. standbys in the mix of songs, pieces such as 'Get Up' or 'I Remember California' which would have felt at home on *Document* or *Lifes Rich Pageant*.

Green provided an interesting and effective launching pad for the next stage in their career; it was time to throw out the old references and rebuild the R.E.M. sound from scratch. Commercially, retreads of *Document* and *Green* would have served Warner Brothers especially well; their avowed intent is, after all, to sell as many records as possible and it's easy to sell things which are familiar. From an artistic point of view, had the band repeated itself at this stage the future would have looked bleaker, as they may have pushed themselves into a corner from which it would have been difficult to escape. As the *Green* tour had questioned their live performance and deconstructed the concert form, their next studio effort had to take the same approach to their songwriting and recording techniques.

It's easy to berate a band for making the same kind of record over and over again. With some it is a case of lack of imagination, an overriding commitment to one area of music or a desire to cash in on a successful format – anyone who's ever heard Status Quo will take the point. The difficulty for many groups, however, is the speed at which they are required to work, particularly in their early years and if they record for a small label. We've already seen the demands that cash flow made on R.E.M., requiring them almost to live on the road, making albums almost as an afterthought. Simple financial mechanics dictated their every move for around eight years until they had completed the *Green* tour, leading to a degree of frustration with a finished product which never quite came up to their expectations.

Signing with Warners freed them from that helter-skelter period of their lives, but imposed different restrictions on them, as Bill explained: 'What's stopping us making a record a year? We'd like to, but the record company won't let us, they see a record's life as eighteen months. They can't conceive of putting them out quicker.' Warners allowed them the luxury of some time off after November 1989 to think hard about the shape the new record might take, giving them the chance to compile a sizeable backlog of songs from which they could later choose the best.

The decision not to take this new record on the road was absolutely pivotal to its tone and to the attitude with which the four approached it. The memory of the *Green* tour had a lot to do with the writing of the album, Bill suggesting that 'after touring for a year we were sick of our usual instruments', Mike putting it a little more forcefully: 'After so many months on tour I didn't want to play bass and I mainly switched to organ. Bill took the bass parts that were needed initially because he had vowed never to play drums again.'

Michael accepted that 'change is inherent and very important for the growth of the band – it would be very easy to pick a formula and be very successful but we prefer to move forward'. One of the greatest difficulties for any band attempting to reappraise its own creative process is that if it consists of the same four people, there are always going to be certain similarities from one record to another. If a song is written from the heart then each subsequent song will be grounded in the same philosophy and principles, even if the mood changes from happy to sad to nostalgic to optimistic. Every writer will have their own fundamental ideas which will alter only very slowly over a long period of time.

As R.E.M. held the songwriting process to be sacrosanct, there was never any question of adding anyone else to the quartet. In order to engineer a radical departure from the previous records some other element would have to be thrown in. Sensibly going back to the departures made on *Green*, they accepted that the 'different' songs such as 'Hairshirt' came about because of the use of unfamiliar instrumentation, which tied in very nicely with their avowed lack of interest in playing their own instruments again. Although additional songwriting help had been spurned, the songs were created with an eye on employing extra hands in the studio as Bill remarked: 'We wanted to experiment and go off into different tangents and possibilities. We wanted to spend a lot of time working on a record that wasn't so guitar-oriented, so we approached songwriting from an organ standpoint which we'd never done before; we wanted to use a lot of strings, outside musicians.' The use of organ as the central composing instrument gave the new songs a thoroughly different texture, but it also saw something of a shift in the roles within the group, at least from an outsider's view.

In the past, Peter Buck had been viewed as the musical core of the group, a function of the guitar-based sound that the band had preferred. Now, Mike seemed to come more to the fore, taking the lead vocal on two of the songs, one of which, 'Near Wild Heaven', got a single release. This new emphasis stressed that R.E.M. is very much a team, and finally gave Mike some media attention, which was normally focused almost exclusively on Michael.

For his part, Peter had regularly spoken of the kinds of records he wanted R.E.M. to make; he is a great theorist, but few of his often outlandish suggestions have ever come to fruition. With *Out Of Time*, as the new album was entitled, he finally came close to realizing the ambition of 'making a baroque-ish record'. The restraint that he showed on guitar was one of the leading factors in making such an approach possible. In addition, having spent almost a year on the road with the band, Peter Holsapple was drafted into the studio band to play guitar on many of the basic tracks, leaving Buck free to play mandolin or acoustic guitar.

This was an important development, as having two guitarists playing together on the original backing tracks alleviated the need for Peter to go back and overdub layer upon layer of guitar on to a song. As Bill explained, 'On this one, because we had Peter Holsapple, we could get all the guitars on the basic track and then move on ... bringing in a second guitarist allowed us to put fewer guitars on.' Ironically, by having an extra guitarist in the studio band, *Out Of Time* became far less of a guitar-fuelled album, and the songs benefited from the extra space that provided. Mike agreed, 'It's got a very sparse lushness. There's so much on it but there's also a lot of breathing space.'

It was important that they changed direction, as Mike admitted before going into the studio: 'We knew it was time to make a bigger record. Not as in a big hit record, not in the sense of selling a lot of copies, I just mean in the sense of encompassing a lot of things, having new things jump out at you.' Tacitly, R.E.M. were accepting that as far as the studio was concerned, they hadn't been as creative as they could have been and that this was the time to break that mould: simply, it was time that they began to make some great rather than very good albums. Bill conceded that getting away from touring made an enormous difference to their writing: 'Knowing that we weren't gonna have to play the stuff onstage freed us up to go out on a limb musically ... the 1990s needed to be a little different.'

The greatest departure for them was the decision to employ strings on many of the songs, which proved to be a stiff challenge.

They were fortunate in having Scott Litt still on board, as his experience in this area was crucial. Back in his days at the Power Station, he had been used to dealing with full orchestras: 'On this album I think at most we only had fifteen string players in, not a huge orchestra because we weren't at all sure about what we'd need where.' In order to assist with the process, Mark Bingham – who Michael had met while working on the Disney project *Stay Awake* on which he sang 'Little April Shower' along with Natalie Merchant – was called in to help with the string arrangements, though both Mike and Michael wrote their own arrangements too.

If the three music writers were giving themselves a difficult task in uprooting a decade's worth of tradition and replacing it with something new, Michael felt that he, too, should play his part in the process. R.E.M. were known largely for *Green* and, perhaps, *Document*, records on which they had taken an unashamedly political stance, while the interviews that surrounded that period were equally unflinching in their level of political engagement. Moving into a new decade, Michael felt that they shouldn't 'make another record that was up-front politically. In the United States particularly when we first spoke out, we didn't realize how needy the public were for public figures who spoke the truth. We're so used to government leaders who talk around everything that when someone speaks very directly, people flock to them' – after all, author Garrison Keillor described Ronald Reagan as 'the president who never told bad news to the American people'. Stipe continued, 'Overnight we became very well known as political activists which is great; as citizens, as individuals and as a group we're very politically active. However we don't want to be categorized as a political band and it was important to me as a lyricist not to grow tired of writing political songs.' The rest of the band welcomed this departure warmly, Bill commenting that 'by doing *Out Of Time*, we got away from jumping on a soap-box stamping our feet'.

The level of interest and commitment of which Stipe spoke was essential to R.E.M.'s political philosophy – they did not want to become a second generation Clash, mouthing empty political platitudes simply because it was expected of them. They would speak on issues when they felt it right, a more potent approach than making points from a sense of obligation. They stepped back from the political arena feeling that, in the climate of the time, no amount of politicizing by a rock band could change attitudes or votes. Instead, a band like R.E.M. had to come at the situation from a different angle. They saw that the most important theme of the late '80s and early '90s was the abject lack of morality in public and personal life. In twisting the subject matter of their songs towards the deeply personal, R.E.M. were getting people to question their own attitudes and behaviour patterns in their own closest relationships. In coaxing people into self-examination on that scale, the hope remained that their world view might be altered too. By writing songs that espoused a greater degree of morality and spirituality, R.E.M. were looking to personal politics as the way forward.

Another reason to disengage was the severe pressure being placed on Stipe, who was becoming a messianic figure to certain sections of the audience. He admitted, 'To be the spokesman of my generation is a pretty wide load to carry and I don't want to be pigeon-holed as a political writer.' In addition, now Stipe was a fully fledged celebrity, it became apparent that he might be able to use that unwanted status. Celebrity furnished him with a platform beyond R.E.M., meaning that if he wanted to make a statement, the press would listen to him and would print at least some of what he had to say. With this extra outlet, Michael was freed from the need to make political comments within the framework of his lyrics. Given this new liberty, he began to cast around for new inspiration and set himself a tough examination of his writing ability: 'I wrote an album of love songs, every song is a love song. Thematically, the record deals with time and memory and love, which is where the title came from – out of memory or out of love didn't make much sense.'

Having written a selection of love songs, often in the first person, Michael wasn't keen on being confronted with the same misunderstandings that had plagued 'World Leader Pretend' on the previous album. Before settling on *Out Of Time*, 'The original title was *Fiction* because I wanted to make it very clear that these songs aren't about me. After that we wanted it to be *Return Of Mumbles* because there are songs on it that are less understandable than the ones on *Document* or *Green*.'

Developing his hyperbolic interview technique in promoting the album, Michael suggested that he had never tackled the love song before, which was patently untrue. Certainly there had never been the concentration on the subject that *Out Of Time* provided, and even here not all the songs were about love. Why the reluctance to tackle *l'amour*? 'I didn't write love songs for ten years because as a teenager I felt really cheated by certain songs that I'd hear on the radio and think, "That's exactly me," then I'd hear the next one and think the same and then a month later hear them again and feel like I'd been had.' It's also likely that since love is the single most used subject matter in the popular song, someone as idiosyncratic as Michael Stipe would have viewed it with something approaching disdain, looking to chart new terrain of his own. Or maybe he just didn't feel up to the task, cloaking those emotions, addressing issues as an easier target for his words. It can't be denied that the precision of his language on *Out Of Time* is a far cry from the faltering vocabulary that occasionally clouds the songs on *Reckoning* or *Fables Of The Reconstruction*.

Michael being Michael, he wasn't going to restrict 'love' to the standard 'boy meets girl, boy loses girl' song. *Out Of Time* explores different facets of the emotion, the strongest song dealing with the strongest bond, that between mother and child. 'Belong' had already been showcased on the *Green* tour where it illustrated that the band were out to simplify their sound still further.

It is a track that stands or falls on the creation of a level of dramatic tension which has then to be sustained throughout the piece, a tension carried by the taut, repetitive bass figure. The song was taken as a sombre commentary on the state of the world, some suggesting that the mother threw herself and her child to their deaths in the face of a world they could no longer cope with as in Peter Gabriel's 'Home Sweet Home'. In fact, the vocal is very specific, far more definite than any previous Stipe lyric; there is no such action either explicit or implied by the track:

I think it's significant to state that it's not a song about defenestration. I took great pains to clarify that. There's an event that has come to the attention of the woman who's the protagonist and she realizes how significant it is to her child and herself and she goes to the window to take a breath. To me its very uplifting and probably the most political song on the record.

Going further, he explained to *Lime Lizard*,

The mother is telling the child her reactions to an event which she is witnessing via the media. The event is major and she is reacting positively to it. The voice is someone else commenting on the sense that the bond between mother and child is the most powerful love of all.

'Belong' is another side of 'Disturbance At The Heron House', though in this case the revolution that has come to the woman's attention is successful. Despite the simplicity of the lyric itself, an absolute model of economy, the song encompasses a range of emotions and deals with several issues, including the incredible nature of the global village, news coming in about events happening maybe half a world away and making a difference to the lives of people not directly affected by it. It studies the relationship between mother and child, as she explains the situation: the child is unable to take it in but is rapt with attention at his or her mother's voice, illustrating that the deeply personal is as important as the global politic. It questions all of our reactions to the news media, asking why this one woman is so moved by events when many of us simply allow things to wash over us without further thought. It even touches upon the way in which people can overcome repressive regimes, the motif of hope from *Green* resurfacing once more.

The dispassionate tone that Michael used on the piece was something different for him and was one of a number of surprises that were in store for R.E.M. *aficionados* over the course of *Out Of Time*. The fans had already been given a pretty good idea that this album was going to be a departure when the first song, 'Radio Song' brought rapper KRS-1 into the fold. Michael had long been an admirer of his and had been looking for an opportunity to work with him for some time. They had done a PSA for C-00 together and then collaborated on a song called 'State Of The World', a hip-hop hybrid that had made extensive use of strings as the rhythmic element, indicative of the direction in which Michael's musical tastes were moving. The introduction of the rap section, particularly the hilarious closing rant, livened up what was otherwise a pretty pedestrian slab of white soul. Bill was certainly not afraid to align himself with the rapper's forthright views on the moribund state of US radio: 'We don't owe radio shit . . . we sneaked through because we had a fan base that couldn't be denied. If you want to get on the radio in America you have to pay. So we'll just have to sell fewer records.'

There was an understandable trace of vitriol in Bill's comment: R.E.M. and their contemporaries had spent many years trying to get their music played on any radio station beyond the confines of the college campuses. Back in 1987, Peter Buck had even become the star of a comic book; in 'Lil'Tee's Peter Buck', this latest superhero came into conflict with the Format Führer whose avowed intent was to ensure that the airwaves were flooded with 'Stairway To Heaven'. Given that around that period Peter had come to resemble one of the vultures from *The Jungle Book*, maybe he had finally found his metier. The crusade to get radio play was acutely observed by cartoonist Jack Logan, for the school of '83 had a really rough time with mainstream radio. It wasn't until R.E.M. recorded 'The One I Love' that they eventually made some impression on the commercial stations, and there's little doubt that their success paved the way for Pearl Jam and Nirvana in the early '90s.

Michael conceded when talking about 'Radio Song', 'Where "Belong" shows there are positive aspects to the global village, I'm writing here about the drawbacks.' The song is an example of their collective disdain for the cloning of the entire entertainment industry into sanitized little packages of safe, homogenous, vacuous junk, forcing those who might be interested in something a little more interesting to scour the independent airwaves and record stores.

Probably the only song that was guaranteed airplay was 'Shiny Happy People', an effervescent romp that screamed 'hit single' from the rooftops. The orchestral section at the beginning and then again midway through the song was destined to dampen down this effect a little but not even a DJ could have mistaken the commercial possibilities of the song. Peter brought the guitar riff to the band, leaving Michael with something of a dilemma, since he did not want to detract from the melody line by singing over it. He also had this problem with 'Endgame', which remained an 'instrumental because I didn't want to muck up the music. I just sang nonsense over the top following the melody.'

Realizing the greater potential of 'Shiny Happy People' Peter eventually twisted his arm. Michael was delighted with the end result, confessing, 'I meant it as an incredibly happy song . . . to me the guitar line was the greatest melody I'd ever heard . . . God the video is just the happiest thing I've ever seen,' obviously having blocked out Peter's contribution to the film, which appeared to pay homage to the stone-faced silent comedian, Buster Keaton. Although Michael appeared to be filled with the joys of spring, there were those who questioned his sincerity especially as, in an unguarded moment, he admitted that ' "Shiny Happy People" [is] so relentlessly upbeat you want to throw up'.

An in-joke or not, the song was worthy of its inclusion on the album for the glorious harmonies on the chorus and the chance to hear the sublime voice of Kate Pierson from the B52s, the instigators of the Athens scene back in the late '70s. Michael was enthusiastic at her participation: 'She's my favourite singer, I just love that nasal adenoid thing, it moves me. We had talked for years about singing together. She used to be in a band called the Sun Do Nuts when she was in school and we talked about regrouping that. These songs seemed like an opportune moment to get together.' With Michael having similarly corrupted sinuses their voices meshed particularly well, the greater clarity of Mike's contribution having already set the tone. It was little surprise that Kate's voice should be so well suited to the song since, according to Bill, 'When the song was being written, Michael heard her part straight away, it wasn't an afterthought. He wrote it with her in mind.' Scott Litt was quick to point out that the harmonies were not always as effortless as they sounded: 'With R.E.M. it's a little hit and miss. Michael sings some parts which ordinarily you wouldn't think of, while Kate just came in and worked out her own ideas, nobody told her what to sing so it just developed into something pretty off the wall. Like a science project!'

Once they had succeeded in luring Kate into the fold for *Out Of Time*, it would have been the height of foolishness not to make further use of her abilities. On 'Me In Honey', a more typical R.E.M. piece, she is especially effective, an emotional backing to Stipe's anguished voice. Michael admitted at the time that it was his perspective on the 10,000 Maniacs song 'Eat For Two', Natalie Merchant's take on unwanted pregnancy. The male protagonist is being shut out of the decision-making process, his frustrated confusion clear in the final plaintive verse. Like a number of the songs on *Out Of Time* – and like the bulk of *Monster* a few years later – 'Me In Honey' concerned a relationship in a state of disrepair, broken hearts strewn everywhere.

As an observer of the world, Michael has concentrated on the grimmer realities of life and has been criticized as being needlessly miserable, but he is not alone in looking for dramatic situations in which to place his ideas and imagination. 'Me In Honey' is a particularly affecting song when looked at in connection with the group's stance amid the pro-choice lobby; they have all been long-term advocates of a woman's right to choose whether she wants to terminate a pregnancy or not and then to receive the appropriate medical treatment in a safe and secure environment. For dramatic purposes, it's not difficult to extend the line of the argument a little further to the point where a woman's choice is not that of her partner; for a writer, that tension is an excellent source of inspiration.

The song took some lyrical twists and turns, but it was another that was swiftly put together, as Peter remembered:

> That was literally a riff Mike played once, I put this guitar line over it and Bill added a drum beat. It was maybe thirty seconds long and it was on the end of a tape of five real songs but Michael fixated on that. Just thirty seconds, one chord. He went, 'That beat, that key, D flat, I've got a song for it,' he said. 'Perfect,' and we had a song.

'Me In Honey' was one of the few songs that did not require any embellishment from a string section but it was clear that most of *Out Of Time* was written with just that in mind. Bill accepted, 'These songs needed help. Let's be honest. We're not above admitting that we need help. We're good but we're not great. Any other record, it may have been kinda weird to have so many people involved but these songs cried out for it. There was no pressure about having to reproduce or replicate these songs live so we thought, "Let's make a wacko record," and bringing in other people made that easier.' The horizons that the decision to stay at home had opened up were considerable, but given that they were still relatively inexperienced in the studio, they required some help in exploring these opportunities to the full. The strings were not in themselves a dramatic departure, having turned up as early as *Fables Of The Reconstruction*, but this was the first time R.E.M. had allowed an entire album to be coloured by them, a move that worked to their advantage.

Peter's urge to make a baroque album was satisfied on 'Low' where the strings are especially central; dense and tense, rolling around a brooding organ and bass combination. Michael shied away from talking about the song except in reference to the line about love seeming silly or shallow, which he used to explain his previous abhorrence of love songs. In the course of a particularly good *NME* interview, Gavin Martin tackled Stipe on 'Low''s similarity to a textbook definition of manic depression. Stipe shrugged off the question with an unconvincing, 'I'd never thought about it that much, it's just a song. It was written on the road and I put together a bunch of nonsense phrases . . . it is as I wrote it in a feverish moment somewhere touring round the world. I think it's kinda funny actually.' Some of its imagery is bleakly amusing but given the trouble that Michael takes with so many of his lyrics, this explanation doesn't ring true.

It's tempting to view the characters who populate the songs as extensions of the four guys in the band, which they are not. However, given Martin's question, the following quote from Bill Berry, looking back to the *Green* tour from a 1994 perspective, is especially interesting:

> Not touring for five years was great, although I missed it, but I think we all really matured. We'd lost our senses of identity . . . it could very well have saved my life. That sounds kinda dramatic but I definitely became closer to my wife. I fell in love with her the moment I saw her but our relationship didn't really start until I got off the road. I tended to be a manic depressive at that point and my wife brought me out of that. I remember finishing the *Green* tour and being almost suicidal, because I'd spent ten years looking at a bottle. You have to get out of that.

'Low' did not make it to the finished record simply on Michael's say-so, as the rest of the band continued to edit his work and throw in their own ideas for the lyrics. One possibility was quickly vetoed by Peter:

> Usually 95 per cent of Michael's stuff goes straight on to record, but there's always one thing where I'll go through his notes and say, 'Michael, I hate this' – there was some kinda new age stuff and I find it so much distasteful hippy bullshit, but he was like, 'Ok, it came up in conversation, we'll leave it.' To me it's Shirley Maclaine territory, let her handle it.

There was no question of editing 'Country Feedback', one of the strongest songs on the record which maintained the sort of psychological brutality that 'The One I Love' had revelled in. Deceptively simple musically, it was a good example of the progression from the previous album and the sympathetic way in which the extra musicians were employed. On this track the arcane sound of the pedal steel guitar played by John Keane was juxtaposed with Peter's ultra-modern 'loud guitar' (as it was credited on the sleeve), providing a striking approximation of the diametric viewpoints in the lyric. In order to carry the emotion of each song's narrative through to its conclusion convincingly, Michael tried to record the vocals in as few takes as necessary, a stern test of his professionalism and Scott Litt's engineering expertise. Michael noted,

> It's a pretty live record . . . I didn't want to sit around singing twelve vocals and then cobble them together, [so] half are first or second takes. The version of 'Country Feedback' was a demo, I only ever sang it once . . . I just had a piece of paper with a few words. I sang it then walked out and came back the next day to hear it. The music as well was played for the first time as we recorded it and I think we decided then and there not to re-record it. It's a very desperate song, from the uglier side. It's pretty much about having given up on a relationship.

It continued the lyrical fascination with the seamier side of life, and the assertion that it was a song born out of desperation was right on the money, akin to the 'prop' theme of 'The One I Love' but this time from the other viewpoint. In pretending that *Out Of Time* was nothing but love songs, R.E.M. might have been trying to shift the media focus, but in reality it is no less political an album that *Green*. The lyrical metaphors in 'Country Feedback' are clear: the character singing looks at his partner with something approaching disgust, drawing energy from his vitriolic lambasting, feeding on his contempt, and yet seems mournful about the passing of the relationship. The force that had broken the relationship apart has a wider interpretation as a comment on our society, as lives are torn apart by agencies beyond the control of individuals who have then to resort to brutality as some kind of psychotic reaction, an escape from the insanity that engulfs them. Whether it is a man driven over the edge by being unable to provide for his family or simply someone's response to a violent world doesn't need to be clarified: the point is made in the obvious frustration at the loss of control, bodies being pushed around by events rather than being able to chart their own destiny. Peter's view was 'Michael came in and shouted this stuff off. It was exactly what was on his mind that day . . . it was real.'

Another vision of the uglier side of love was the international hit 'Losing My Religion', or 'Oh Life' as the Israelis would have it. This elicited controversy in the same way as 'World Leader Pretend', a useful trick for a first single from the album. With the 'spotlight' line such a vibrant part of the chorus, listeners immediately assumed that it was a song about Stipe himself, since he spent so much time in the spotlight himself – it was reported that he later wished he'd sung 'that's me in the kitchen' to make the point about the everyman perspective, but this may be a piece of disinformation. Certainly Peter felt that the song might have been one of the more personal efforts on the record.

However, Michael ploughed on with the story that it was a step further down the line from The Police's 'Every Breath You Take', a song abut unrequited love of any sort. That led to further theories, most notably expounded by Marcus Grey in his book *It Crawled From The South*, that it was a reaction to the phenomenon of celebrity stalking and the murder of John Lennon by a deranged fan. There may have been something of this: Stipe himself had been exposed to the downside of celebrity – Peter noted that when you sold 100,000 records, your fans wanted to chat about music, but at the 1,000,000 mark 'you get people who sit at home and their radio talks to them'. The many interpretations of the song provided much of its attraction.

One thing that Michael did want to make perfectly clear however was that it was a secular song, as he told *Hot Press*:

In Georgia 'losing my religion' is a very common phrase. It means that you're at the end of your rope or you're fed up. Literally the phrase means something so powerful that it could challenge your spiritual convictions, but it's used casually. A waitress who has had a very busy night and a very rude table would walk into the kitchen and the cook would say, 'How was your table?' and she would say, 'I almost lost my religion!'

For Scott Litt, the song posed particular difficulties once it became clear that it would be a single. 'It was a bit of a struggle because of the nature of the song, we had to make it sound full enough but not too pop,' though the instrumentation is so bizarre that it would have been hard to turn it into a pop record – certainly it was the first time a song written on a mandolin had been a hit since the early seventeenth century. The video also played its part in the process, going on to win the group an armful of awards around the world, most notably from MTV. Even now, if you watch MTV for a couple of hours, there's every chance 'Losing My Religion' will appear.

The video broke new ground for R.E.M. and showed the shifting character of the group and their desire to reduce the emphasis on Michael's role a little in favour of the rest of the group. For three or four years, Michael Stipe had increasingly become the face of R.E.M., an occupational hazard for lead singers, while the others were progressively pushed into the background. Michael's role was actively encouraged in some respects since none of the others were keen on the limelight, but presentationally it caused difficulties since the burden of expectation was thrown on to Stipe. *Out Of Time* saw a concerted effort to present the group as a united front. Interviews became a group experience and all four members actually began to appear on film, turning Mike, Bill and Peter into personalities in their own right, lightening Michael's load.

Some considered the simplicity of the 'Losing My Religion' and 'Shiny Happy People' films to be a cop-out and a compromise when compared with the idiosyncratic films that accompanied 'Fall On Me' or 'Finest Worksong'. It's quite true that they are easier on the eye and far simpler for a wider audience to absorb but that was partly to do with the material they had; to put some pseudy clip with 'Shiny Happy People' would have been pretentious in the extreme.

'Losing My Religion' is a wholly different animal, and might have carried an 'artistic' video in the sense the critics meant it. Nevertheless, the film produced was very rich in colour and imagery and it would be hard to construct a case for it being a cop-out. It was banned in Ireland because of a crucifixion sequence, though apparently there was also some disquiet at the alleged homo-erotic content. It stood apart from run-of-the-mill videos, leapt out of the television screen and added a different dimension to the song. Michael had finally succumbed to the dread concept of lip-syncing for the first time since 'Wolves, Lower' in 1982. 'We'd pushed video as far as we could without lip-syncing,' he argued. 'I've been a real outspoken opponent of it because it's a fake, but I saw some videos that really spoke to me and I had to reassess my opinion. What I came up with is yes, it is fake, but videos are fake, TV is fake but what can come through is the emotion.' Michael himself put in a powerful performance as the epitome of frustration, justifying his decision.

Out Of Time offered the world the chance to reevaluate R.E.M.. Naturally, Michael was always at the fore of each album by virtue of providing the group with its voice, but on *Out Of Time* the guiding light seems to be Mike Mills. He proved himself a more than capable lead vocalist on 'Near Wild Heaven' and 'Texarkana', the harmonic, summery quality of the former ensuring its release as a single. His sharp lyrics offer a simpler version of regret and missed opportunity which dovetail nicely with Michael's work to convey that oddly warm feeling of loss and alienation in which they specialize. But his contribution went much further than that; if, superficially at least, *Document* had been Peter's record, *Out Of Time* was ostensibly Mike's, his keyboard parts offering the structural framework to songs that could otherwise have gone off in many disparate directions.

Out Of Time suggests in some regards a lack of involvement from Michael Stipe – he sings the lead on only eight of the eleven tracks, 'Endgame' being an instrumental, and also wrote eight lyrics. It's reasonable to surmise that either the challenge of writing eleven love songs proved to be too much or, more likely, his involvement in other projects restricted the time he had available to work on the album. He was far more involved in filming than at any other time, both with C-00 and in compiling a home video entitled *This Film Is On . . .*, the title taken from a line in 'Country Feedback'. This package featured an accompanying video for each song on *Out Of Time* and was in the main a return to the more obscurist vision of yore. *Q* were bemused by it, saying 'weird isn't quite the word', but it proved more imaginative and better value for money than the standard hit video package which often comes in at less than thirty minutes. With that on his plate, Michael also co-ordinated the album's packaging, a job which he said 'almost killed me', adding to the feeling that he was spreading himself too thinly, requiring Mike to take up some of the slack. The attempt to make them appear more of a group entity in the future was therefore essential, freeing up some of Michael's time to concentrate on more important work, rather than promotional chores.

Recorded at Bearsville in New York and then mixed at Prince's Paisley Park complex, *Out Of Time* caused conflicting emotions inside the group when it was finished. With deadpan humour,

Michael asserted that the record would redefine the course of pop history, but there was a degree of uncertainty about its commercial potential. Not quite the huge departure it was reported as being, it was still a bold step away from the guitar-driven rock band that had come to prominence in the late '80s. Bill recalled the final playback: 'It was kinda odd, we sat around chatting and making final comments about what we'd just finished and the unanimous consensus was that even though we were proud of it, this record we'd just done was commercially gonna be a flop . . . we just didn't hear a single on it.' Failure to hear 'Shiny Happy People' seems a tad unlikely, but Mike reinforced the point when he commented, 'We had a great deal of confidence in the record as a piece of work, but I'd be lying if I said I ever thought it was a sure-fire chart thing.' Peter bluntly confessed, 'Okay, we're not gonna sell any records. Fuck it y'know you do what you think is right and stand by it.' The reviews, however, suggested that their approach had been worth it. Mark Cooper in *Q* wrote, 'This brooding departure offers them at their most reflective, challenging and intriguing,' *Sounds* called it 'a moral victory for independence and self-sufficiency in the face of the corporate beast that would so love to shackle R.E.M.', while *Melody Maker* felt it was a 'stunning baroque beauty fashioned from dark, frank lyric testimony and the wilful chaos of the band's switched instrument fever'. But doubts still remained as to its commercial viability.

On release, *Out Of Time* became the first record by a rock group to top the *Billboard* charts in over a year, turning the same trick in scaling charts across the world, its phenomenal success completely eclipsing that of *Green*. There are any number of contributory factors to its popularity. The groundwork R.E.M. did with Warners in promoting *Green* was now coming to fruition, and the new converts they'd reached on that tour were all going out to pick up the new album in its first few weeks of release. In this sense it was further vindication of the decision to join Warners, their impressive distribution and promotional network ensuring that the new record was available everywhere and marketed properly. Allied to that, in 'Losing My Religion', the first track to be released in most countries, they had finally come upon a single that was quintessential R.E.M. rather than the more atypically dumb sound of 'Stand'. It gave a better picture of the breadth of their vision, and, when coupled with the video, it came to represent a group that had many facets. With such a successful single in the bag, it was almost inevitable that the album would follow suit.

The single biggest factor in its rise to the top has to be the music itself, but timing was vitally important too. Its release coincided with the Gulf War, hitting the shops as the bombs were hitting Baghdad. In a time of such turmoil, a period of chaos and terrible uncertainty, music in general provided both a soundtrack and a reassuring form of escape. Where R.E.M. held the trump card was in the timeless nature of this new music. Its traditional framework was a source of comfort in strange days, injecting an important air of continuity into a year where there suddenly seemed to be no absolutes to cling to any more. It was a feeling borne out by the way in which they promoted the record; having refused to do live shows, they went on a 'TV tour' which covered Europe and the US, playing new and old songs in an acoustic format, the most celebrated of these shows being the MTV *Unplugged* special. Seeing these five figures – Peter Holsapple was recruited once again to play guitar while Buck dealt with mandolin duties – plainly enjoying their music provided an anchor for the audience. *Out Of Time* was an album that was completely in tune with its times, an example of the 'Sergeant Pepper' effect.

That *Unplugged* show was hugely popular and remains the best example of the genre, the gentle atmosphere indicating the depth of their material and the quality of the musicians, Michael Stipe's voice seeming almost supernatural at times. There's an old maxim that only the very best songs can handle the acoustic treatment, the spartan setting cruelly exposing any flaws in composition. *Unplugged* proved that above all else, R.E.M. were very good indeed, worthy of entering the songwriting pantheon.

They did play a few selected shows during the year, one in Virginia and a couple at London's Borderline Club off Charing Cross Road under the *nom de plume* Bingo Hand Job – Bill, Mike, Michael and Peter became the Doc, Stinky, the Reverend Bingo and Raoul for the occasion. These London shows were necessary in order to secure the requisite work permits to enter the country and play a session for Radio 1 and BBC2's *The Late Show*. Playing almost in revue, Billy Bragg and Robyn Hitchcock among others were called on to provide assistance, provoking very different reactions. Steve Sutherland in *Melody Maker* complained that '[they] unravel credibility so far in sixty minutes that ten years of accumulated admiration dissipate into disappointment', though Roy Wilkinson informed *Sounds* readers that 'it would be futile to try and recall a more fulfilling concert'. Peter Buck was more interested in a bootleg of the event that was available within days: 'I think you can hear people snorting cocaine, sniffing and wheezing, talking and ordering drinks. I kinda like that.' The greatest weakness of the event, however, was the exhumation of the Troggs' 'Love Is All Around', which after its inclusion on the 'Radio Song' single ultimately provided Wet Wet Wet with a number one and the population at large with a five-month migraine.

Despite the huge global success of the record, they chose not to recant on their no-touring principle, although the temptation must have been strong with several hundred thousand extra sales guaranteed and the world's stadia just waiting to be filled. Remarkably perhaps, music remained their guiding light in the midst of all this commercial success, Bill's verdict on touring being that 'the monster got too big, it's like a military operation now, it's insane. We feel like a studio band right now,' a view with which Peter heartily concurred: 'I think we're doing our best work at the moment, we're kinda on a roll . . . all through we were demoing songs for the next record. I think not touring will be the best thing in the world for us.' There was already a surfeit of material ready and they were itching to start writing again; on their return from six months of promotional duties, they began work on their next record almost immediately.

11

CACTUS FIELD HIPPIES

The success of *Out Of Time* was welcome vindication of R.E.M.'s collective decision to leave college behind more than a decade earlier. Many years of hard work had finally been translated into financial reward, buying the group the security to do whatever they wanted to in future. The general feeling was that if a relatively downbeat album like *Out Of Time* could be so successful, there were now no limits to what they could go on to do.

The initial premise for the album that became *Automatic For The People* was a rock collection that could be taken out on the road. After six months of intermittent writing, the material R.E.M. arrived at was pretty sombre fare, not at all what they had been looking for. Nevertheless the songs they had promised to provide them with their best set yet; the decision was taken pretty early on, certainly prior to recording, that they would not tour and would follow the same guiding principles that shaped *Out Of Time*. *Automatic* would present each song as a separate entity with the demands of the road given no opportunity to restrict R.E.M.'s collective imagination.

The enormous popularity of *Out Of Time* meant that the band were writing and rehearsing only sporadically. From the autumn of 1991 through to the spring of 1992, they seemed to be perpetually attending award ceremonies to pick up gong after gong. Peter's truculent disregard for the whole idea persisted and so it generally fell to Bill, Michael and Mike to provide acceptance speeches. The MTV awards were an especially glittering occasion for them as 'Losing My Religion' virtually swept the board, winning six categories including Best Video; Peter made his excuses and just arrived in time for the party. Michael used the MTV platform to make a number of points; each time he visited the podium to accept another trophy he stripped off layers of T-shirts to reveal slogans such as 'Rainforest', 'Choice', 'Love Knows No Colour', 'Alternative Energy Now', 'Handgun Control', 'The Right To Vote' and 'Wear A Condom'.

The Grammys, which took place in February 1992, were another beanfeast which required their attendance; the relative pecking order among awards shows was borne out when Peter actually turned up for this one, although it was under protest: 'My mom and wife wanted to go so I went but I did it for them. And I said, "Ok if I'm going to the Grammys I'm going to wear my pyjamas." Everybody started laughing and I said, "I'm fucking serious!" Then the day before, we were in the limo and everyone was going, "Now Peter, I know you promised to wear your pyjamas and we really hope you do, but if you don't we're not going to think you chickened out." Those were fighting words, I was bound and determined to wear my pyjamas.' God only knows what the press would have made of things if Michael had worn pyjamas – presumably it would have been judged a triumphantly cryptic statement – but Peter's decision was seen as typically brattish rock star behaviour; lurid emerald-green pyjamas decorated with an assortment of gambling motifs were just the sort of clothes that many of the gathered throng might have been happy to pay several thousand dollars for had they come from a fashionable designer. Peter got the same effect without any effort, and in exchange for pocket money. Not that R.E.M. were ideologically averse to spending some money, as Mike explained, 'Michael wears really expensive clothing. It's just that he doesn't wear it the way it should be worn. He'll walk into a ritzy store and they'll be pretty rude to him until they realize he's wearing a $800 suit that his dog has slept on.'

Although the Grammys – for which R.E.M. had seven nominations – were dominated by Natalie Cole's 'Unforgettable', R.E.M. picked up three trophies, firmly placing them at the centre of the celebrity world, a position with which they were increasingly uncomfortable. Michael made the comment that 'the very weird religion of celebrity in the United States really scares me, it's like we're creating Gods, fake heroes because we don't have any real ones'. If not the most original of statements, it does illustrate the speed at which R.E.M. had suddenly entered mainstream consciousness, taking us back to the argument about 'Losing My Religion' being a celebrity stalking song. As a band, and in the light of Kurt Cobain's suicide, R.E.M. were indeed fortunate that they had had the chance to mature as people away from the media glare before they were thrust into it. However prepared they were though, the reality was still disconcerting for individuals who enjoyed the opportunity for solitude to work on new musical ideas. Even Athens offered less of an escape than previously, since it was now on the map as the home of R.E.M., increasing the intake at the university among kids who wanted to meet their favourite group. The band took the unwanted attention pretty well, though Bill and Mike were living further out of town by now and Peter was starting off on a road that was to eventually take him out of Athens for good.

With all the distractions now put to one side, 1992 offered the chance to write and record a follow-up to *Out Of Time*. The idea was to move away from any hint of a formula, but, as the band reacted instinctively to the music that was coming out of them, the new material proved to be both a continuation and progression from the *Out Of Time* mood. The success they had had seemed to play a part in their introspective attitude, their sudden status as popular figures forcing them to look at themselves as individuals to measure the change in their attitudes, if any. The nostalgic, wistful flavour to some of the music suggests that the group were struggling to come to terms with their new identity as major mainstream commercial artists, regretting in some ways the passing of their early days on the road. By implication, it was also a period where they mourned the passing of their youth and questioned their beliefs as they grew older. Bill admitted, 'It's so weird to think those days are gone. For all the power and money that we've got now it still makes me sad to think that it's never gonna be like it was. I'm not living in a dream world and I don't want to live in the past but it's kind of sad that it's changed to the point where something as simple as touring has become so incredibly complicated.'

Michael caught the mood too, with lyrics that are bittersweet in tone, often dealing with death and the passage of time. However, his lyrics are very resilient, with a resolve that simply and compassionately points out that there is strength to be gained from the death of others and that life is there to be lived.

Having compiled a backlog of around thirty-five songs, the main task for Michael was to choose those which inspired lyrics or for which he already had some appropriate words. Some songs inevitably fell by the wayside in recording, as Peter eventually complained: 'There were a couple I loved so bad I wish he'd finished them. He had one called "The Devil Rides Backwards On A Horse Called Maybe", it was a great title and it fit the chorus too.' Having whittled the material down to manageable levels, all that remained was to put the tracks on to tape. Peter told Q about the US tour that ensued: 'The main idea was to track in Bearsville which has a huge great drum room, great for recording live, then overdubs in Criteria, Miami ... mixed in Seattle at Bad Animals because it had the kind of board we liked and we always wanted to visit there ... we decided to waste some money and go to Daniel Lanois' studio in New Orleans; just let's go down and not work ourselves to death, see if we can get into the flow of things and capture something.'

That attitude was new to a band who, until *Out Of Time*, had generally tried to bash out records in the quickest possible time. It was obviously a function of financial security but the approach and the music that ensued was also a reflection of their leap off the treadmill. With a more relaxed lifestyle, R.E.M. were able to reflect on their previous work and their lives. The thoughtful sound of *Automatic For The People* makes it clear that a lot of hard work had gone into writing and recording, a lot of theorizing had made it possible – yet they had not lost the life in the songs, had not worked them to death. There was a strong sense of continuity in the record but much of that had come from planning, rather than honing every last note to perfection in the studio. *Automatic For The People* sounds like well-crafted intuition, another contradiction, even if it was not without its little crises, as Peter explained: 'Probably from beginning recording to halfway through we're as tight as we ever are, everyone's really excited and you can see this whole thing coming. About halfway, that's when people start diverging on opinions and we start fighting, and then mixing is like a tug of war.'

The title was chosen to show their confidence in the record. The slogan was taken from the local Weaver D. soul-food restaurant; when you make an order there, his reply is, 'It's automatic.' To Mike, this represented the album: 'We've made a record, we think it's good and you can have it if you want it.' Not a particularly hyped-up attitude, but indicative of the self-contained way in which R.E.M. have come to work. *Automatic For The People* might be taken as a deliberate step back from the success of *Out Of Time*, an attempt to defuse the celebrity bomb – after all, 'Here's another song about death' is not normally the way you sell lorry-loads of records. Buck was very clear about the priorities for the group from here: 'I think U2 tend to go for it more than we do. I had the feeling when I bought the first U2 record that they understood where they wanted to go a lot better than we did. For us, fame and being on the world platform is a not really necessary by-product of what we want to do.'

Michael chose not to do interviews for the record, retreating from even greater fame which might well have impinged on his ability as a writer. Stipe's views were generally formed by his outsider's perspective, so to be at the hub of the media world might have changed the way he thought. Even so, his refusal to do interviews was also part of the R.E.M. cycle; for *Document*, Peter handled most of the interviews, for instance. As lyricist, Michael was inevitably quizzed closely about the nature of the songs; by stepping outside the interview format he maintained the air of mystery that was so important to him as a songwriter, while keeping his feet on the floor, freeing him from the intemperate praise of journalists everywhere. Given the superficially downcast feeling to the record, the interviews that he would have had to weather this time would have been in even greater depth than ever before – not an ordeal to which he was willing to subject himself. R.E.M. had seen U2 consumed and almost destroyed by fame and fortune until they regrouped and chose to cope with it by satirizing the whole idea through Zoo TV. In their turn, R.E.M. avoided the celebrity trap by simply ignoring the whole process, carrying on with their lives as normal.

In keeping with the low-key promotion, there were no television appearances, and only a curtailed international promotional tour was undertaken by Mike and Peter, who, as usual, was happy to talk to anyone and everyone. The first single from the album, 'Drive', was scarcely designed to follow up the success of 'Shiny Happy People' or 'Losing My Religion', either. A sombre track which sets the tone for the forthcoming album, it reprised their collective opposition to George Bush in its opening line, the juxtaposition of crack, smack and Bushwacked making a point on the White House's policy on drugs. Any more explicit connection between the former head of the CIA and drug dealing was entirely coincidental. Probably. What it did show was that in an election year, R.E.M. – while not returning to the political polemic of

Document – were still willing to point the finger at those failing to serve their country.

'Drive' is one of those R.E.M. songs that almost didn't happen, as Peter explained: 'I had it on a cassette of demos and I always fast forwarded through it, I thought it was the most boring thing I'd ever heard. Then Michael had these lyrics which defined the song.' Musically it is dark, but the defiant lyrical idea turns that atmosphere on its head, with its refusal to give up in the face of almost unbearable pressures to the contrary. In this regard it is the ideal opener, for each song on the album has its kernel of hope, couched in melancholic tones. In 'Drive', allied to the politics there was, according to Mike, 'a hopeful message . . . telling kids to take control of their own lives,' a serious reprise of 'Stand'.

'Ignoreland', on the other hand, steams along on an adrenalin rush of vitriol, a throwback to the basic anger of *Document* and containing one of Stipe's finest lyrics. A catalogue of the lies told by the Republicans to win power, a vehement attack on their duplicity, musically it jars against the rest of the album, and both Mike and Michael subsequently wondered whether it was right to include it on the album.

Michael's voice is very matter-of-fact, a little detached but plainly incensed, with the distorted instrumentation adding to the overall effect, Mike's fuzz bass line lending an almost demented air. Written at a point when Bush looked as though he might well go on to win a second term, its desperation is palpable. Harking back to 'Finest Worksong', Stipe asks the question how anyone could 'be all you can be' in a country where you have 'throw up on your shoes'? Peter made it clear that Michael was acting on the group's behalf when he told *Q*,

In America . . . we're pretty much able to ignore reality. We have this great ability to pretend there's nothing wrong, that we're still a superpower and it doesn't matter if we kill a couple of hundred thousand people. Oh and Reagan lowered taxes. In fact, taxes were raised twelve times during his reign. He lowered rich people's taxes – he and George Bush made me rich, but my mom's taxes went up. She's a secretary. Most people are able to ignore all that and vote overwhelmingly for these guys who just out and out lie to you.

If there is an air of introspection about *Automatic For The*

People, the political dimension is in the mix too, sparking that sense of resignation, of acceptance and of defiance. All of those elements combined to push the group into a more outspoken place in the election campaign than ever before. They gave whole-hearted support to the Rock the Vote project, which tried to ensure that as many people as possible were registered to vote, and Michael started to appear on the platform with the Democrats, introducing Bill Clinton's running mate Al Gore at one party rally. Peter was less sure of their role in the political process, accepting that they all had their own individual right to donate money or make appearances but still insisting, 'I'm pretty cynical about politics at the presidential level. Michael did a lot of stuff, I voted for Clinton, I think he's an honest person, I think Al Gore is an honest person and anything would be better than Bush. That said, I don't think I'd ever sit down with any president.' Given that Buck is the professional cynic in the band, it's not too surprising to hear him talk in those terms, but it does expose a dichotomy at the heart of the group's political activity. Creatively, this is an important source of musical friction, pulling the songs in a number of directions at once, which is generally beneficial for the group.

The divergence over policy was made clearer at a fundraiser for the Democrats attended by Al Gore. Gore's wife, Tipper, had been a prominent member of the Parents Music Resource Centre (PMRC), better known as the 'Washington Wives' who had been attempting to bring about censorship, or at the very least, stickering of records. Peter was particularly opposed to that campaign, as he made clear in no uncertain terms:

> I respect Al Gore a lot, his record on the environment is good but I think [Tipper and the PMRC] is something to be worried about. She's very dangerous because she's empowered these right-wing cranks, she gave them a voice, legitimized them, they still use her name . . . I didn't mean to be rude to them but I didn't want her to think that just because we didn't write 'Cop Killer' we're on her side. I told her, 'I think you're aligning yourself with some very dangerous people. It's all very well to think that what you're doing is labelling records but after that it's book burnings.' She's a nice lady and real rational but she looked like I'd slapped her.

One track, ushered in by a block of backing voices reminiscent of

'I'm Not in Love' by 10CC was 'Star Me Kitten'. Its lush texture is in sharp contrast to the sentiment of the song – real title 'Fuck Me Kitten'. Peter explained to *Melody Maker*,

> We didn't want to have 'fuck' on the outside of the record sleeve … they were shooting this movie in Seattle [while we were mixing] and Meg Ryan came by and she just loved the song but she said, 'When I grew up, if the word "fuck" was in the title and it was on the cover, I couldn't buy it in my town.' You want to reach people, you don't want someone to arbitrarily say, 'You can't hear this.'

Michael's vocal is chilling, employing the measured tones of Anthony Hopkins in *Silence Of The Lambs* to monstrous effect. Mike's view was, 'Michael's just saying, "Yeah, relationships are tough and ours may not be the best but go ahead. What are you waiting for? Fuck me!"' Of all the songs on *Automatic*, this points the way towards what they would be doing next, not in a musical context, but in the way Michael sings through a deranged character. As Peter noted, 'It's a real perverse love song, demented, but it's an endearing term. It's not about cats.'

The biggest departure from days of yore on *Automatic For The People* is an obvious lack of ensemble playing, something which Peter acknowledged: 'It's kind of like the *White Album*, we didn't do a lot of playing together. We never played "Sweetness Follows" or "Nightswimming" as a band. Bill wrote "Everybody Hurts" and he's hardly on it.' The songs are often made to sound fuller by the judicious use of string instruments, the arrangements this time being provided in part by John Paul Jones of Led Zeppelin fame. This collaboration was a fortuitous accident, according to Buck: 'Scott Litt met him one night and just asked him. I'd liked his stuff since I was a kid. It's easy to hate Led Zeppelin because of their imitators but for me they were a psychedelic blues band.' Mike Mills' role in R.E.M. has been compared with that of Jones in Zeppelin and there are striking similarities which ensured that the two worked well together.

The string arrangements on *Automatic* are more fully realised than on *Out Of Time*, in part thanks to Jones, but also because the band themselves were feeling more confident with the form. The cello part on 'Sweetness Follows', for instance, is absolutely central to the song, creating a strong baroque flavour which matches the doleful lyrical tone, with Peter's guitar feedback adding a different wash of colour to the mix. Peter admitted, '[The song] would be too saccharine if it didn't have that discordant cello back there.' As a further example of Michael's fascination with death and the rituals that surround it, 'Sweetness Follows' is deeply affecting, the mournful timbre of his voice giving it a resonant nobility. It does not actively preach the concept of faith or an afterlife but it does achieve a powerful spirituality, with Stipe apparently singing about the redemptive powers, the necessity to mourn and to allow real feelings to be exorcised. Allan Jones called the song 'harrowing ... the blackest, bleakest moment R.E.M. have committed to record' in his *Melody Maker* review but it could just as easily have been construed as a message of solidarity to anyone going through a painful loss.

'Try Not To Breathe' is, ironically, a little more airy, working its own magic around a beautifully simple acoustic guitar motif, the space progressively filled by Mike's work on keyboards and backing vocals. 'Embellishment is something I do,' he admitted, and on this occasion it is especially successful. The lyrical inspiration came from Peter this time: 'When I was doing the demo, I had this little microphone right in front of me and I was breathing really loud and it was making too much noise. I said, "I'll try not to breathe," and Michael took that as a title ... like an exercise he tried to think about why someone would try not to breathe. It's about an old man who's imagining himself dead and holding his breathe to try to imagine what it's like to be gone.' Michael later pointed out that it is an old woman rather than a man, but the gist remains the same.

Like so many of their best songs, it embraces both a lyrical and musical dichotomy; musically, it is almost serene, but there is a disturbing undercurrent from Buck's distorted electric guitar as Michael's voice changes in tone from welcoming death to reassuring those left behind that life goes on, imparting the wisdom of age.

There is little ambiguity in 'Everybody Hurts', Michael having tackled the lyric with the same determined precision that had benefited 'Belong'. Peter applauded this example of the lyricist's craft, noting that it was written to reach those that might be considering suicide: 'He wanted that song to reach teenagers and not be misunderstood. You don't want something that needs a maths degree to go through when you're trying to reach a seventeen-year-old and say, "It's ok, things are tough, but they get better." There's not a line out of place in there.' Michael was especially proud of his work: claiming that the blue ribbon on his chest; the prize at the end of the night, is the ability to say "God, I did it, I wrote a song that a lot of different people from a lot of different backgrounds with a lot of different ways of thinking can call their own and respond to emotionally and intellectually."' It struck a universal chord and went on to become perhaps the most popular song on the record, deservedly so.

For such an emotional piece, it started out as something of a joke, according to Peter: 'We all switched instruments. Mills played drums, I played bass and Bill played guitar and the demo was just the worst thing . . . we had to stop at one point, we were laughing so hard.' Michael heard the tape, however, and felt that it fitted some words that he'd been working on, and the very straightforward 'Everybody Hurts' was the finished result. The video that accompanied it on its inevitable single release was shot in a huge gridlock on a section of freeway, but it did its job well, catching the mood of the song beautifully as hundreds of people left the isolation of their stationary cars to come together. The shot of Michael singing 'hold on' from the central reservation was the most powerful musical image of the year and helped win them yet another armful of MTV statuettes in the 1993 poll. As a beacon of hope that would be seen by countless disaffected youngsters across the world, the song served its purpose a hundred times over. Peter was less impressed, however: 'We closed the freeway in San Antonio for three days to shoot it. You have to ask yourself, "Was it worth it?"'

This seemingly unwavering focus on the issues of death, loss, memory and love meant questions were asked about the source of inspiration. Each band member answered that they all had friends who were afflicted with AIDS, and many fans and observers felt that this was the reason such a pall had descended on the band. This was compounded by Michael's ambiguous sexuality, the fact that he went to the Grammys sporting a 'White House Stop AIDS' cap, the assertion that R.E.M. would not tour *Automatic For The People*, Anton Corbijn's austere, Beckett-like sleeve photography which captured an especially mournful-looking Stipe, Stipe's refusal to do interviews and his skinny physique. Soon, certain sections of the media concluded that AIDS was an issue that must have hit very much closer to home. According to the press, Michael was about to follow Freddie Mercury to the grave as another AIDS-riddled rock star.

The evidence was as selective and spurious as that which had pronounced Paul McCartney dead in the late 1960s. A glance through Corbijn's book *Famousz Photographs 1976.88* shows that his black and white photography is always powerful and concentrates on conveying personality rather than surface, so there is nothing new in his subjects looking severe. Stipe had regularly shied away from interviews in the past, as has already been noted. Finally, he is perennially thin, and has been ever since R.E.M. first emerged: in fact, the inner sleeve photograph on *Automatic*, of him with Peter Buck, actually presents him in robust physical shape.

Never allowing facts to get in the way of a good story, the press and the music industry rumour-mongers got to work: *Automatic For The People* would be the last record, Michael wouldn't see out the year, they were stockpiling tracks *à la* Queen and Mercury for future release once Michael was gone. As the facts have subsequently shown, it was all complete nonsense, though Stipe's refusal to issue a statement quelling the stories was odd. It was left to Mike and Peter to put out the tabloid fire, the exasperated Buck asking, 'What can you say about it? We've all been tested, we have tons of insurance, millions of dollars worth. Not that it's anybody's business, or that I care one way or the other what people think, but I know Michael passed the test just two months ago and one of the reasons we know is that we have this God-like insurance.' Trying to find a bright side amid the gossip, he added, 'As bad as it is to have these rumours, if it makes kids think a little bit more about their actions, that's fine.' As they had feared, fame meant that R.E.M. were easy game for these scurrilous accusations, showing just how sensible their decision was to take a low-key approach to the new project.

It wasn't until a year or so later that Michael made a comment on the subject:

> I thought it was incredibly misguided. The record is much more about mortality generally but AIDS is something that we all have to deal with ... 'Try Not To Breathe', for instance, was written from the point of view of an eighty-seven-year-old woman ... I'm sexually ambiguous, I always have been. I've always written gender-fuck songs that are specifically unspecific.

However, Stipe was slightly chastened by the episode, in particular over his disregard for those fans who had been desperately worried about the state of his health.

> I did not realize there was genuine concern, which doesn't say much for me. As a cynical pop star I just thought people were sticking their nose in where it didn't belong . . . I really felt like if I answered it would make it seem like being HIV positive or having AIDS was something to be embarrassed of or ashamed of, I just thought that calling a press conference with my doctors behind me would stigmatize people with AIDS. I naively thought, 'Maybe this'll change the way some people think.'

Essentially, the experience taught Michael and R.E.M. that the message they felt they were getting across by virtue of their actions would be distorted to match the media's agenda. Stipe's attempt at silent solidarity with AIDS sufferers was twisted into a silent admission of illness. It was a painful lesson for all the group.

If Michael was fascinated with mortality in 1992, Peter had his own personal difficulties which might have had something to do with the downbeat tone of the record. Mike took up some of his responsibilities, perhaps guiding the music in a different direction, while Peter's persistence with acoustic instruments helped shape the rest of the accompaniment. The lack of loud guitar gave strings and keyboards leeway to become the dominant sounds on the record.

Peter was already expressing his personal disenchantment in veiled terms when he spoke to *Vox* about *Automatic For The People*. Telling Steve Malins that he'd spent most of the previous year travelling, he added, 'I could very easily wipe out the entire past and start all over right now and it wouldn't bother me at all. I could very easily get in a plane and fly somewhere and never talk to anyone I know again. I'd probably feel lonely for a week or two but I'm kind of a no-nonsense person, I don't think about the past,' an assertion belied by the doggedly nostalgic tone of the album. Given Buck's famous wanderlust, his attachment to the spirit of the road that persisted even beyond R.E.M.'s long years of touring, the idea of being tied to one place was anathema. And his wife, Barrie, was co-owner of the 40 Watt Club, she wasn't exactly free to take off whenever she felt like it.

Buck admitted in 1994 that throughout part of the *Out Of Time* process and beyond into *Automatic For The People*,

I pretty much spent two years in bed. All I did was drink wine and lay in bed. I'd get up and practise every night and then go back to bed. I never left my house and then I figured out what I wanted to do with my life and did it. I made a lot of changes. But it was kinda fun, I'd recommend it to anyone. If you feel depressed, take a two-week vacation and don't leave your bed. Order pizza, drink wine, it's a great thing.

Given his penchant for exaggeration, it's probable that he wasn't quite so isolated; after all he had a hand in two R.E.M. albums, did the *Out Of Time* promotional tour and also travelled a great deal. However, his waistline increased dramatically and it was very clear that he wasn't getting a great deal of exercise. The upshot of it all was that his marriage was over, in turn affecting the kind of music he was writing, adding to the melancholic atmosphere of *Automatic*. Ultimately, Peter sorted out his own problems, going to live in New York briefly and then moving on to Seattle:

I decided to get out of Athens because for me it's a town where I am inextricably linked with being in R.E.M.. Seventy-year-old women know who I am and they know the gossip about me. I got very tired about that in a way the other guys haven't . . . it was a great experience to get away from the road for a while – I've been through some serious dealing with adulthood in the '90s.

Most observers agreed that *Automatic For The People* is a very 'mature' record, with some excellent moments of pop, too, such as 'Man On The Moon' or 'The Sidewinder Sleeps Tonite', both hit singles. 'Man On The Moon' touches on one of Michael's heroes, comedian Andy Kaufman, best known as Latka in *Taxi*. Back in 1988 Stipe told *Melody Maker* that Kaufman was

incredible, a very risky performer. I think he died from cancer but a lot of his fans are still wondering whether his death was staged because that was certainly the kind of humour he dealt with. It was incredibly black comedy, so it would seem to a lot of people that his final joke would be to stage his own death and get away with it. I think comedy may have died with Andy Kaufman, he was the king.

On the subject of kings who may or may not be dead, Michael's thoughts naturally went to the king of rock'n'roll, Elvis Presley. As Mike elaborated later, 'Man On The Moon' is 'a situation where Andy Kaufman meets up with Elvis in Heaven, only Heaven happens to be a truck-stop . . . Michael's just got this funny take on faith and beliefs, trying to understand if what you're seeing is the real thing.'

Michael had taken to referring to himself as a satellite receiver over the years and a lot of the work that the band was doing seemed to have started with fragments picked out of the ether, be it news stories, old songs or bits of conversation. 'Monty Got A Raw Deal' for instance is about – insofar as any of Michael's lyrics are 'about' anything so specific – the actor Montgomery Clift. According to Peter, 'It came about because there was someone who was a photographer on the set of *The Misfits* who came by the studio. He had photos from it and he was talking about it. How much of the song is real, how much of it is about Montgomery Clift and how much is about fame, I couldn't tell you.' What Buck could be certain of was just how the song was written: 'I wrote the main riff on my bouzouki in the hotel room in New Orleans. I don't know what the couple next door were doing – it sounded like an orgy. It was about three in the morning and what sounded like four different radios going on at the same time, a lot of people and banging. But this is New Orleans, what do you expect? You can't complain so I sat up and played.'

On its release, *Automatic For The People* was hailed as a masterpiece by all sections of the media, yet many asked if it was their swan song. The ostensibly funereal tones of some of the material clearly overwhelmed some observers, outweighing the clever pop that was also on offer. Presumably the bookending of the record with 'Drive' and 'Try Not To Breathe' at the beginning and 'Nightswimming' and 'Find The River' at the end created first and final impressions that were so powerfully evocative they dwarfed all else. Those two closing songs form one of the strongest endings to any record in rock's history; as the elegiac closing strains of 'Find The River' die away you just have to pause and take a breath.

'Nightswimming' originally came together at the end of the *Out Of Time* sessions, but was never completed satisfactorily. The idea of it never reaching an album was too terrible to contemplate, so its appearance on *Automatic* was timely. Indeed, it was fortuitous that the band did keep it back, for it matches the mood of *Automatic* quite perfectly, an aching, yearning piece of nostalgia that embodies the theme of mortality. Mike recalled for *Vox*,

Twenty or thirty of us would go skinny-dipping at two in the morning – you know, build a fire and get naked. There was a possibility of the sheriff coming up, we were drinking and doing who knows what and we could have gone to jail. Whereas now, no-one does it any more except once in a while we take a friend up there to show them, and even if you do go to swim, it's still not like it used to be because no-one knows about it and there's really no chance of anyone coming down and bothering you.

Within the lyric, Stipe conveys all of that regret for the passing of time and those magical moments, evoking such sadness yet simultaneously advocating living life to the full to make the most of such times. It is very clearly a band recollection, yet only Stipe and Mike actually appear on it; the collective voice being carried by just part of the band is very reminiscent of The Beatles, especially the *White Album*, a connection specified by the orchestral tune-up that opens the song.

To follow the wistful sorrow of 'Nightswimming' with 'Find The River' is almost too much, a closing lament. Reviewing the album in *NME*, Dele Fadele perceptively noted, 'This whole scenario [of loss] eventually coming to everybody, you think it's just too bleak, until you remember how you can be washed clean by the river, made whole again, reborn. Then there's more hope. . . .' And at its heart, *Automatic For The People* is a beautiful, hopeful record; the final song reiterates 'strength' and 'courage', and rejoices in the resilience of humanity. That theme is present even in the enormous backing harmonies, as Mike explained in *Q*:

I asked everybody to sing a background part for the chorus without hearing any of the other guys. Mine was really emotional and Bill's was totally the opposite, cool and low-key. They really worked together. That's the kind of thing that keeps it from being too processed; that lets you know that it's not being machined to death, that there are human beings doing it.

Automatic For The People is a deeply human, extraordinarily intimate record. Michael Stipe's propensity for writing lyrics with myriad interpretations is at its very best, coupling seamlessly with the most emotionally charged music that R.E.M. had yet achieved.

Every listener can immerse him or herself in the record and emerge at the other end with their own pictures, their own memories and their own emotions. *Automatic For The People* stands as one of those very rare pieces of work that every listener can claim as their own personal property away from the hype, the accepted interpretations and the reams of reviews. For that alone, it will come to be seen as one of those Top Twenty all-time great albums that Peter was so keen to make. Maybe there isn't a better album out there.

In the public mind, *Automatic For The People* continued the changes in perceptions of R.E.M.. If *Out Of Time* had pegged them as intelligent musicians who were unlikely to trash hotel rooms, *Automatic* bestowed an odd kind of kudos upon them, to the point where they were almost viewed as keepers of the American way of life, as a Rockwell vision of decent, travelling minstrels rather than the Orwellian harbingers of *Document*. 'Nobility' is a word already used to describe them in this chapter but it bears repetition given that it's a term not often used in connection with rock'n'roll. R.E.M. had come to stand for honest integrity, an odd reputation for a rock band to have.

On Bill Clinton's election to the White House, an Inauguration Gala took place in January 1993. The great and the good were gathered to pay homage to the new president; in among the showbiz glitterati such as Sidney Poitier, Lauren Bacall and Whoopi Goldberg stood Michael Stipe, ready to give a reading to the assembled crowd. He quoted from Woody Guthrie's 'This Land Is Your Land' and closed by saying, 'Let us sort out the music from the sound.' Amid such world celebrities whose fame Stipe had come to rival, Michael cut an everyman figure, representing the interests and aspirations of America's ordinary people. In the shadow of the home of the American president, Michael Stipe personified nothing more than the same kind of decency and determination to stand up for what's right that James Stewart embodied for an earlier generation. Mr Stipe had gone to Washington, but this was no Frank Capra movie.

Michael Stipe's appearance at the gala showed the public's great affection for R.E.M., far greater than that lavished on any comparable rock act. It also indicated the way in which both *Out Of Time* and, more especially, *Automatic For The People* had captured a changing mood in the US and had come to represent the times for a lot of people. As far as it went, this was the greatest of compliments. But what was next? Mike felt, 'One more record this slow would probably kill us. I think we're all ready to work on faster, more driving songs.'

12

THE SUPREME BONER

The quest was on to find a suitably different direction for the album following *Automatic For The People*. One of the great benefits of signing to a label like Warner Brothers is the ancillary facilities they offer; when R.E.M. wanted to take a break together to discuss the future, they were offered the use of a company house in Acapulco, not an unattractive bonus. In an attempt to map out their strategy, they spent some time together there, relaxing and talking over the future.

In the early days it had been very much the group against the world as they put all their collective energy into getting a deal, getting an audience and building that until it was commercially viable. Once the money started coming in, however, the business side of the operation commanded a disproportionate amount of time, while financially the band members were freer to pursue their own interests. Michael was increasingly involved in film projects, for example, accepting that 'the bigger you become as a band the more money and possibilities you have at your disposal'. Peter was sorting out his domestic situation and playing guitar with anyone and everyone, and Bill was becoming a gentleman farmer. Although they were still committed to the future of R.E.M., these other matters reduced the time they had available for a group which was no longer the be-all and end-all of their lives. With *Automatic For The People* that sort of dislocation reached its peak, as almost half the songs did not feature a group performance.

Mike had already hinted that this new album had to be a little more musically direct, but it was common practice for the band to say an album would take one form, only for something else to take its place, so little credence was given to these remarks. However, Bill weighed in with a similar idea:

I would have been out of the band basically if we'd made the trilogy of melancholy sullen records. *Automatic For The People* was supposed to rock but those songs didn't come out of us – it was a fine record but I pretty much told everybody, 'This record rocks or I leave!' . . . we decided that we wanted to limit the amount of overdubs as much as possible. You're left with very few elements so it makes sense to whack it out a bit.

With amps set to a Spinal Tap-like '11', the scene was set for *Monster*.

The studio phase of R.E.M.'s career was, temporarily at least, coming to a conclusion, as Peter admitted:

We hadn't been functioning as a band and we felt that it was time that we did the whole thing again, a band recording, a tour and videos emphasizing the performance side of the group . . . over the years there seems to have been a trajectory where we started out as a live band, recorded things in a live manner and then, over the last three records – *Green* through *Automatic* – it has been less and less a band and more and more one or two people playing together then layering stuff on top. Bill brought in 'Everybody Hurts' and he wasn't even on the basic track which was me, Mike and a drum machine. We felt like we wanted to work again as a band.

One of the catalysts for their urge to go back on the road seemed to be the electrifying performance they gave at the 1993 MTV awards, where they stole the show from Neil Young in performing a funked-up version of 'Drive' and the inevitable 'Everybody Hurts'. That brief appearance indicated a band that still knew how to work a live crowd and a group for whom live performance was a central part of their life force. They were right to retreat when they did, making two very fine studio-based records as a result, but now was the time to inject some new life into R.E.M. by treading the boards once more.

Ironically for a group that had come up through the live school, for many of their fans who had only heard of them over the last couple of records they were a studio folk group who played acoustically. But Bill was adamant: 'We're a noisy rock'n'roll band y'know, that's what we do best.' By now Bill and Peter had come through personal difficulties and were looking towards the future; Mike was keen to get back on the road too, so things were very definitely moving towards that driving rock music of which Bill had spoken.

The band compiled a whole range of material in preparation for the new record, writing forty-five songs by Peter's estimation. Some of this caught the tail end of the *Automatic* atmosphere, as Peter revealed: 'There's a whole album of really good acoustic stuff that's kinda similar to *Automatic* that I hope we don't throw away.' But now was no longer the time for such muted statements, especially since the idea was to take the new songs out on tour; Michael was looking for noisy songs, 'so I don't have to worry about pitch. I can just get up there and yell, which I kinda like.' Roadworthiness was not the only consideration that mattered though: their ninth studio effort had to stand up alongside two of the very best albums of the decade so far.

On both *Out Of Time* and *Automatic For The People*, Mike Mills was generally regarded as the architect of the band's sound, a sweeping generalization, even if much of that work did bear his stamp most clearly. To continue the generalizations, *Monster* was to see the return of Peter Buck as the defining force. Four years on from the *Green* tour, Buck was finally pining for loud electric guitar, an instrument he had barely played since they came off the road.

Monster became a celebratory album and Peter was very definitely in that mood. After making the alterations to his life that he felt were necessary, his demeanour was transformed, as he told *Hot Press*: 'I'm really good at change but first I have to figure out what I want first. For two years I spent most days drinking wine. There were eight months especially where I just thought, "Fuck it!"' Getting off the booze, Peter solved most of his problems by moving to Seattle – 'nobody knows who the fuck I am, they've got Eddie Vedder living there' – and with the help of his second wife Stephanie. With his life on an upward curve – Stephanie gave birth to twins during the recording of *Monster* – Buck was intent on making some noise and having some fun after a dark period. The trauma of touring and trying to drown out a screaming crowd, followed by a few years in the studio led Buck to admit, 'I just forgot the pleasure of turning up really loud and playing.'

Even back in the early days when R.E.M. were a raw rock'n'roll group, the guitar sound was melodic rather than a sandblasted shriek. Peter put the new sound down to an equipment purchase. 'I just bought an amp which had a great tremolo on it and as stupid as that sounds Bill immediately wrote "I Took Your Name" and I wrote "Crush With Eyeliner" within about an hour of buying it.' *Monster* is drenched in guitar noise, effects and feedback; it was something of a change in tack but all the better for it. However good *Out Of Time* and *Automatic* had been, many of R.E.M.'s older fans had been waiting a long time for Peter to plug in again. *Monster* shows that R.E.M. were a band so confident and on such a creative roll that they now chose only to work in extremes where, of course, all the very best work is done. It's nonsense to suggest that *Monster* is noise terrorism like that produced by Einsturzende Neubaten or even Michael's own Tanzplagen, but then few find any redeeming qualities in that style. The task which R.E.M. continued to set themselves was to take the basic song format and push it to the very limits, leaving what is still recognizably a song with a melody line, but only just.

The circumstances surrounding the creation of *Monster* were not particularly auspicious. All four band members had taken a proper holiday in the aftermath of *Automatic*, the first extended break they had allowed themselves in over a decade, and during this period they all found that life outside the group's tunnel vision had its compensations. Michael found the time to develop a film project that he had long held dear. Hooking up with Oliver Stone to provide the requisite Hollywood muscle, he spent much of 1993 'going back and forth to Los Angeles to work on an entire feature film. It's a road movie, there are no actors and a first-time director. It's called *Desperation Angels*. Three guys take off on a road trip and kind of discover America, or rather the America after Reagan and Bush. The film is political, it's not funny, it will be very controversial.' Despite giving a lot of his time to the idea, it was taken out of development in 1994, much to his bitter disappointment. 'It was top-shelved, in other words deemed too dark, too underground, too political'.

Michael's outside interests provided a hurdle to overcome, while another was Peter's move to Seattle, which could easily have disrupted songwriting duties. To alleviate the problem, Peter returned to Athens for a few weeks, Bill explaining the new process:

This was the first record where he didn't live in Athens so we couldn't just spend months and months going in for an hour or two a day to write, which is the way we always worked. This time we had this really strong work ethic where we had to go in and work for eight or nine hours. At first I dreaded it because it sounded like a job, but very quickly those eight hours turned into twelve because we were having so much fun playing with tremolos, singing through strange microphones. We never applied ourselves that hard before.

The fiercest blow dealt to the group was a deeply personal one – the death of actor River Phoenix in October 1993. Michael took the loss badly:

River was like my little brother and his death was the most profound loss I've ever experienced in my life. I had to sit back and look at everything around me in a different light. *Automatic For The People* dealt with passage, mortality, we really covered that and we needed to do a record that was really different because I felt that we had reached kind of a zenith with that. River's death prevented me writing for five months. When I did I wrote 'Crush With Eyeliner', 'What's The Frequency, Kenneth?' and 'Circus Envy'.

On hearing of Michael's grief at Phoenix's death, many would have anticipated a record that followed very closely in the tracks of *Automatic For The People*. However, it's readily understandable that Michael would not have wanted to submerge himself in a record that could only serve as a painful reminder of loss. Instead he looked towards an affirmation of life, and the excitement of existence rather than the pain of parting. The consequence was a record which could be seen as therapeutic, and which he took to describing as 'cut-up-thrash-punk-rock, in your face, kind of sexy and fuck off'. Sadly the death of River Phoenix was not the only traumatic loss that he and the band would have to endure before completing the album.

In April 1994 came the news that Nirvana's Kurt Cobain had committed suicide in Seattle. All of R.E.M. had got to know Cobain, Stipe calling him an 'ally'. Sadly, his suicide had a grim inevitability to it, following a drug overdose a few weeks earlier. His reason had been clouded by the darkest emotions over those last few months, and many people had tried to offer him help, but as Mike noted, 'If someone is determined to take that course, then there's nothing you can do.' Michael had proposed that the two should work together on a soundtrack for an independent movie being made by the Starn brothers who had worked on the *Out Of Time* album sleeve: 'It was an attempt to get him out of the place he was in. I was talking to him up until he disappeared. I had this project that these people had come to me with and they said that their ideal would be to have either me or Kurt do the music for the film. I sent him plane tickets but he just didn't want it.'

Cobain approached his own suicide so purposefully that Stipe wanted to make it clear that he should 'not become the patron saint of suicide or the patron saint of heroin', while Peter was more forceful in the press:

Suicide is such a wilful, solipsistic act, it's shocking it still shocks me. He brought a lot of baggage with him, it wasn't just about fans. He let himself be in a position where he wasn't happy with things and drugs are the worst thing in the world to exacerbate that ... I want everyone to know what a terrible, dirty little thing suicide is, I see Krist [Novoselic] and Dave [Grohl] all the time, they're never gonna be the same.

Many reasons have been put forward suggesting why someone so apparently successful in his chosen profession should take his own life and this is not the place to rehash those arguments. Kurt Cobain is dead and should be allowed to rest in peace rather than providing ammunition for newspaper circulation wars. Suffice it to say that Kurt Cobain had problems not purely related to music and fame, which were compounded by his heavy use of heroin. The demands of the money-making music industry allowed no time or compassion for his personal difficulties, as Peter expressed with disgust, 'There's just this machine that rolls and rolls and you have to try to take control ... they did tours when they didn't want to and that kinda thing, they never learned to say no.'

Michael was careful not to apportion blame for the suicide to anyone or anything, but he did make one telling remark about the unbearable demands that we put on rock stars who are often little more than teenagers. 'By the time I became "the voice of a generation" in '87 or '88, we had five or six records under our belt. I'd been through it, although I didn't experience the tabloid media circus that surrounded those guys ... if I'd gotten the attention on

Murmur that he got on *Nevermind*, I wouldn't be around to tell the tale; I would've died.' R.E.M.'s approach to *Monster* was affected by the tragedy, which might seem trivial in the light of Cobain's death. Michael said, 'When he died after River's death, I fucking threw my hands up and said, "I've got to get this out," and "Let Me In" came out of it which was written to Kurt, for Kurt and about Kurt . . . I had to express the frustration that I had, trying to pull him out and not succeeding.' 'Let Me In' evolved into a virtual duet, with Michael backed by a fierce hail of guitar noise from Peter that conjured up the rawness of some of Nirvana's work. In keeping with the rest of *Monster*, Michael's voice was a murmur, though the plaintive refrain made his target perfectly clear, angry frustration ringing in his voice.

Frustration was the keynote in the aftermath of Cobain's death for, in comforting Cobain's widow Courtney Love, Stipe soon found himself a tabloid target again. Love was allegedly pregnant, and the press couldn't make up their minds whether Michael was the father or whether it might be Lemonhead Evan Dando or Trent Reznor of Nine Inch Nails. The fact that Love was not pregnant was widely ignored since it would have ruined the story. Michael laughed it off in the same way he had the AIDS rumours, but it provided further proof that the press now treated him as their property.

Michael responded to this treatment in the robotic strains of 'King Of Comedy', a venomous diatribe against the world of commerce in general, and the music business in particular. The song seems riddled with the ghost of Cobain, especially in the final dramatic declamation, 'I'm not commodity.' As with *Out Of Time*, Stipe was at pains to tell the world, 'I'm definitely writing in different voices . . . I created a lot of personas. Very creepy personas as well . . . on *Monster* I stay closer to the surface than on *Automatic*.' He conceded, 'I know exactly what's going on tape by the time it goes down. I know in "King Of Comedy" how much playfulness there is with the image people have of me. Hopefully it's a shared joke.'

The theme of media stereotypes, the technological revolution and its attendant commercial rape is probed further by 'What's The Frequency, Kenneth?', the first single and first track on the album. Heralded by ringing guitar, it is Stipe's attack on the media invention of Generation X and the attempt made by the establishment to understand, commodify and thereby neuter it. The genesis of the song was explained by Peter Buck:

There's a famous newscaster in America, Dan Rather, he's very stolid and sincere – really straight guy – and he was beaten up one day. And he claimed two men ran up to him and started pounding him mercilessly and then they'd stop and go, 'What's the frequency Kenneth?' and then beat him some more. It didn't make any sense y'know, 'What the fuck are you talking about, what exactly is going through your mind there?'

Once the phrase had entered the American consciousness, Michael took its completely incomprehensible character as a metaphor: 'It's this guy who's desperately trying to understand what motivates the younger generation and who has gone to great lengths to try and figure them out and at the end of the song it's completely fucking bogus.' Michael described the song as 'a comment on the media and a better comment than *Natural Born Killers*, which I thought sucked' – though maybe he was sucking sour grapes after the demise of *Desperation Angels*. Later Stipe admitted, 'I still respect Oliver Stone and I went to see *Natural Born Killers* with great expectations. But what I got instead was just the first drug movie of the '90s. There's no story, just a lot of show.' On further consideration and having condemned the actions of the establishment, Michael accepted, 'I'm completely fascinated by media culture and by the media and I don't mind being a part of it. I kinda enjoy it to a degree. I'm a bit of a starfucker.' With its theme of the growth in the mass media, 'What's The Frequency, Kenneth?' ploughed a similar furrow to U2's Zoo TV tour and *Zooropa*, while 'King Of Comedy' was, superficially at least, very close to 'Numb' from the same record. At this stage, R.E.M. were being criticized for following the blueprint that U2 had already used to reinvent themselves. *Monster* sounded strikingly modern by R.E.M. standards, and anyone with a copy of *Achtung Baby!* would already be familiar with a number of *Monster*'s components, such as the obsession with twisted relationships, and the joy or pain of sex. R.E.M. had been likened to U2 before, and there is a degree of similarity; when *The Joshua Tree* turned U2 into the world's biggest band, they appeared to be an ascetic group of miserable blokes who had no idea of how to enjoy their good fortune. Much the same was said of R.E.M. when their 'death' album, *Automatic For The People* began to sell in similar quantities.

Monster sprang from the same sort of reaction that *Achtung*

Baby! had, and represented a throwing off of the shackles, an attempt to lighten the load and inject a little humour into the mix. It also moved away from the focus on global issues. Anyone writing a song like 'Crush With Eyeliner' was clearly a bit of a joker and somebody whose opinions on Bosnia were worth no more than those of the average man or woman in the street. *Monster* was simply another part in the continuing R.E.M. saga, no more, no less. Students of the band should have seen it coming, as part of R.E.M.'s tradition of reinvention – they were Southern storytellers from *Murmur* to *Fables*, they were electric political polemicists from *Lifes Rich Pageant* through *Document* and into *Green*, where an acoustic phase took hold, running through to *Automatic For The People*. That had reached its logical conclusion, so the return to their rock roots was overdue. Having covered love and death on the previous two records, sex was now the inevitable source of inspiration for a Michael Stipe uncomfortable with those James Stewart analogies. Mike also welcomed the change in emphasis, noting that 'a lot of the songs are very life-affirming and positive in a way. Sex itself is sort of an affirmation.'

Michael realized that Peter and Bill had triggered the change with 'I Took Your Name' and 'Crush With Eyeliner'. 'That tremolo is pretty swaggering,' he confessed. 'It set the pace.' For all four though, *Monster* provided the opportunity to reacquaint themselves with the reasons they were excited by music in the first place, and was a very necessary revitalization of their collective enthusiasm, so easily lost in a sea of commercial decisions. Mike felt that 'it was time to muddy it back up' and Michael's voice was mixed down accordingly, recapturing the enigmatic sound that had played such a large part in the band's development. Michael felt that 'a lot of the album is referring back to Iggy and The Stooges and Patti Smith and Television and stuff like that', though the most apparent influence was The Stones, maybe via The New York Dolls, Peter confirming that 'it has a kinda glam feel to it'.

'Crush With Eyeliner' was described by Stipe as 'a paean to The New York Dolls, with reference to *Frankenstein*, which, of course, is one of their songs'. To the wider public, that song – along with 'I Took Your Name' and 'Star 69' – was a tribute to The Rolling Stones, sounding almost as if they might have got on to *Exile On Main Street*. Down to the whooping backing vocals, the influence of The Glimmer Twins was pretty apparent, as Peter recycled the very best of Keith Richard's trademark licks. You could almost see Buck lurching into the studio with a guitar slung over his shoulder, cigarette in the corner of his mouth, bottle of Jack Daniels in one hand, gypsy scarves in the other ready to drape over a handy table lamp to set the mood. Since R.E.M.'s inception, Peter had been telling the world that Keith Richard was one of his greatest influences, rather than Roger McGuinn of The Byrds, and finally the proof was there.

The appearance of Thurston Moore from Sonic Youth on backing vocals for 'Crush With Eyeliner' made the comparisons with The Stones all the more apparent, creating an undercurrent of malevolence. Moore – who had worked with Mike Mills in the Backbeat band, providing the soundtrack for the film about the life of original Beatle Stuart Sutcliffe – brings his own kind of myth to a recording session, Sonic Youth's cartoon violence and Manson obsession adding a certain weight to his already menacing tones. *Monster* had been turned into a creepshow by Michael's adoption of numerous personae, so the presence of Moore contributed a little extra authenticity.

Monster proved that R.E.M. had their collective ear to the ground and were not immune to the changing character of their country, and especially its rising tide of violence. Talking to *Vox*, John Seawright, a local Athenian poet noted,

Ten years ago you'd think nothing of walking anywhere in town at night, from one party to another at two in the morning sometimes miles across town. People would sit around in vacant lots all night and just talk. But not any more. The atmosphere is quite different now, the attacks are not robberies, it's young kids who increasingly don't see anything else to do. It's just making the town a little more like any other town in America.

This mood made its presence felt in *Monster*, while the USA's seemingly unarrested decline into chaos was noted by many commentators reflecting on Bill Clinton's two years in the White House. Stipe's response was sharp: 'Clinton is an incredible radical and so's his wife. They've been hurled into a position of incredible compromise, a position that's so much more complex than any of us have any idea . . . the one thing Clinton can't say to the media and the American public is that he's got handed a really rotten deal from the last twelve years.'

Those twelve years had spanned the whole of R.E.M.'s musical career. In that time, only *Fables Of The Reconstruction* had been a real problem to record, but *Monster* had its moments, too. The project was beset with external difficulties which turned recording into a logistical nightmare. Mike was rushed into hospital with appendicitis, Michael had a tooth abscess, Bill was out of action for a fortnight with a severe case of 'flu, while on a happier, but no less disruptive note, Peter became the proud father of twin daughters. *Monster* got its name because, according to Mike, 'It threatened to consume us all,' and there were dark mutterings surrounding the whole recording process. Mike told *Select* midway through recording that 'we have to begin working as a unit again which we haven't been doing very well lately', and Peter chipped in with, 'It would get to the stage where we would mix something for three days and not even one of us would like it.'

These complications were partly as a result of their not having worked as a unit for so long, but also the unsettling nature of the songs was not designed to soothe the savage beast. Peter admitted, 'The lyrics are creepy, Michael's singing in character and a lot of the characters aren't really nice people it seems.' The point is made on 'I Took Your Name', which features an obsessive, power-crazed protagonist. *Mojo*'s David Cavanagh called it a 'pale rewrite of "Turn You Inside Out"' and there are parallels between the two, but 'I Took Your Name' focuses on the misuse of power, rather than simply recognizing its existence. 'I Took Your Name' is much heavier in sound and intent, clearly designed to light up the football stadia of the world, but still has its subtleties, the tolling bell in the background ominously prophetic. Though Iggy Pop is name-checked, 'I Took Your Name' is closer in tone to The Stones' 'Sympathy For The Devil' than anything by The Ig.

Obsession becomes possession on both 'You' and 'Strange Currencies'. 'Strange Currencies' is a musical retread of 'Everybody Hurts' with the weird quotient upped, but lyrically it couldn't be more different. Starting where 'Losing My Religion' left off, 'Strange Circumstances' and 'You' take matters further; having lost his religion, Michael's character has now fallen over the precipice, convincing himself that everything will work out if only the object of his affection would pay him some attention and listen to what he has to say.

'Star 69' takes its name from the way crank callers are traced in the US – by pushing those three buttons, you get the number of your last caller. This time the rampantly paranoid Stipe character is apparently on the receiving end. A little more obvious is 'I Don't Sleep, I Dream', in which Michael's emotional detachment is disconcerting, running through sexual positions and practices like an M.O.T. checklist, even if he grandly, or perhaps ironically, called the song 'nothing if it's not some sonic version of the dream state'. As far as the public is concerned, this was Stipe's first foray into the blatantly sexual, and it was, frankly, a little shocking. Michael had, after all, been saddled with an almost pious, wholly sexless image in the wake of *Automatic*, a sage with no bodily functions of which to speak. By 1992 the idea of Michael Stipe exchanging fluids seemed as likely as catching the Pope mainlining in Madonna's dressing room. Along with Morrissey, Michael was assumed to be a celebrity celibate.

'Tongue' put a stop to all that nonsense, as the title might suggest. The song is a beguiling Motown ballad, with Michael revealing a delicate Smokey Robinson falsetto and a roguish humour that was less than PC. A recently self-confessed flirt, in 'Tongue' Michael exposed his newly minted philosophy, 'Anyone can get laid, it's just a matter of lowering your standards enough.'

Monster stands up as an excellent album that would make any sane person's list of the top five records of the year. It is a little too tremolo-reliant in places, and the band were a little too quick to turn up the volume rather than develop a song further in others. A few tracks are clearly designed for live performance rather than repeated playing in the comfort of your own home, but 'Bang And Blame', 'What's The Frequency, Kenneth?', 'Let Me In', 'Strange Circumstances' and 'Tongue' form a handful of songs that any group would be proud to call their own. On its release, Peter Buck exclaimed, 'I kind of hope this album upsets people, I want people to take it home and go, "What?"' Buck got his wish as *Monster* premiered to some of the poorest reviews in their career. In *Mojo*, David Cavanagh sugared the pill with, 'When R.E.M. are great they make birdsong sound phony. But *Monster* remains a harsh dispatch, full of self-important Biro scribbles and ironic inverted commas.' *Select*'s Roy Wilkinson averred that with this 'fraught, sometimes claustrophobic beast . . . R.E.M. have come to at least the strong impression of an impasse'. Gavin Martin in *Vox* put his finger on the inspiration for the new sound made by 'bone-crunching, crotch-kicking, slavering beasties; R.E.M. are back with material that should withstand any amount of vexation their long-awaited world tour can throw at them', but it was *Q*'s Stuart Maconie who inadvertently summed up the real source of disappointment: 'It's grossly unfair to use a group's own triumphs to browbeat them, but we have to measure *Monster* by the standards R.E.M. have recently set. From that point of view it often feels one-dimensional and obscure.' Basically, it was seen as less good than their last album, ergo it wasn't any good at all – an understandable, if erroneous, view.

Monster was not as good a record as *Automatic For The People* in the eyes of many, and certainly it lacks that depth and subtlety, but it did see the group reaching out in a different direction, something to be applauded, particularly as it resulted in such a confident and assured album. Most significantly, it marks the final stage of Michael Stipe's progression from the timid mumbler of *Murmur* to a writer able to stand shoulder to shoulder with that other great chronicler of life in all its paranoid, twisted glory, Lou Reed. It is only because critics were preoccupied with making comparisons with *Automatic* that this observation was not more widely noted, for Stipe's characterizations are as vivid as anything rock's greatest curmudgeon might invoke. *Monster* was quickly dismissed as not up to scratch, the *NME* year-end critics poll placing it fourteenth behind The Prodigy, Beastie Boys, Oasis and Orbital.

Monster was also overshadowed by the announcement that R.E.M. were to go back on the road again, touring the world right through 1995. In Britain, indoor shows were announced – all 100,000 tickets were snapped up the day they went on sale, blowing up Sheffield's telephone exchange in the process, so further outdoor shows were added to meet the demand. The group approached the tour with mixed feelings, Bill and Peter the most obviously animated at the prospect. Peter was, of course, laying the most ambitious of plans, such as recording a new album in various hotel rooms around the world to short-circuit critical expectations, *à la Zooropa*: 'We wanna be more ambitious, not just get on the bus, play, get on the bus and then play. There's a way to do it to make it exciting and that might be to record.' In the same breath however, he was saying that this time around, life on the road would be a little less hectic: 'My family are gonna be with me every second. It'll be interesting because the last time we went out we were younger and a little wilder and our idea of a great time was to go and find the nearest bar that was kinda cool and we'd stay there until we were the last ones in the bar. That's not the way it works now.'

One thing that does not change with R.E.M. is their attitude to sponsorship. Peter made it very plain that, no matter what the costs might be, 'we're very much opposed to any form of sponsorship . . . I think it makes you look like an utter schmuck . . . I can't see myself playing from the heart and soul and then telling people to drink whatever. I find it really revolting.'

Ticket sales have made it abundantly clear that the world is ready for R.E.M.. The more worrying question from a fan's point of view is whether or not R.E.M. are ready for the world. Since their last junket with *Green*, the group's following has grown exponentially, and R.E.M. now find themselves in the tabloid press as well as the Sunday supplements. Their every move will be scrutinized in the way that Michael Jackson, Madonna, U2 or Prince are watched, the paparazzi will be out to get them and every show will come complete with its own media circus of movie stars and supermodels who want to be seen at *the* show. It's unlikely that Michael will end up engaged to Claudia Schiffer, perhaps, but given the way that Peter and Bill usually react to the superstar bullshit, tempers may start to fray. For the tour Mike and Michael are both apparently honing new images, and the all-new Michael Stipe will have much to contend with in the coming year. It's to be hoped that his new, seemingly more relaxed persona will deal with it with the confidence and style he and the rest of the group have used to come through a decade of madness. At least Peter's not worried: 'We're pretty good at avoiding the rock'n'roll traps. Nobody's married a supermodel yet.'

13

LET US SORT OUT THE MUSIC FROM THE SOUND

Only a churlish observer would try to denigrate the achievements of R.E.M., but it would be excessive to suggest that they have redefined the course of popular music. Their success has been in taking rock'n'roll back to its theoretical roots in a similar way to the punk movement in the '70s. By giving the music back to ordinary people, by succeeding on their own terms and by eschewing compromise wherever possible, R.E.M. have embraced all of rock's guiding principles. The vital ingredient in R.E.M.'s rise is, of course, their songwriting, rather than their musical ability.

The major error made by countless bands as the 1970s began was equating incredible technical proficiency with an interesting and entertaining sound. Looking back, all that bands such as ELP produced was sound without any discernible trace of music. As Michael Stipe noted in a different context, 'Let us sort out the music from the sound.' R.E.M. have been doing this very successfully for fifteen years now.

Songwriting ability is not the only reason for R.E.M.'s success. They have also managed to avoid the biggest problems caused by ego, thanks to their keen interest in the minutiae of rock history. Peter Buck in particular has always understood better than most why bands disintegrate. His suggestion to split writing and royalties equally was the most inspired moment in their career, ensuring that no-one could profit from the band more than the others, thereby avoiding tiresome power struggles. Most important, though, is the fact that the four individuals who make up the group are level-

189

headed and take fame for the fickle joke that it is. Celebrity has never interested them; all their goals have been musical ones, their greatest ambition to make the best records they possibly can.

Their collective friendship has also been instrumental in carrying them through. Each is happy to go on the record to testify to that bond, Michael first: 'We like each other, we love each other, we respect each other. We have the typical unnecessary battles and fights and screamings about this and that but it's all part of the process. We realize that without debate and without democratic decision you have oligarchy and none of us is interested in that.'

You might think it's easy for Michael Stipe to be content with his lot, as he gets all the credit, which is very true. Like all singers, he is always considered to be the most interesting and intriguing member of the troupe. From the point of view of Bill, Mike and Peter though, this is a positive advantage, since it keeps them well out of the limelight. Rational to the last, Mike makes a telling remark, 'We've made it a point since the very beginning to let everybody know that R.E.M. is a four-piece band and that everybody counts equally . . . I know what I contribute to the band so the hell with everybody else.'

Roles become narrowly defined over the years within many bands, but R.E.M. seem happy to shift between instruments, changing musical emphasis and direction at whim, which is one of the features that endears them to their audience.

Humour has also been an important part of the mix, both musically and socially, drawing them closer together in the face of outrageous reviews. Peter remembered one in particular: 'Some of the worst reviews we've had have been so funny you have to laugh. One Dutch guy wrote, "I'm so fed up of these cactus field hippies coming over to Holland." What on earth is a cactus field hippy? I still think of that review with pleasure.'

Their close friendships with each other have created a unique musical chemistry. Bill sees that chemistry as having its roots in their resistance to personal change in spite of stardom's attractions: 'It's uncanny how much we haven't changed. Peter's still cynical. Mike's still a great sports fan and Michael still eats roots and seeds and stuff.' It's a prosaic description of one of the world's finest rock groups but that's pretty much their strength, the ability to reduce issues into simple truths that communicate directly with millions of people.

What does the future hold for R.E.M.? It's too early to say if

Monster represents a staging post on their way to a new musical style, whether it's a full stop in their career or merely the raucous rock'n'roll album that was required to get them back on the road. What it does prove is that they still have plenty of ideas, a deft touch in the studio and the desire to push their own boundaries further and further back.

How long can they continue? What is there left for them to do? The answer to the first question is easy – they'll go on for exactly as long as they want. The second question is harder. Commercially, there is nothing left to achieve; they've already sold far more records than they ever dreamed would be possible back in the days of sold-out shows at Tyrone's in Athens. But the musical landscape is more difficult to interpret. With pop and rock's increasing fragmentation as the years go by, it's impossible for any group to influence the world in the way that Elvis, The Beatles or The Stones did in the '60s. Music is now too compartmentalized to be the global phenomenon it once was, and members of R.E.M. could gain greater satisfaction from working in a different sphere. For example, fans might worry that Michael's ambitions in film could impinge on the future of R.E.M.. Michael dismisses the idea: 'I consider myself extremely lucky not only to be in a band that I consider to be a really great band but also to be able to work with other guys who I really respect. To still want to work with them and have our relationships is pretty extraordinary.'

All four band members have interests beyond the group now and these extracurricular activities may well prolong the life of R.E.M.. By having R.E.M. as just one aspect of their lives, the band retains its allure, its excitement. Each time they get back together, it's a fresh experience. Bill admits that his life away from the band couldn't be more different, but it revitalizes his enthusiasm for R.E.M.: 'I'm a hay farmer now, I have to worry about rainfall and fertilizer, keeping oil in the tractor. But I get on the tractor and it's like all my problems go away. It's been great therapy for me.'

Peter's response to the question of whether or not the end is nigh is pragmatic. 'I just can't imagine breaking up a really good band and putting a new one together. What's the point? I like to work in a functioning group, I like the sense of growth and compromise you get when you're working with people you've known for a long time . . . we still fall out, we yell at each other or sulk but that's OK too. When we start making bad records, that's when I'll quit.' The fatalistic Michael Stipe is a little more resigned to the idea that the group will eventually come to a grinding halt, but then again, 'It's like the end of *Blade Runner*. Who cares?'

R.E.M. has always been a mix of the magical, the mundane, the brilliant and the bizarre. Peter has all the best stories, so the last word goes to him in reminiscent mood, telling *Q* about a Hallowe'en show in Honolulu in 1984.

It was a costume show and at the very last countdown Adolf Hitler pulled open his jacket and he had a four-foot-long rubber penis bouncing up and down. He won by acclamation; Adolf Hitler as well-endowed flasher beat out a woman who wore nothing but a wrap, a naked space alien with antennae. She was going to win but you couldn't beat Hitler with a massive prong. It was 120 degrees and we had to follow that. What a career.

UK DISCOGRAPHY

Singles

RADIO FREE EUROPE
Radio Free Europe (edit) / There She Goes Again
August 1983

TALK ABOUT THE PASSION
Talk About The Passion / Shaking Through / Carnival Of Sorts
(Box Cars)
November 1983

SO. CENTRAL RAIN (I'M SORRY)
So. Central Rain (I'm Sorry) / King Of The Road / Voice Of
Harold / Pale Blue Eyes
March 1984

(DON'T GO BACK TO) ROCKVILLE
(Don't Go Back To) Rockville / Wolves, Lower / 9–9 / Gardening
At Night (live)
June 1984

CAN'T GET THERE FROM HERE
Can't Get There From Here (3.10 edit) / Bandwagon / Can't Get
There From Here (3.39 edit) / Burning Hell
July 1985

WENDELL GEE
Wendell Gee / Crazy / Ages Of You / Burning Down / Driver 8
(live)
October 1985

FALL ON ME
Fall On Me / Rotary Ten / Toys In The Attic
July 1986

SUPERMAN
Superman / White Tornado / Femme Fatale
March 1987

IT'S THE END OF THE WORLD AS WE KNOW IT (AND I FEEL FINE)
It's The End Of The World As We Know It (And I Feel Fine)
(2.59 edit) / This One Goes Out (live) / It's The End Of The
World As We Know It (And I Feel Fine) / Maps And Legends
(live)
August 1987

THE ONE I LOVE
The One I Love / Last Date / Disturbance At The Heron House
(live)
November 1987
Chart: 51

FINEST WORKSONG
Finest Worksong (LP Version) / Time After Time, Etc (live) /
Finest Worksong (Lengthy Club Mix) / Finest Worksong (Other
Mix) / It's The End Of The World As We Know It (And I Feel
Fine)
April 1988
Chart: 50

THE ONE I LOVE
The One I Love / Fall On Me / So. Central Rain
October 1988

STAND
Stand / Memphis Train Blues / (The Eleventh Untitled Song)
January 1989
Chart: 51

ORANGE CRUSH
Orange Crush / Ghost Riders / Dark Globe
May 1989
Chart: 28

STAND
Stand / Pop Song '89 (Acoustic) / Skin Tight (live)
August 1989
Chart: 48

LOSING MY RELIGION
Losing My Religion / Rotary Eleven / After Hours (live) / Stand
(live) / Turn You Inside-Out (live) / World Leader Pretend (live)
February 1991
Chart: 19

SHINY HAPPY PEOPLE
Shiny Happy People / Forty Second Song / Losing My Religion
(Live Acoustic) / I Remember California (live) / Get Up (live) / Pop
Song '89 (live)
May 1991
Chart: 6

NEAR WILD HEAVEN
Near Wild Heaven / Pop Song '89 (Live Acoustic) / Half A World
Away (live) / Tom's Diner (live) / Low (live) / Endgame (live)
August 1991
Chart: 27

THE ONE I LOVE
The One I Love / Crazy / This One Goes Out (live) / Maps And
Legends / Driver 8 (live) / Disturbance At The Heron House (live)
September 1991
Chart: 16

RADIO SONG
Radio Song / Love Is All Around (live) / Shiny Happy People
(Music Mix) / You Are The Everything (live) / Orange Crush
(live)/ Belong (live)
November 1991
Chart: 28

IT'S THE END OF THE WORLD AS WE KNOW IT (AND I FEEL FINE)
It's The End Of The World As We Know It (And I Feel Fine)
(2.59 edit) / Radio Free Europe (Hib-Tone Version) / Radio Free
Europe (IRS Version) / Time After Time, Etc (live)
December 1991
Chart: 39

DRIVE
Drive / World Leader Pretend / First We Take Manhattan / It's A
Free World, Baby / Winged Mammal Theme
September 1992
Chart: 11

MAN ON THE MOON
Man On The Moon (edit) / Turn You Inside-Out / Arms Of Love /
Fruity Organ / New Orleans Instrumental No. 2
November 1992
Chart: 18

THE SIDEWINDER SLEEPS TONITE
The Sidewinder Sleeps Tonite / Get Up / The Lion Sleeps Tonight /
Fretless / Organ Song / Star Me Kitten (Demo)
February 1993
Chart: 17

EVERYBODY HURTS
Everybody Hurts (edit) / Pop Song '89 / New Orleans Instrumental
No. 1 (Long Version) / Mandolin Strum / Dark Globe / Chance
(Dub)
March 1993
Chart: 7

NIGHTSWIMMING
Nightswimming / Losing My Religion (live) / World Leader
Pretend (live) / Belong (live) / Low (live)
July 1993
Chart: 27

FIND THE RIVER
Find The River / Everybody Hurts (live) / World Leader Pretend
(live)
November 1993
Chart: 54

WHAT'S THE FREQUENCY, KENNETH?
What's The Frequency, Kenneth? / What's The Frequency,
Kenneth? (K Version) / Monty Got A Raw Deal (live) / Everybody
Hurts (live) / Man On The Moon (live)
Chart: 9

BANG AND BLAME
Bang And Blame / Losing My Religion (live) / Country Feedback
(live) / Begin The Begin (live) / Bang And Blame CK version
October 1994
Chart: 15

CRUSH WITH EYELINER
Crush With Eyeliner / Fall On Me (live) / Me in Honey (live) /
Finest Worksong (live) / Crush With Eyeliner (instrumental
version)
Chart: 23

Albums

MURMUR
Radio Free Europe / Pilgrimage / Laughing / Talk About The
Passion / Moral Kiosk / Perfect Circle / Catapult / Sitting Still /
9–9 / Shaking Through / We Walk / West Of The Fields
August 1983

RECKONING
Harborcoat / 7 Chinese Brothers / So. Central Rain (I'm Sorry) /
Pretty Persuasion / Time After Time (Annelise) / Second Guessing /
Letter Never Sent / Camera / Don't Go Back To Rockville /
Little America
April 1984
Chart: 91

FABLES OF THE RECONSTRUCTION
Feeling Gravity's Pull / Maps And Legends / Driver 8 / Life And
How To Live It / Old Man Kensey / Can't Get There From Here /
Green Grow The Rushes / Kohoutek / Auctioneer (Another
Engine) / Good Advices / Wendell Gee
June 1985
Chart: 35

LIFES RICH PAGEANT
Begin The Begin / These Days / Fall On Me / Cuyahoga / Hyena /
Underneath The Bunker / The Flowers Of Guatemala / I Believe /
What If We Give It Away? / Just A Touch / Swan Swan H /
Superman
August 1986
Chart: 43

DEAD LETTER OFFICE
Crazy / There She Goes Again / Burning Down / Voice Of Harold /
Burning Hell / White Tornado / Toys In The Attic / Windout /
Ages Of You / Pale Blue Eyes / Rotary Ten / Bandwagon / Femme
Fatale / Walter's Theme / King Of The Road / Wolves, Lower /
Gardening At Night / Carnival Of Sorts (Box Cars) / 1,000,000 /
Stumble
May 1987
Chart: 60

DOCUMENT
Finest Worksong / Welcome To The Occupation / Exhuming
McCarthy / Disturbance At The Heron House / Strange / It's The
End Of The World As We Know It (And I Feel Fine) / The One I
Love / Fireplace / Lightnin' Hopkins / King Of Birds / Oddfellows
Local 151
September 1987
Chart: 28

EPONYMOUS
Radio Free Europe / Gardening At Night / Talk About The
Passion / So. Central Rain / (Don't Go Back To) Rockville / Can't
Get There From Here / Driver 8 / Romance / Fall On Me / The
One I Love / Finest Worksong / It's The End Of The World As We
Know It (And I Feel Fine)
October 1988
Chart: 69

GREEN
Pop Song '89 / Get Up / You Are The Everything / Stand / World
Leader Pretend / The Wrong Child / Orange Crush / Turn You
Inside-Out / Hairshirt / I Remember California / Untitled
November 1988
Chart: 27

OUT OF TIME
Radio Song / Losing My Religion / Low / Near Wild Heaven /
Endgame / Shiny Happy People / Belong / Half A World Away /
Texarkana / Country Feedback / Me In Honey
March 1991
Chart: 1

THE BEST OF R.E.M.
Carnival Of Sorts / Radio Free Europe / Perfect Circle / Talk
About The Passion / So. Central Rain / (Don't Go Back To)
Rockville / Pretty Persuasion / Green Grow The Rushes / Can't
Get There From Here / Driver 8 / Fall On Me / I Believe /
Cuyahoga / The One I Love / Finest Worksong / It's The End Of
The World As We Know It (And I Feel Fine)
October 1991
Chart: 7

AUTOMATIC FOR THE PEOPLE
Drive / Try Not To Breathe / The Sidewinder Sleeps Tonite /
Everybody Hurts / New Orleans Instrumental No. 1 / Sweetness
Follows / Monty Got A Raw Deal / Ignoreland / Star Me Kitten /
Man On The Moon / Nightswimming / Find The River
September 1992
Chart: 1

MONSTER
What's The Frequency, Kenneth? / Crush With Eyeliner / King Of
Comedy / I Don't Sleep, I Dream / Star 69 / Strange Currencies /
Tongue / Bang And Blame / I Took Your Name / Let Me In /
Circus Envy / You
September 1994
Chart: 1

SOURCES

The following publications, television and radio broadcasts have all been helpful in the compilation of this book. We have not quoted from all of these and nor is it a complete list of all the material uncovered in research. Each of the following had something worthwhile to say:

Books

It Crawled From The South, Marcus Grey (Guinness)
Remarks – The Story Of R.E.M., Tony Fletcher (Omnibus)
R.E.M. Behind The Mask, Jim Greer (Sidgwick & Jackson)

Magazines

Atlanta Constitution: 'R.E.M. Remade For MTV', Steve Dollar, 5 September 1991

Chronic Town: An R.E.M. fanzine

Creem: 'Local Heroes', Robert Gordon, April 1991

Cut: 'Wielding A Subtle Sledgehammer', David Belcher, April 1989

Details: 'R.E.M.', Brantley Bardin, April 1991

Fretless: An R.E.M. fanzine

GQ: 'The Boys Are Back In Gowns', Neil McCormick, October 1994

The Guardian: 'Rulers Of The Campus', Mark Cooper, 25 September 1987; 'Green and Keen In Rural America', Adam Sweeting, 28 February 1991

Hot Press: 'R.E.M. Take On The World', Liam Fay, 29 June 1989; 'Stipe Making Sense', Paul Byrne, 27 June 1991; 'It's Only Rrrrrock'n'roll . . .' , Liam Fay, 2 November 1994

Lime Lizard: 'Rapid Ear Movement', Lynne Aldridge, April 1991

Melody Maker: *Murmur* LP review, David Fricke, 7 May 1983; 'Murmur Mystery', David Fricke, 26 November 1983; Live review, Camden Dingwalls, Allan Jones, 3 December 1983; *Reckoning* LP review, Ian Pye, 14 April 1984; 'Days of Reckoning', Adam Sweeting, 21 April 1984; Live review, Edinburgh Caley Palais, Tom Morton, 24 November 1984; 'Passionate Friends', Tom Morton, 1 December 1984; Live review, Dublin SFX Centre, Helen Fitzgerald, 15 December 1984; 'The Black Mountain', Helen Fitzgerald, 27 April 1985; 'Eat Of The Night', Allan Jones, 15 June 1985; *Lifes Rich Pageant* LP review, Mat Smith, 6 September 1986; 'Southern Accents', Tom Morton, 6 September 1986; *Dead Letter Office* LP review, Allan Jones, 9 May 1987; *Document* LP review, Allan Jones, 12 September 1987; 'Welcome to the Occupation', 12 September 1987; Live review, Columbus Ohio, Paul Mathur, 7 November 1987; News report, 15 October 1988; 'Heroes', Peter Buck, 22 October 1988; *Eponymous* LP review, Mat Smith, 29 October 1988; 'Strangers In A Strange Land', Steve Sutherland, 29 October 1988; 'Buckshot and Blues', Steve Sutherland, 5 November 1988; *Green* LP review, David Cavanagh, 12 November 1988; 'Heroes', Michael Stipe, 24 December 1988; News report, 24 December 1988; 'All-American Alien Boys', David Stubbs, 27 May 1989; Live review, Wembley Arena, Ted Mico, 1 July 1989; 'The Return Of R.E.M.', David Fricke, 6 October 1990; 'Bucking The System', David Fricke, 15 December 1990; *Tourfilm* video review, Steve Sutherland, 12 January 1991; 'The Final Countdown', Harold DeMuir, 2 & 9 March 1991; *Out*

Jones, 21 December 1991; 'Time After Time', Allan Jones, 4 January 1992; 'Desperation Angels', David Fricke, 26 September 1992; 'Remote Control', David Fricke, 3 October 1992; *Automatic For The People* LP review, Allan Jones, 3 October 1992; 'Rebellious Jukebox', Peter Buck, 19 December 1992; 'Return Of The Grievous Angels', Mat Smith, 2 October 1993; 'Monsterway To Heaven', David Stubbs, 12 November 1994

Mojo: *Monster* LP review, David Cavanagh, October 1994; 'Fables of The Four-Headed Monster', Dave DiMartino, Jim Irvin and Mark Ellen, November 1994

New Musical Express: *Murmur* LP review, Richard Grabel, 3 September 1983; 'Making Loud Murmurs', Richard Grabel, 5 November 1983; *Reckoning* LP review, Mat Snow, 21 April 1984; 'Four Guys Bucking For The Sainthood', Barney Hoskyns, 21 April 1984; 'Remedial Treatment', Mat Snow, 4 May 1985; R.E.M. interview, Andy Gill, 6 July 1985; *Lifes Rich Pageant* LP review, Andy Gill, 16 August 1986; 'Bucking The System', Danny Kelly, 5 September 1987; *Eponymous* LP review, Edwin Pouncey, 29 October 1988; *Green* LP review, Sean O'Hagan, 12 November 1988; 'Another Green World', Sean O'Hagan, 24 December 1988; 'It's The End Of The World As We Know It (And Don't We Feel Fine)', Jack Barron, 5 August 1989; *Out Of Time* LP review, Terry Staunton, 16 March 1991; 'Reconstruction Time Again', Gavin Martin, 23 March 1991; 'Stipe Making Sense', Roy Wilkinson, 1 June 1991; *Automatic For The People* LP review, Dele Fadele, 3 October 1992; 'Georgia's Best', Terry Staunton, 2 January 1993; 'The Ones I Love', Emmanuel Tellier, 25 December 1993; 'The Most Brilliant Talented Human Being Alive Today', John Mulvey, 17 September 1994; 'Bucking The System', John Mulvey, 24 September 1994; *Monster* LP review, Keith Cameron, 24 September 1994

Observer: 'The Power Of Post-yuppie Pop', Jon Savage, 21 May 1989

Pulse: 'R.E.M. 1992', Ira Robbins, October 1992

Q: *Document* LP review, Mark Cooper, October 1987; 'Tab-happy', Adrian Deevoy, November 1987; 'Welcome To The Funny

Farm', Adrian Deevoy, December 1988; *Green* LP review, Andy Gill, December 1988; *Tourfilm* video review, Martin Aston, February 1991; 'The Home Guard', Andy Gill, April 1991; *Out Of Time* LP review, Mark Cooper, April 1991; *This Film Is On . . .* video review, Adrian Deevoy, November 1991; 'Touched! Chuffed! Etc!', Mat Snow, January 1992; 'Plink! Plink? Plink!', Mat Snow, October 1992; 'Lyrically Dark, Musically Oddball', Mat Snow, November 1992; *Automatic For The People* LP review, Phil Sutcliffe, November 1992; 'Tune In, Cheer Up, Rock Out', David Cavanagh, October 1994; *Monster* LP review, Stuart Maconie, November 1994

Rolling Stone: *Lifes Rich Pageant* LP review, Anthony DeCurtis, 28 August 1986; 'R.E.M. In The Real World', Steve Pond, 3 December 1987; 'A Loose Weird Effort', Anthony DeCurtis, 27 August 1987; 'R.E.M.'s Brave New World', Anthony DeCurtis, 20 April 1989; 'Number 1 With An Attitude', Jeff Giles, 27 June 1991; 'Monster Madness', Anthony DeCurtis, 20 October 1994

Select: 'The Reluctant Celebrity', Mark Kemp, February 1991; 'The Trouble With Michael', David Cavanagh, November 1992; 'Super Fly Guys', Clark Collis, November 1994; *Monster* LP review, Roy Wilkinson, November 1994

Sounds: '20/20 Visionaries', Tim Sommer, 4 June 1983; 'Murmur's Boys', Sandy Robertson, 17 September 1983; 'The Day Of Reckoning', Bill Black, 28 April 1984; 'Return Of The Rickenbackers', Sandy Robertson, 8 December 1984; 'Fable Rapping', Jack Barron, 13 July 1985; *Lifes Rich Pageant* LP review, Edwin Pouncey, 16 August 1986; 'The Secret File Of R.E.M.', Roy Wilkinson, 12 September 1987; *Document* LP review, David Quantick, 12 September 1987; *Eponymous* LP review, Keith Cameron, 29 October 1988; 'Michael Stipe's Greatest Zits', Keith Cameron, 29 October 1988; *Green*, LP review, Roy Wilkinson, 12 November 1988; 'Revolution Starts In The Bathroom Mirror', Keith Cameron, 26 November 1988; 'Pop Corn And Orange Crush', Roy Wilkinson, 24 June 1989; 'The Buck Stops Here', Roy Wilkinson, 1 July 1989; *Out Of Time* LP review, Keith Cameron, 9 March 1991; Live review, London Borderline, Roy Wilkinson, 23 March 1991; 'Love And Other Four Letter Words', Roy Wilkinson, 23 March 1991

Sources

Sunday Times: 'Is It Only Rock'n'Roll?', Robert Sandall, 4 October 1992

The Times: 'Talking Heads', David Sinclair, 7 November 1992

Top: 'R.E.M.', Peter Clark, October 1987

Vox: 'Finest Worksongs', Parke Puterbaugh, February 1992; 'Shy Men Of Athens', Steve Malins, November 1992; 'Southern Comfort', Martin Townsend, September 1993; 'They Think It's All Ogre', Erik Van Den Berg, November 1994; *Monster LP* review, Gavin Martin, November 1994

Radio

Should We Talk About The Government? Warner Brothers promotional interview, 1988
Radio 1 *Saturday Sequence* interview, 10 June 1989
Radio 1 *Into The Night* interview, 13 March 1991
Radio 1 *Evening Session*, 26 September 1994

Television

Livewire, US TV, October 1983
Pageantry, IRS promotional film, 1986
Green, Warner Brothers promotional film 1988
Green video press kit, 1988
Talk About The Passion, MTV, 1988
Rapido, UK TV, April 1989
Transmission, UK TV, 1989
Rai Uno, Italian TV, 1989
VPRO, Dutch TV, 1989
MTV News – Tourfilm, December 1990
Timepiece, video press kit, April 1991
MTV News – Q Awards, November 1991
Entertainment Tonight, US TV, 1991
Rapido, UK TV, 1991
Villalux, Dutch TV, 1991
The New Music, Canadian TV, 1991

Rockumentary, MTV, 1991
Videomusic, Italian TV, 1991
Onrust, Dutch TV, 1991
Unplugged, MTV, 1991
Late Show, UK TV, 1991
MTV News – Grammys, February 1992
MTV News – BPI Awards, February 1992
BPI Awards, UK TV, February 1992
MTV News – C-00, February 1992
MTV News – Vote Clinton, October 1992
Past, Present & Future, MTV, 1992
MTV News – *Rock For Choice*, January 1993
Naked City, UK TV, August 1993
MTV News – MTV Awards, September 1993
Peel Slowly & See, UK TV, December 1993
The Big E, UK TV, 1993
VH1 Feature, UK TV, October 1994
VH1 – Q Awards, November 1994

Books For Rock Fans

Books From Citadel Underground: Classic Books of the Counterculture— Challenging Consensus Reality Since 1990

Bob Dylan: Portraits From the Singer's Early Years by Daniel Kramer oversized paperback $16.95 (#51224)

Conversations With the Dead: The Grateful Dead Interview Book by David Gans paperback $14.95 (#51223)

Deadheads: Behind the Scenes With the Family, Friends, and Followers of the Grateful Dead by Linda Kelly paperback $14.95 (#51687)

Death of a Rebel: A Biography of Phil Ochs by Marc Eliot paperback $14.95 (#51555)

Rock Folk: Portraits From the Rock 'n Roll Pantheon by Michael Lydon; introduction by Peter Guralnick paperback $9.95 (#51206)

Wanted Man: In Search of Bob Dylan Edited by John Bauldie paperback $9.95 (#51266)

(Ask for a FREE Citadel Underground brochure)

The Art & Music of John Lennon, by John Robertson paperback $12.95 (#51438)

The Best Rock 'n Roll Records of All Time: A Fan's Guide to the Stuff You Love by Jimmy Guterman paperback $12.95 (#51325)

Bonnie Raitt: Just in the Nick of Time by Mark Bego hardcover $22.50 (#72315)

The Classic Rock Quiz Book: From the Animals to Frank Zappa by Presley Love paperback $12.95 (#51689)

Deadheads: Behind the Scenes With the Family, Friends, and Followers of the Grateful Dead by Linda Kelly paperback $14.95 (#51687)

Death by Rock and Roll: The Untimely Deaths of the Legends of Rock by Gary J. Katz paperback $9.95 (#51581)

ELVIS! The Last Word by Sandra Choron & Bob Oskam paperback $ 8.95 (#51280)

The Eric Clapton Scrapbook by Marc Roberty oversized paperback $16.95 (#51454)

The Jimmy Buffett Scrapbook by Mark Humphrey with Harris Lewine oversized paperback $18.95 (#51461)

The Last Days of John Lennon: A Personal Memoir by Fred Seaman hardcover $19.95 (#72084)

Off the Charts: Ruthless Days and Reckless Nights Inside the Music Industry by Bruce Haring paperback $19.95 (#72316)

R.E.M.: From *Chronic Town* **to** *Monster* by Dave Bowler & Bryan Dray paperback $12.95 (#51724)

Rock Lyrics Quiz Book by Presley Love paperback $10.95 (#51527)

Rock Names: From ABBA to ZZ Top—How Rock Bands Got Their Names by Adam Dolgins paperback $10.95 (#51617)

Rockonomics: The Money Behind the Music by Marc Eliot paperback $12.95 (#51457)

The Show Must Go On: The Life of Freddie Mercury by Rick Sky paperback $10.95 (#51506)

Sophomore Slumps: Disastrous Second Movies, Albums, Songs and TV Shows by Chris Golden paperback $14.95 (#51584)

The Worst Rock 'n Roll Records of All Time: A Fan's Guide to the Stuff You Love to Hate by Jimmy Guterman & Owen O'Donnell paperback $14.95 (#51231)

Prices subject to change; books subject to availability